SCOTTISH PLACE-NAMES

SCOTTISH PLACE-NAMES

THEIR STUDY AND SIGNIFICANCE

W. F. H. Nicolaisen

B. T. BATSFORD Ltd. London

ISBN 0 7134 5234 X

Printed in Great Britain by
Billing & Sons Ltd, Worcester
for the publishers B T Batsford,
4 Fitzhardinge Street, London W1H 0AH

Contents

Illustrations

Preface

This book has been for over 20 years in the making. It was in the autumn of 1951 that I first began to study place-names systematically, narrowing my interest a few years later to an investigation of Scottish place-nomenclature, particularly river-names. From 1956 to 1969, the task of building a Scottish Place-name Survey as part of the School of Scottish Studies in the University of Edinburgh kept me continuously and closely in touch with toponymic research in Scotland, and the inevitable result of my own activities in that field was a variety of publications on the subject, making their appearances over the years in a number of journals and congress transactions, too scattered to allow any one reader to see them all or to create even the vaguest impression of the deliberate building of a cumulative corpus of information and inter-related studies. Only the 32 'Notes on Scottish Place-Names' published regularly in the journal *Scottish Studies* from 1958 to 1969, and the series of 122 monthly one-page articles, printed under the general heading of 'The Story Behind the Name' in *The Scots Magazine* from August 1960 to January 1971, displayed a sense of thematic cohesion and continuity; but even they were far from comprehensive and did not call for the kind of systematic approach which is demanded by a rounded study of this, or any, topic.

In the course of the last few years, I have been asked several times to bring together these scattered publications in a single volume, in order to make them more accessible to the general reader. I have, however, resisted such suggestions because a loosely textured anthology of a selection of my own writings from 1957 onwards would have been far from satisfactory, at least from my own point of view, since some of the things I said in print in the late 50s and early 60s still bear the unmistakable stamp of the beginner and would have looked somewhat immature and out of place beside some of the later products. Also the lack of inner cohesion would have remained.

I have therefore preferred to write a book which would aim at a cohesive and systematic, although not a comprehensive, account of the study of Scottish place-names, while at the same time permitting me to incorporate at least some of my earlier publications, or portions of these. Readers who know parts of my published work will, for that reason, undoubtedly recognise certain ideas, arguments, materials, and passages, but will, it is hoped, also notice that nothing has gone into this book without the kind of careful revision necessary to create an organic whole, on the one hand, and to say things in the most felicitous and convincing way, on the other. Much of this book, however, is new and not based on anything I have said in print elsewhere, chiefly because there were still many areas and aspects, within this field of study, on which I had never had the chance to concentrate, but also because the study of names in general has come of age in the last decade and has ceased to be the handmaiden of linguistics. It is hoped that the seams between the old and the new have become totally unrecognisable.

The major part of the book relies on two main principles or methodological approaches, i.e. the distribution of Scottish place-names in space and time. The outward expression of these basic notions are numerous maps and the organisation of chapters IV to IX. Critics may detect here an overemphasis, in this respect, at the expense of other approaches. Be that as it may, this method is deliberately employed in this volume to lead away from the traditional, exclusive search for linguistic etymologies and lexical meaning, and to utilise the visual impact which only a map can have, both as the cartographic end product of a study in distribution and as the starting point of new avenues of research. In this respect, maps are so much better than name-lists, and the fascination of place-names lies as much in their extralinguistic potential as in their embeddedness in language.

Since no book on Scottish place-names written in the 1970s can, or wants to, ignore the work of previous scholars, a brief word is called for at this point to explain the handling of such earlier works. My general indebtedness to them is acknowledged in the bibliography on pp. xiv-xxii which, while much more than just a list of references, contains every publication which has proved useful in the preparation of this volume. In some instances, particular allusions and direct quotations are included in the text. The latter are always attributed to their authors, however, usually without detailed reference to the specific work in which they occur. It is assumed that they are to be found in the relevant publications cited in the bibliography. I am aware of the scholarly code which requires fuller references than the ones I have given, but within the context of this book a whole series of footnotes seemed to be both inappropriate and distracting, and it is my experience that they are normally ignored by the general reader, anyhow.

Similarly, whenever a modern name is documented by an earlier spelling, only the date of that spelling is mentioned but not the source which provides it. Although in some cases it does matter in which particular source a spelling occurs, this kind of evaluation does not usually enter into any of the arguments put forward in this volume. Whereas it is important *when* a particular early form is found, the question as to *where* it occurs is mostly secondary for our purposes. Naturally, the discussion of the name *Falkirk* in Chapter I and the problems investigated in Chapter II call for an exception to this general rule. The source abbreviations used in those portions of the text are based on those proposed in the 'List of Abbreviated Titles of the Printed Sources of Scottish History to 1560' which was published as a supplement to the *Scottish Historical Review* (October 1963). Whenever appropriate, I have extended the abbreviations in order to make them more transparent even without consultation of the exact title.

The following publications of my own have, in revised versions, been .completely or partly incorporated in, or form the basis of, these chapters:

Chapter I: 'Scottish Place-names: 31. *Falkirk*'. *Scottish Studies* 13 (1969) 47-59.

Chapter II: 'Early Spellings and Scottish Place-names'. *Edinburgh Studies in English and Scots* (London, 1971) 210-233.

Chapter III: 'Some Problems of Chronology in Southern Scotland'. *Proceedings of the Ninth International Congress of Onomastic Sciences* (London, 1966) 340-347. Louvain 1969.
'Scottish Place-names: 24. *Slew-* and *sliabh*'. *Scottish Studies* 9 (1965) 91-106.

Chapter IV: 'Fashions in Street Names'. *The Scots Magazine* 89, No. 3 (June 1968) 233.
'Personality Towns'. *The Scots Magazine* 91, No. 2 (May 1969) 143.
'Scottish Place-names: 10. The Type *"Burn of-"* in Scottish Hydronymy'. *Scottish Studies* 3 (1959) 92-102.
'Scottish Place-names: 15. Names Containing the Preposition *"of"*. *Scottish Studies* 4 (1960) 19-205.
'Scottish Place-names: 25. *"Hill of-"* and *"Loch of-"* '. *Scottish Studies* 9 (1965) 175-182.
'Why Friockheim?' *The Scots Magazine* 75, No. 6 (September 1961) 531.
'Friockheim'. *The Scots Magazine* 77, No. 3 (June 1962) 201-202.
'Place-names in Bilingual Communities'. *Names* 23 (1975) 167-174.

Chapter V: 'Anglo-Saxons and Celts in the Scottish Border Counties'. *Scottish Studies* 8 (1964) 141-171.
'Scottish Place-names: 28. Old English *wīc* in Scottish Place-names'. *Scottish Studies* 11 (1967) 75-84.

Chapter VI: 'Norse Settlement in the Northern and Western Isles:

Some Place-name Evidence'. *The Scottish Historical Review* **48**, 1 (April 1969) 6-17.

'Life in Scandinavian Lewis'. *The Scots Magazine* **78**, No. 4 (January 1963) 329.

'The Post-Norse Place-names of Shetland'. Forthcoming.

'Norse Place-names in South-west Scotland'. *Scottish Studies* **4** (1960) 49-70.

'Scottish Place-names: 22. Old Norse *pveit*, etc.' *Scottish Studies* **8** (1964) 96-103.

'Scottish Place-names: 23. The Distribution of Old Norse *býr* and *fjall.*' *Scottish Studies* **8** (1964) 208-213.

'Scottish Place-names: 29. Scandinavian Personal Names in the Place-names of South-east Scotland'. *Scottish Studies* **11** (1967) 223-236.

Chapter VII: 'Gaelic Place-names in Southern Scotland'. *Studia Celtica* **5** (1970) 15-35.

'Place-names of the Dundee Region'. In: S.J. Jones (editor), *Dundee and District,* British Association for the Advancement of Science (Dundee, 1968) 144-152.

'Of Churches and Saints'. *The Scots Magazine* **88**, No. 6 (March 1968) 590.

'The Distribution of Certain Gaelic Mountain-names'. *Transactions of the Gaelic Society of Inverness* **45** (1969) 113-128.

'Scottish Place-names: 32. Gaelic *tulach* and *barr*'. *Scottish Studies* **13** (1969) 159-166.

Chapter VIII: 'The Picts and the Pits'. *The Scots Magazine* **88**, No. 1 (October 1967) 74.

'Place-names of the Dundee Region'. See Chapter VII.

'Gaelic Place-names in Southern Scotland'. See Chapter VII.

'Anglo-Saxons and Celts in the Scottish Border Counties'. See Chapter V.

'*P*-Celtic Place-names in Scotland: A Reappraisal'. *Studia Celtica* **7** (1972) 1-11.

'Scottish Place-names: 30. Fintry'. *Scottish Studies* **12** (1968) 179-182.

Chapter IX: 'The Waters of Glenlivet'. *The Scots Magazine* **84**, No. 4 (January 1966) 338-339.

'Scottish Place-names: 13. Some Early Name-Forms of the Stirlingshire *Carron.*' *Scottish Studies* **4** (1960) 96-104.

'Scottish Place-names: 14. Avon'. *Scottish Studies* **4** (1960) 187-194.

'Great Britain and Old Europe'. *Namn och Bygd* **59** (1971) 85-105.

'Scottish Place-names: 26. Blackadder and Whiteadder'.

Scottish Studies **10** (1966) 78-87.
'Die alteuropäischen Gewässernamen der britischen Hauptinsel'. *Beiträge zur Namenforschung* **8** (1957) 211-268.

I am most grateful to the various editors and publishers concerned for so kindly and readily permitting me to make use of these publications of mine for the purposes of this book.

As will be obvious after a brief perusal, the particular approach adopted for this volume would have been ineffective without an adequate number of relevant distribution maps. In this respect, too, I have been very fortunate. Maps 1-3, 5-10, 14-17, and 19-21 were prepared by myself and are reproduced from *An Historical Atlas of Scotland c. 400-c. 1600*, edited by Peter McNeill and Ranald Nicholson, with the permission of the Trustees of the Conference of Scottish Medievalists. The same Trustees and Dr. Isabel Henderson also gave me permission to reproduce Map 18 from the *Historical Atlas*, and Professor Stuart Piggott kindly allowed me to include Map 4 which is here reproduced from *The Prehistoric Peoples of Scotland* (London, 1962), p. 129. These visual aids are an important feature of this book, and my special thanks are due to the generosity of those who made their reproduction possible.

It would be impossible, on the other hand, to thank all those who, in the last 25 years, have, in one way or another, influenced my thinking, listened to my questions, given me good advice, and encouraged me in my work. Their number is very large, and any attempt to list them all would be futile; it would be so easy to miss out somebody. I must, however, with deep gratitude mention my earlier mentors, the late Professor Hans Krahe of the University of Tübingen and Mr. Angus Matheson of the University of Glasgow who guided a beginner's precarious steps, and the late Dr. O. K. Schram whose knowledge and kindliness kept me from faltering in later years. My appointment to the School of Scottish Studies in 1956 made my personal interest in Scottish place-names official, so to speak, and several members of the Advisory Committee of the School showed a continuing and encouraging interest in my work: Professors Gordon Donaldson, Kenneth H. Jackson, Angus McIntosh, Stuart Piggott, and J. Wreford Watson, as well as the late Professor Sidney Newman. My colleagues, too, and especially Mr. Ian A. Fraser, gave me much needed support and help on numerous occasions. It is certainly not the fault of these good people if I have not heeded their advice and the views expressed in this book are, of course, my own responsibility. I can only hope that the result of my work will do some justice to those formative years in the University of Edinburgh from 1956 to 1969, without which this volume would not exist.

State University of New York
at Binghamton, 1976 W. F. H. Nicolaisen

Bibliography

The literature on Scottish place-names is very extensive, in view of the fact that the study of names touches on so many different disciplines. It is therefore impossible to provide a comprehensive bibliography in this context. In the selected list of publications which follows, only works have been included which have been helpful in the preparation of this volume; the inclusion of any book or article in the list does not constitute a qualitative judgment.

Alexander, William M.; *The Place-Names of Aberdeenshire*. Third Spalding Club. Aberdeen, 1952.

Anderson, A.O.; *Early Sources of Scottish History 500 to 1286*. 2 vols. Edinburgh, 1922.

Anderson, Marjorie O.; 'Lothian and the Early Scottish Kings'. *The Scottish Historical Review* **39** (1960) 98-112.

Armstrong, A.M., Mawer A., Stenton, F.M., and Dickens, Bruce.; *The Place-names of Cumberland*. 3 vols. English Place-name Society, Vols XX-XXII. Cambridge, 1952.

Arnold, Thomas (ed); *Symeonis Monachi Opera Omnia*. Vol II. Rolls Series 75. London, 1885.

Bannerman, John; 'The Dál Riata and Northern Ireland in the Sixth and Seventh Centuries'. In: *Celtic Studies – Essays in Memory of Angus Matheson 1912-1962*. (Eds) James Carney and David Greene. London, 1968, 1-11.

Barclay, Robert S. (ed); *The Court Book of Orkney and Shetland 1612-1613*. Kirkwall, 1962.

Barclay, Robert S. (ed); *The Court Books of Orkney and Shetland 1614-1615*. Scottish History Society, Fourth Series, Vol 4. Edinburgh, 1967.

Barrow, G.W.S.; 'Treverlen, Duddingston and Arthur's Seat'. *The Book of the Old Edinburgh Club* **30** (1959) 1-9.

Barrow, G.W.S.; *The Border – An Inaugural Lecture*. University of Durham, 1962. Reprinted in a revised version as 'The Anglo-Scottish Border'. *Northern History* **1** (1966) 21-42.

Beveridge, Erskine; *The 'Abers' and 'Invers' of Scotland.* Edinburgh, 1923.

Black, George F.; *The Surnames of Scotland.* New York, 1946.

Blair, P. Hunter; 'The Origins of Northumbria'. *Archaeologia Aeliana,* Fourth Series, **25** (1947) 1-51.

Blair, P. Hunter; 'The Bernicians and their Northern Frontiers'. In: *Studies in Early British History.* (Ed) N.K. Chadwick. Cambridge, 1954, 137-172.

Blair, P. Hunter; *An Introduction to Anglo-Saxon England.* Cambridge, 1962.

Brøgger, A.W.; *Ancient Emigrants.* Oxford, 1929.

Cameron, Kenneth; *The Place-names of Derbyshire.* 3 vols. English Place-name Society, vols XXVII-XXIX. Cambridge, 1959.

Cameron, Kenneth; *English Place-names.* London, 1961.

Chadwick, H.M. *Early Scotland.* Cambridge, 1949.

Chadwick, Nora K.; 'The Name Pict'. *Scottish Gaelic Studies* **8** (1958) 146-176.

Chadwick, Nora K.; 'The Conversion of Northumbria: A Comparison of Sources'. In: *Celt and Saxon.* (Ed) N.K. Chadwick. Cambridge 1963, 138-166.

Chadwick, Nora K.; *Celtic Britain.* London, 1963.

Chalmers, George; *Caledonia.* Vol I. London, 1807. Vol III. London, 1824.

Christison, D.; 'On the Geographical Distribution of Certain Place-names in Scotland'. *Proceedings of the Society of Antiquaries of Scotland* **27** (1892-3) 255-280.

Clouston, J. Storer (ed); *Records of the Earldom of Orkney 1299-1614.* Publications of the Scottish History Society. Second Series, Vol 7. Edinburgh, 1914.

Cramp, R.; 'The Anglican [*sic*] Sculptured Crosses of Dumfriesshire'. *Transactions of the Dumfriesshire and Galloway Natural History and Antiquarian Society,* Third Series, **38** (1961) 9-20.

Dalrymple, Sir David; *Annals of Scotland from the Accession of Malcolm III surnamed Canmore, to the Accession of Robert I.* Edinburgh, 1776.

Dauzat, Albert; *La Toponymie Française.* Paris, 1946.

Diack, Francis C.; 'Place-names of Pictland'. *Revue Celtique* **38** (1920-21) 109-132; **39** (1922) 125-174.

Diack, Francis C.; *The Inscriptions of Pictland.* Aberdeen, 1944.

A Dictionary of the Older Scottish Tongue; Eds Sir William A. Craigie, A.J. Aitken. Chicago, 1931-.

Dilworth, Anthony; 'Strathavon in Banffshire, Srath Athfhinn or Srath Abhainn?' *Scottish Gaelic Studies* **9**, 2 (1962) 136-145.

Dixon, Norman; *The Place-names of Midlothian.* Typescript Ph.D. Thesis. Edinburgh, 1947.

Dodgson, John McNeal; 'The -ing- in English place-names like Birmingham and Altrincham.' *Beiträge zur Namenforschung* (Neue Folge) 2 (1967) 221-245.

Dodgson, John McNeal; 'Various Forms of Old English -ing in English Place-names'. *Beiträge zur Namenforschung* (Neue Folge) 2 (1967) 325-396.

Dodgson, John McNeal; 'Various English Place-name Formations Containing Old English -ing.' *Beiträge zur Namenforschung* (Neue Folge) 3 (1968) 141-189.

Donaldson, Gordon (ed); *The Court Book of Shetland 1602-1604.* Scottish Record Society 84. Edinburgh, 1954.

Ekwall, Eilert; *Scandinavians and Celts in the North-west of England.* Lunds Universitets Årsskrift N.F. Aud 1, Bd 14, Nr 27. Lund, 1918.

Ekwall, Eilert; *The Place-names of Lancashire.* Manchester, 1922.

Ekwall, Eilert; *English River-names.* Oxford, 1928.

Ekwall, Eilert; *The Concise Oxford Dictionary of English Place-names.* Fourth Edition. Oxford, 1960.

Ekwall, Eilert; *English Place-names in -ing.* Second edition. Lund, 1962.

Ekwall, Eilert; *Old English wīc in Place-names.* Nomina Germanica 13. Lund, 1964.

Eyre-Todd, George; *History of Glasgow.* Vol III. Glasgow, 1934.

Feilitzen, Olof von; *The Pre-Conquest Personal Names of Domesday Book.* Nomina Germanica 3. Uppsala, 1937.

Forbes, Alexander Robert; *Place-names of Skye.* Paisley, 1923.

Förster, Max; *Der Flussname Themse und seine Sippe.* München, 1942.

Fraser, Ian A.; 'The Place Names of Illeray'. *Scottish Studies* 17 (1973) 155-161.

Fraser, Ian A.; 'The Place Names of Lewis — The Norse Evidence'. *Northern Studies* 4 (1974) 11-21.

Fraser, J.; 'The Question of the Picts'. *Scottish Gaelic Studies* 2 (1927) 172-201.

Fraser, J.; 'Pet(t) in Place-names'. *Scottish Gaelic Studies* 5 (1942) 67-71.

Geipel, John; *The Viking Legacy.* Newton Abbot, 1971.

Goblet, Y.M.; *A Topographical Index of the Parishes and Townlands of Ireland.* Dublin, 1932.

Gray, Alexander; *The History of Islay Place Names.* Glasgow, n.d.

Henderson, George; *The Norse Influence on Celtic Scotland.* Glasgow, 1910.

Henderson, Isabel; *The Picts.* London, 1967.

Holder, Alfred; *Alt-celtischer Sprachschatz.* Vol 1 (A-H). Leipzig, 1896.

Inglis, H.R.G. (ed); *The Early Maps of Scotland.* Revised Edition. Royal Scottish Geographical Society. Edinburgh, 1936.

Jackson, K.H.; 'The "Gododdin" of Aneirin'. *Antiquity* 13 (1939) 25-34.

Jackson, K.H.; 'Common Gaelic – The Evolution of the Goedelic Languages'. *Proceedings of the British Academy* 1951, 71-97.

Jackson, K.H.; *Language and History of Early Britain.* Edinburgh, 1953.

Jackson, K.H.; 'Two Early Scottish Names'. *Scottish Historical Review* 33 (1954) 14-18.

Jackson, K.H.; 'The British Language During the Period of the English Settlements'. In: *Studies in Early British History.* (Ed) N.K. Chadwick. Cambridge, 1954, 61-82.

Jackson, K.H.; 'The Britons in Southern Scotland'. *Antiquity* 29 (1955) 77-88.

Jackson, K.H.; 'The Pictish Language'. In: *The Problem of Picts.* (Ed) F.T. Wainwright. Edinburgh, 1955, 129-166.

Jackson, K.H.; 'The Sources for the Life of St Kentigern'. In: *Studies in the Early British Church.* (Ed) N.K. Chadwick. Cambridge, 1958, 273-357.

Jackson, K.H.; 'Edinburgh and the Anglian Occupation of the Lothian'. In: *The Anglo-Saxons.* Studies... presented to Bruce Dickins. London, 1959, 35-42.

Jackson, K.H.; 'On the Northern British Section in Nennius'. In: *Celt and Saxon.* (Ed) N.K. Chadwick. Cambridge, 1963, 20-62.

Jackson, K.H.; 'Angles and Britons in Northumbria and Cumbria'. In: *Angles and Britons.* (Ed) H. Lewis. Cardiff, 1963, 60-84.

Jakobsen, Jakob; *The Place-names of Shetland.* London, 1936.

Jensen, Gillian Fellows; 'English Place-names such as Doddington and Donnington'. *Sydsvenska Ortnamnssällskapets Årsskrift(1974)* 26-65.

Johnson-Ferguson, Col. Sir Edward; *The Place-names of Dumfriesshire.* Dumfries, 1935.

Johnston, James B.; *Place-names of Scotland.* Edinburgh, 1892. Second edition, Edinburgh, 1903. Third edition, London, 1934.

Johnston, James B.; *The Place-names of Berwickshire.* Edinburgh, 1940.

Kermack, W.R.; 'The English Settlement in Tweeddale and Lothian'. *The Scottish Educational Journal,* 15 October 1937.

Kermack, W.R.; 'Early English Settlement, South-west Scotland'. *Antiquity* 15 (1941) 83-86.

Kirby, D.P.; 'Strathclyde and Cumbria: A Survey of Historical Development to 1092'. *Transactions of the Cumberland and Westmorland Antiquarian and Archaelogical Society* 62 N.S. (1962) 77-94.

Kneen, J.J.; *The Place-names of the Isle of Man.* Douglas, 1925-1929.

Krahe, Hans; 'Alteuropäische Flussnamen'. *Beiträge zur Namenforschung* 5 (1954) 201-220.

Krahe, Hans; *Sprache und Vorzeit.* Heidelberg, 1954.

Krahe, Hans; 'Die Oder und die Eder'. In: *Sprachgeschichte und Wortbedeutung* – Festschrift Albert Debrunner. Bern, 1954, 223-239.

Krahe, Hans; *Unsere ältesten Flussnamen.* Wiesbaden, 1964.

Kuhn, Hans; 'Ablaut, *a* und Altertumskunde'. *Zeitschrift für vergleichende Sprachforschung* **71** (1954) 129-161.

Lewis, Henry, and Pedersen, Holger; *A Concise Comparative Celtic
Grammar,* Göttingen, 1937.

Lewis, H. (ed.); *Angles and Britons.* O'Donnell Lectures. Cardiff, 1963.

Lorimer, W.L.; 'The Persistence of Gaelic in Galloway and Carrick'.
Scottish Gaelic Studies **6** (1949) 113-136, and **7** (1953) 26-46.

MacBain, Alexander; 'The Norse Element in the Topography of the
Highlands and Isles'. *Transactions of the Gaelic Society of Inverness*
19 (1893-4) 217-245.

MacBain, Alex.; *Place-names Highlands and Islands of Scotland.* Stirling,
1922.

MacDonald, Angus; *The Place-names of West Lothian.* Edinburgh, 1941.

MacKenzie, W.C.; *Scottish Place-names.* London, 1931.

MacKinlay, James Murray; *Influence of the pre-Reformation Church
on Scottish Place-names.* Edinburgh, 1904.

MacKinlay, James Murray; *Ancient Church Dedications in Scotland.
Non-scriptural Dedications.* Edinburgh, 1914.

MacQueen, John; 'Welsh and Gaelic in Galloway'. *Transactions of the
Dumfriesshire and Galloway Natural History and Antiquarian Society*
32 (1953-54) 77-92.

MacQueen, John; 'Kirk- and Kil- in Galloway Place-names'. *Archivum
Linguisticum* **8** (1956) 135-149.

MacQueen, John; *St Nynia.* Edinburgh, 1961.

MacQueen, John; 'The Picts in Galloway'. *Transactions of the Dumfriesshire and Galloway Natural History and Antiquarian Society* **39**
(1962) 127-143.

MacQueen, John; 'The Gaelic Speakers of Galloway and Carrick'.
Scottish Studies **17** (1973) 17-33.

Marstrander, Carl J.S.; 'Det norske landnåm på Man'. *Norsk Tidsskrift
for Sprogvidenskap* **6** (1932) 40-355.

Marstrander, Carl J.S.; 'Remarks on the Place-names of the Isle of Man'.
Norsk Tidsskrift for Sprogvidenskap **7** (1934) 287-334.

Marstrander, Carl J.S.; 'Celtic River-names and River-goddesses'. *Norsk
Tidsskrift for Sprogvidenskap* **7** (1934) 344-346.

Marwick, Hugh; *The Orkney Norn.* Oxford, 1926.

Marwick, Hugh; *The Place-names of Rousay.* Kirkwall, 1947.

Marwick, Hugh; *Orkney Farm-names.* Kirkwall, 1952.

Marwick, Hugh; *The Place-names of Birsay.* (Ed) W.F.H. Nicolaisen.
Aberdeen, 1970.

Mawer, Allen; 'The Scandinavian Kingdom of Northumbria'. *Saga-Book
of the Viking Club* **7**, 1 (1911) 38-64.

Mawer, Allen; *The Place-names of Northumberland and Durham.*
Cambridge, 1920.

Maxwell, Sir Herbert; *Studies in the Topography of Galloway.* Edinburgh, 1887.

Maxwell, Sir Herbert; *Scottish Land-names.* Edinburgh, 1894.

Maxwell, Sir Herbert; *The Place-names of Galloway.* Glasgow, 1930.

McNeill, Peter and Nicholson, Ranald (eds) *An Historical Atlas of Scotland c. 400 – c. 1600.* St Andrews, 1975

Meid, Wolfgang; 'Indo-European and Celtic'. *Proceedings of the Third International Congress of Celtic Studies, Edinburgh 1967.* Edinburgh, 1968, 45-56.

Menzies, Gordon (ed); *Who are the Scots?* London, 1971.

Miller, John Pringle; *Interesting and Local Place-names [in Lanarkshire]; How They originated.* Collection of cuttings from the *Hamilton Advertiser* 1931-32, supplemented by typescript. Royal Scottish Geographical Society.

Miller, P.; 'Notes on the Derivation and Meaning of the Place-name of Falkirk, as ascertained from charters and other historical documents'. *Proceedings of the Society of Antiquaries of Scotland* 27 (1892-3) 58-65.

Moir, D.G. (ed); *The Early Maps of Scotland.* Third edition. Edinburgh, 1973.

Nicholson, E.W.B.; *Keltic Researches.* London, 1904.

Nicolaisen, W.F.H.; For publications by the author, relevant to, or incorporated in, this book, see Preface, pp. xi-xiii.

Oftedal, Magne; 'The Village Names of Lewis in the Outer Hebrides'. *Norsk Tidsskrift for Sprogvidenskap* 17 (1954) 363-408.

Oftedal, Magne; 'Norse Place-names in the Hebrides'. *Annen Viking Kongress, Bergen 1953.* Ed. Kjell Falck. Universitetet i Bergen Årbok 1955, Historisk-antiquarisk rekke Nr 1. Bergen, 1955, 107-112.

Olsen, Magnus; *Farms and Fanes in Ancient Norway.* Oslo, 1928.

Piggott, Stuart; *Ancient Europe.* Chicago, 1965.

Pokorny, Julius; *Zur Urgeschichte der Kelten und Illyrier.* Halle, 1938.

Pokorny, Julius; *Indogermanisches Etymologisches Wörterbuch.* Vol I. Bern, 1959.

Price, Liam; *The Place-names of Co Wicklow.* Dublin, 1945-1949.

Price, Liam; 'A Note on the Use of the Word *Baile* in Place-names'. *Celtica* 6 (1963) 119-126.

Radford, C.A.R.; 'From Prehistory to History'. In: *The Prehistoric Peoples of Scotland.* (Ed) Stuart Piggott. London, 1962, 125-154.

Reaney, P.H.; *The Origin of English Place-names.* London, 1960.

Rygh, O.; *Norske Gaardnavne.* Forord og Indledning. Kristiania, 1898.

Scherer, Anton; 'Britannien und das "alteuropäische" Flussnamensystem'. *Britannica* – Festschrift für Hermann M. Flasdieck. Heidelberg, 1960, 241-250.

Scherer, Anton; 'Der Ursprung der "alteuropäischen" Hydronymie'. *VII Congresso Internazionale di Scienze Onomastiche – Atti e Memorie* 2. Firenze, 1963, 405-417.

Schmid, Wolfgang P.; *Alteuropäisch und Indogermanisch.* Akademie der Wissenschaften und der Literatur zu Mainz – Abhandlungen der geistes– und sozialwissenschaftlichen Klasse, Jahrgang 1968, Nr 6. Mainz, 1968.

Scottish National Dictionary; (Eds) William Grant, David D. Murison. Edinburgh, 1931.

Searle, William George; *Onomasticon Anglo-Saxonicum.* Cambridge, 1897.

Sedgefield, W.J.; *The Place-names of Cumberland and Westmorland.* Manchester, 1915.

Sedgefield, W.J.; 'Methods of Place-name Study'. In: *Introduction to the Survey of English Place-names.* English Place-name Society. Vol I, Part 1. Cambridge, 1925, 1-14.

Senex *et alia*; *Glasgow: Past and Present.* Glasgow, 1884.

Sharp, L.W.; *The Expansion of the English Language in Scotland.* Typescript Ph.D. Thesis, Cambridge, 1927.

Skene, William F.; *Celtic Scotland.* Vol II. Second edition. Edinburgh, 1887.

Small, Alan; 'The Historical Geography of the Norse Viking Colonization of the Scottish Highlands.' *Norsk Geografisk Tidsskrift* 22 (1968) 1-16.

Smith, A.H.; *The Preparation of County Place-name Surveys.* London, 1954.

Smith, A.H.; 'Place-names and the Anglo-Saxon Settlement'. *Proceedings of the British Academy* 42 (1956) 67-88.

Smith, A.H.; *English Place-name Elements.* 2 vols. English Place-name Society. Vols XXV-XXVI. Cambridge, 1956.

Smith, A.H.; *The Place-names of the West Riding of Yorkshire.* 8 vols. English Place-name Society, Vols XXX-XXXVII. Cambridge, 1961-63.

Sommerfelt, Alf; 'On the Norse form of the name of the Picts and the date of the first Norse raids on Scotland.' *Lochlann* 1 (1958) 218-222.

Stewart, John; 'Shetland Farm Names'. In: *The Fourth Viking Congress, York, August 1961.* (Ed) Alan Small. Aberdeen University Studies 149. Edinburgh, 1965, 247-266.

Stewart, John; 'The Place-names of Shetland'. In: *The Shetland Book.* (Ed) A.T. Cluness. Lerwick, 1967, 136-140.

Strom, H.; *Old English Personal Names in Bede's History.* Lund, 1939.

Sveinsson, Einar Ól.; 'Þingvellir – the place and its history'. *Þriðji Víkingafundur, Third Viking Congress (Reykjavík, 1956).* Árbók hins íslenzka fornleifafélags, fylgirit, 1968 74-76.

Thomas, Charles; 'The Interpretation of the Pictish Symbols'. *Archaeological Journal* 120 (1963) 31-97.

Thomas, Charles; *Britain and Ireland in Early Christian Times A.D. 400-800.* London, 1971.

Thomas, R.J.; *Enwau Afonydd a Nentydd Cymru.* Cardiff, 1938.

Wagner, Heinrich; 'Indogermanisch — Vorderasiatisch — Mediterranes'. *Zeitschrift für vergleichende Sprachforschung* 75 (1958) 58-75.

Wainwright, F.T. (ed); *The Problem of the Picts.* Edinburgh, 1955.

Wainwright, F.T. (ed); *The Northern Isles.* London, 1964.

Watson, Charles B. Boog; 'Notes on the Names of the Closes and Wynds of Old Edinburgh'. *The Book of the Old Edinburgh Club* 12 (1923) 1-156.

Watson, William J.; *Place-names of Ross and Cromarty.* Inverness, 1904.

Watson, William J.; 'Some Sutherland Names of Places'. *The Celtic Review* 2 (1905-6) 232-242, 360-368.

Watson, William J.; 'Topographical Varia'. *The Celtic Review* 5 (1908-09) 337-342.

Watson, William J.; 'The Picts: Their Original Position in Scotland'. *Transactions of the Gaelic Society of Inverness* 30 (1919-22) 240-261.

Watson, William J.; *The History of the Celtic Place-names of Scotland.* Edinburgh, 1926.

Watson, William J.; 'The History of Gaelic in Scotland'. *Transactions of the Gaelic Society of Inverness* 37 (1934-36, published 1946) 115-135.

Whittington, G., and Soulsby, J.A.; 'A Preliminary Report on an Investigation into *Pit* Place-names'. *Scottish Geographical Magazine* 84 (1968) 117-125.

Williamson, May Gordon; *The Non-Celtic Place-names of the Scottish Border Counties.* Typescript Ph.D. Thesis. Edinburgh, 1942.

Sources

Only sources actually quoted in the text have been included in this list which is based on the 'List of Abbreviated Titles of the Printed Sources of Scottish History to 1560' (Supplement to the *Scottish Historical Review*, October 1963), but has been augmented by several items outside the scope of that compilation.

Acts of Council *The Acts of the Lords of Council in Civil Causes.* (Eds) T. Thomson and others. Edinburgh 1839 and 1918-

Acts of Lords Auditors *The Acts of the Lords Auditors of Causes and Complaints* (Ed) T. Thomson. Edinburgh, 1839.

Acts of Parliaments of Scotland *The Acts of the Parliaments of Scotland.* (Eds) T. Thomson and C. Innes. Edinburgh, 1814-75.

Anglo-Saxon Chronicle *Anglo-Saxon Chronicle: Two Saxon Chronicles Parallel.* 2 vols. (Eds) J. Earle and C. Plummer. Oxford, 1892-99.

Annals of Lindisfarne *Annales Lindisfarnenses.* Monumenta Germaniae Historica, Scriptorum, Vol XIX. Hanover, 1866.

Annals of Tigernach *The Annals of Tigernach.* (Ed) Whitley Stokes. *Revue Celtique* **16** (1895) 374-419; **17** (1896) 6-33, 116-263, 337-420; **18** (1897) 9-59, 150-303, 374-391.

Annals of Ulster *Annals of Ulster. . . . ; A Chronicle of Irish affairs, AD 431 to AD 1540.* (Eds) W.M. Hennessy and B. MacCarthy. 3 vols. Dublin, 1893-1901.

Anonymous Life of St Cuthbert *Anonymous Life of St Cuthbert.* In: *Two Lives of St Cuthbert.* (Ed) B. Colgrave. Cambridge, 1940.

Antiquities of Aberdeen and Banff *Illustrations of the Topography and Antiquities of the shires of Aberdeen and Banff.* 4 vols. Aberdeen, 1847-69.

Arbroath Liber *Liber S. Thome de Aberbrothoc.* Bannatyne Club. Edinburgh, 1848-56.

Bain, Calendar of Documents *Calendar of Documents relating to Scotland.* (Ed) J. Bain. Edinburgh, 1881-88.

Bede *Historia Ecclesiastica Gentis Anglorum.* In: *Baedae Opera Historica.*

(Ed) C. Plummer. 2 vols. Oxford, 1896.

Blaeu *Geographiae Blavianae Volumen Sextum quo Liber XII, & XIII, Europae Continentur.* Amsterdam, 1662.

Brechin Registrum *Registrum Episcopatus Brechinensis.* Bannatyne Club. Edinburgh, 1856.

Calendar of State Papers *Calendar of State Papers relating to Scotland (1509-1603).* (Ed) M.J. Thorpe. London, 1858.

CDS See Bain, *Calendar of Documents.*

Chronicle of Melrose *The Chronicle of Melrose* (Facsimile Edition). (Eds) A.O. Anderson and others. London, 1936.

Chronicon De Lanercost *Chronicon de Lanercost.* Bannatyne Club. Edinburgh, 1839.

Coldingham Correspondence *The Correspondence, Inventories, Account Rolls and Law Proceedings of the Priory of Coldingham.* (Ed) J. Raine. Surtees Society. London, 1841.

Coldstream Chartulary *Chartulary of the Cistercian Priory of Coldstream.* Grampian Club. 1879.

Commissariot Record of Lauder *The Commissariot Record of Lauder.* Scottish Record Society. Edinburgh, 1903.

De Situ Albaniae (1165) In: *Chronicles of the Picts, Chronicles of the Scots,*... (Ed) W.F. Skene. Edinburgh, 1867, 135-137.

Dryburgh Liber *Liber S. Marie de Dryburgh.* Bannatyne Club. Edinburgh, 1847.

Dunfermline Registrum *Registrum de Dunfermelyn.* Bannatyne Club. Edinburgh, 1842.

Ecclesmachan Kirk Session Records In: H.M. Register House, Edinburgh.

ER See *Exchequer Rolls.*

ESC See Lawrie, *Early Scottish Charters.*

Exchequer Rolls *The Exchequer Rolls of Scotland.* (Eds) J. Stuart and others. Edinburgh, 1878-1908.

Glasgow Registrum *Registrum Episcopatus Glasguensis.* Bannatyne and Maitland Clubs. Edinburgh, 1843.

Henry of Huntingdon, Historia Anglorum *Henrici Archidiaconi Huntendunensis Historia Anglorum.* (Ed) Thomas Arnold. London, 1879.

Hiberniae Delineatio *Hiberniae Delineatio* (c. 1672). In: *A Topographical Index of the Parishes and Townlands of Ireland....* (Ed) L.J.J. Goblet. Dublin, 1932.

Historia Post Bedam *Historia post Bedam.* In: *Chronica Magistri Rogeri de Hovedene.* (Ed) William Stubbs. Vol 1. Rolls Series 51. London. 1868.

Historia Sancti Cuthberti *Historia Sancti Cuthberti,* by Symeon of Durham. In: *Symeonis Monachi Opera Omnia.* Vol 2. (Ed) Thomas Arnold. Rolls Series 75. London, 1885.

Historical Mss Commission (Drumlanrig) *Reports of the Royal Comm-*

ission on Historical Manuscripts. Mss of the Duke of Buccleuch at Drumlanrig. London, 1897.

Historical Mss Commission (Roxburghe) *Reports of the Royal Commission on Historical Manuscripts. Mss of the Duke of Roxburghe.* London, 1894.

Historical Mss Commission (Wedderburn) *Reports of the Royal Commission on Historical Manuscripts. Mss. of Col. D. Milne Home of Wedderburn.* London, 1902.

Holyrood Liber *Liber Cartarum Sancto Crucis.* (Ed) Cosmo Innes. Bannatyne Club. Edinburgh, 1840.

Inchcolm Charters *Charters of the Abbey of Inchcolm.* (Eds) D.E. Easson and A. Macdonald. Scottish History Society. Third series. Vol 32. Edinburgh, 1938.

Index British Museum *Index to Charters and Rolls in the British Museum.* (Ed) H.J. Ellis and F.B. Bickley. 2 vols. London, 1900-12.

Instrumenta Publica *Instrumenta Publica sive Processus super Fidelitatibus et Homagiis Scotorum Domino Regi Angliae Factis 1291-96.* Bannatyne Club. Edinburgh, 1834.

John Leland, Collectanea *Joannis Lelandi Antiquarii de rebus Britannicis Collectanea.* Editio Altera. London, 1770.

Kelso Liber *Liber S. Marie de Calchou.* Bannatyne Club. Edinburgh. 1846.

Kirk Session Records of Dalmeny In: H.M. Register House, Edinburgh.

Laing Charters *Calendar of the Laing Charters 854-1837.* (Ed) J. Anderson. Edinburgh, 1899.

Lawrie, Early Scottish Charters *Early Scottish Charters prior to 1153.* (ed) A.C. Lawrie. Glasgow, 1905.

Life Bishop Wilfrid *The Life of Bishop Wilfrid by Eddius Stephanus.* (Ed) Bertram Colgrave. Cambridge, 1927.

Livingston Kirk Session Records In: H.M. Register House, Edinburgh.

Manx Manorial Roll *The Manorial Roll of the Isle of Man 1511-1515,* (Ed) William Cubbon. London, 1924.

Melrose Liber *Liber Sancte Marie de Melros.* Bannatyne Club. Edinburgh, 1837.

Melrose Regality Records M*elrose Regality Records.* 3 vols. Scottish History Society, Second series. Vol 6. Edinburgh 1914-17.

Memoirs of Sir John Clerk of Penicuik *Memoirs of Sir John Clerk of Penicuik, Baronet, 1676-1755.* Scottish History Society. First series, Vol 13. Edinburgh, 1893.

Mercator, Map of British Isles (1564) In: *Drei Karten von Gerhard Mercator.* Berlin, 1891.

Midcalder Kirk Session Records In: H.M. Register House, Edinburgh.

Midlothian Charters *Charters of the Hospital of Soltre, of Trinity College, Edinburgh, and other Collegiate Churches in Midlothian.*

Bannatyne Club. Edinburgh, 1861.

Morton Registrum *Registrum Honoris de Morton.* Bannatyne Club. Edinburgh, 1853.

MS Royal Charters *HM Royal Charters.* H.M. General Register House, Edinburgh. 2 vols.

National Mss of Scotland *Facsimiles of the National Manuscripts of Scotland.* London, 1867-71.

Newbattle Registrum *Registrum S. Marie de Neubotle.* Bannatyne Club. Edinburgh, 1849.

North Berwick Charters *Carte Monialium de Northberwic.* Bannatyne Club. Edinburgh, 1847.

Nowell, Map of Scotland (*c.* 1564) Three manuscript maps of Scotland by Laurence Nowell, Bishop of Lichfield, England. In: British Museum MS. Cott. Dom. A. XVIII.

Old English Bede *The Old English version of Bede's Ecclesiastical history of the English people.* (Ed) Thomas Miller. Early English Text Society **95, 96, 110, 111.** 4 vols. London 1890-1898.

Ortelius, Map of British Isles See: Abraham Ortelius. *Theatrum Orbis Terrarum.* Antwerp, 1570. Reprinted Amsterdam, 1964.

Parish Registers *Parish Registers of Aberdeenshire.* H.M. Register House, Edinburgh.

Poll Book of Aberdeenshire *List of Pollable Persons within the Shire of Aberdeen* (Ed) John Stuart. Spalding Club. 1844.

Pontifical of St Andrews *Pontificale Ecclesiae Sancti Andreae.* (Ed) C. Wordsworth. Edinburgh, 1885.

Proceedings Calder Baronial Court Proceedings of the Baron Court of Calder Comitis, In: H.B. McCall, *The History and Antiquities of the Parish of Mid-Calder.* Edinburgh, 1894.

Protocol Book Johnsoun *Protocol Books of Dominus Thomas Johnsoun* 1528-78. Edinburgh,1917.

Ptolemy Claudius Ptolemaeus (2nd cent. AD) See: *Geography of Claudius Ptolemy.* (Ed) Edward Luther Stevenson. New York, 1932.

Register of Sasines for Dumfries *Index to the Particular Register of Sasines for the Sheriffdom of Dumfries and the Stewartries of Kircudbright and Annandale.* 1931.

Register of the Great Seal *Registrum Magni Sigilii Regum Scotorum.* (Eds) J.M. Thomson and others. Edinburgh, 1882-1914.

Register of the Privy Seal *Registrum Secreti Sigilli Regum Scotorum.* (Eds) M. Livingstone and others. Edinburgh, 1908-.

Register Privy Council *The Register of the Privy Council of Scotland.* (Eds) J.H. Burton and others. Edinburgh, 1877-.

Retours *Inquisitionum and Capellam Domini Regis Retornatarum, quae in publicis archivis Scotiae adhuc servantur, Abbrevatio.* (Ed) T. Thomson. 1811-16.

Robertson, Index *An Index, drawn up about the year 1629, of many Records of Charters.* (Ed) W. Robertson. Edinburgh, 1798.

Roger de Hoveden *Chronica Magistri Rogeri de Howedene.* 4 vols. Rolls series 51. (Ed) William Stubbs. London, 1868-71.

RMS See *Register of the Great Seal.*

Scalachronica *Scalachronica.* (Ed) Sir Thomas Gray. Maitland Club. Edinburgh, 1836.

St Andrews Rentale *Rentale Sancti Andree.* Scottish History Society. Second series. Vol 4. Edinburgh, 1913.

Stevenson, Illustrations of Scottish History *Illustrations of Scottish History from the Twelfth to the Sixteenth Century.* (Ed) Joseph Stevenson. Maitland Club. Glasgow, 1834.

Symeon of Durham *Symeonis Monachi Opera Omnia.* 2 vols. Rolls series 75. (Ed) Thomas Arnold. London, 1882-85.

Whitby Cartulary *Whitby Cartulary.* 2 vols. Surtees Society. Vols 69 and 72. Durham, 1879-81.

William Roy's Military Survey See: R.A. Skelton, *The Military Survey of Scotland 1747-1755.* The Royal Scottish Geographical Society. Special Publication no 1. (Edinburgh, 1967). Reprinted from the *Scottish Geographical Magazine* **83** (1967).

County Abbreviations

In order to conform with Scottish and Welsh practice, the names of English counties have been abbreviated by a three-letter system. These abbreviations were introduced in *The Names of Towns and Cities in Britain* by W. F. H. Nicolaisen, Margaret Gelling, and Melville Richards (B. T. Batsford Ltd, London, 1970). Practically all of them differ therefore from the abbreviations used by the English Place-name Society and Ekwall. For technical reasons it has been impossible to include also the new region and district designations created in the recent administrative reorganisation of the country.

ABD	Aberdeenshire	DEN	Denbighshire
AGL	Anglesey	DEV	Devon
ANG	Angus	DMF	Dumfriesshire
ARG	Argyllshire	DNB	Dunbartonshire
AYR	Ayrshire	DOR	Dorsetshire
BDF	Bedfordshire	DRB	Derbyshire
BNF	Banffshire	DRH	Durham
BRE	Brecknockshire	ELO	East Lothian
BRK	Berkshire	ESX	Essex
BTE	Bute	FIF	Fife
BUC	Buckinghamshire	FLI	Flintshire
BWK	Berwickshire	GLA	Glamorgan
CAI	Caithness	GLO	Gloucestershire
CAM	Cambridgeshire	GTL	Greater London
CHE	Cheshire	HMP	Hampshire
CLA	Clackmannanshire	HNT	Huntingtonshire
CMB	Cumberland	HRE	Herefordshire
CNW	Cornwall	HRT	Hertfordshire
CRD	Cardiganshire	INV	Inverness-shire
CRM	Carmarthenshire	IOM	Isle of Man
CRN	Caernarvonshire	IOW	Isle of Wight

KCB	Kirkcudbrightshire	RAD	Radnorshire
KCD	Kincardineshire	RNF	Renfrewshire
KNR	Kinross-shire	ROS	Ross and Cromarty
KNT	Kent	ROX	Roxburghshire
LAN	Lanarkshire	RUT	Rutland
LEI	Leicestershire	SFK	Suffolk
LIN	Lincolnshire	SHE	Shetland
LNC	Lancashire	SHR	Shropshire
MDX	Middlesex	SLK	Selkirkshire
MER	Merionethshire	SOM	Somerset
MLO	Midlothian	SSX	Sussex
MON	Monmouthshire	STF	Staffordshire
MOR	Morayshire	STL	Stirlingshire
MTG	Montgomeryshire	SUR	Surrey
NAI	Nairnshire	SUT	Sutherland
NFK	Norfolk	WAR	Warwickshire
NTB	Northumberland	WIG	Wigtownshire
NTP	Northamptonshire	WLO	West Lothian
NTT	Nottinghamshire	WLT	Wiltshire
ORK	Orkney	WML	Westmorland
OXF	Oxfordshire	WOR	Worcestershire
PEB	Peebles-shire	YOE	Yorkshire (East Riding)
PEM	Pembrokeshire	YON	Yorkshire (North Riding)
PER	Perthshire	YOW	Yorkshire (West Riding)

Other Abbreviations and Symbols

c.	*circa* 'about'
fem.	feminine
Gael.	(Scottish) Gaelic
gen.	genitive
ibid.	*ibidem* 'in the same place'
i.e.	*id est* 'that is'
masc.	masculine
ME	Middle English
Mod E	Modern English
Mod Sc	Modern Scots
n.d.	no date
OE	Old English
O. Ir.	Old Irish
ON	Old Norse
O.S.	Ordnance Survey
p	personal name
par.	parish
s.a.	*sub anno* 'under the year'
*	unrecorded hypothetical form
<	developed from
>	developed into
→	(river) flowing into
- (above vowel)	indicates vowel length
∪(above vowel)	indicates short vowel (not normally marked)

Additional Information

P.28   Mordington BWK: An alternative derivation of the first element may be OE *mōr-ping* 'moorland-assembly', as in the district name Morthen YOW (*Mordinges* 1164-81, *Morthyng* 1200-10).

P.36   Paxton BWK: It would be more correct to say that monothematic names are *frequently* earlier than dithematic ones.

P.44   The following should be added to the list of *sliabh*-names:
Coll: *An t-Sliabh*.
Iona: *Sliabh Siar* (now always Staonaig), *Sliabh Meadhonach* (locally simply *Sliabh*).
The appropriate three dots should be added to the distribution map (Map 1, p.43).

P.76   Twynholm KCB and *Penninghame* WIG: The spellings *Tuinham* (for Twynholm) and *Peningham* (for Penninghame) in *Bagimond's Roll* of 1287 not only predate the evidence so far available by more than three centuries, they also strongly suggest that these two names are genuine examples of compound names in OE *-hām* and *-ingahām*, respectively. They therefore significantly strengthen our toponymic evidence for an early Anglian presence in Galloway. See also p. 72.

P.113-14   Humbie: In addition to *Hunda-býr* 'Hundi's farm', derivation from ON *húrn* 'hump, hill' or ON *Hundr* 'dog' is also possible.

P.115   Colinton MLO, etc.: *Kolbeinn* is also a very common personal name in Norway: this may have some bearing on the Irish origin proposed.

P.118   *Bóndi, Tóki*, and *þór-*: Since these three names also occur in Denmark, they are not as indicative of West Scandinavian origin as some authorities allege. The main argument is, however, not affected by this altered emphasis.

P.134   Balnakiel SLK: I have been informed that an earlier name *The Birks* was changed to *Balnakiel* about 1926, after the estate and farm of Balnakiel SUT. The next owner (*Cat*herine Strick*land*) called it *Catlands*, but the present convent reverts to *St. Mary's, Balnakiel*. Locally the current name is simply *Balnakiel*. As a recently imported name, it not only solves the puzzle to which I referred but should also be removed from the list on p.124 and from Maps 11 and 14.

    I am grateful to those readers who kindly provided or made me aware of some of the above information.

November 1978   W.F.H.N.

1
Introduction

The need for a new book on Scottish place-names has been apparent for a long time. This does not mean that there are no books on the subject; indeed, there are many, and any library wishing to have a complete collection of them normally needs several shelves to accommodate them all. It does not mean either that there are no good books on Scottish place-names. The selected bibliography included in this volume shows that there are a number which are of excellent quality, both in their scholarship and in their presentation. What our initial statement does indicate, however, is the lack of a book which will make an attempt to cover all parts of Scotland equally well and which will incorporate the considerable amount of information brought to light since the early 30s when the publication of the third edition of James B. Johnston's *Place-names of Scotland* (London, 1934) and of W.C. Mackenzie's *Scottish Place-names* (London, 1931) signalled the last endeavour to tackle the interpretation of our Scottish place-nomenclature on what one might call a national scale. In fact, if we add to these two titles Sir Herbert Maxwell's *Scottish Land-names* (Edinburgh, 1894), we have a complete list of all the books ever published on the place-names of Scotland, without geographical, linguistic, or typological restriction. This rather meagre trinity does not make it easy for the enquirer into the subject, or for the potential supplier of reliable information to get what he is after, and many a quest consequently ends in predictable frustration, even if the aid of the numerous more limited accounts of Scottish toponymy is employed in addition.

Perhaps we should be even more outspoken at this point and emend our first statement to read: The need for *two* new books on Scottish place-names has been apparent for a long time; one, a dictionary, which will replace James B. Johnston's *Place-names of Scotland*, despite the date of the third edition basically a book which in contents and attitude reflects the date of its first publication − 1892; and another which will set forth in continuous narrative the nature of Scottish place-name evidence, as well as the problems, methods, and results of its study. Personally, this writer feels rather strongly that one book cannot do both jobs − certainly cannot do both of them well − and since the organisation and comprehensiveness of a Dictionary of Scottish

Place-names demand methods of preparation which are both time-consuming and dependent on the exhaustive study of all the available evidence, it is preferable, as well as practical, that we should attend to the second task first: the narrative account. The *Dictionary*, already a long time in the making, will then have to look after itself and will hopefully make its appearance not too many years after the publication of this volume. In a way, this procedure may give the impression of putting the proverbial cart before the equally proverbial horse. Undeniably there are good reasons why the existence of evidence in dictionary form makes it very much easier for an interpretative study to be written (as Kenneth Cameron probably found when he wrote his *English Place-names,* having available Ekwall's *Concise Oxford Dictionary of English Place-names,* as well as several volumes of the county series of the English Place-name Society). There are, on the other hand, equally good reasons why the absence of such a dictionary should be the guarantee that a narrative account will be something more than, or at least something different from, the mere re-arrangement of evidence alphabetically presented. This book, therefore, being denied the assistance of a reliable dictionary, will have to find ways and means of developing its own methodology and approaches and will have to stand unquestionably and precociously on its own feet.

It will also turn to advantage what might in other respects be regarded as a severe disadvantage, by deliberately avoiding anything — apart from the index and certain lists in the text — which might be construed as an echo of an alphabetical order. We have become such slaves of the alphabet that frequently we forget its very nature of mere convenience, and tend to look upon the sequence A, B, C to X, Y, Z as something which in some way classifies or categorizes beyond the order which it imposes on words, letter by letter, from the first to the last — and that only within our own language; for we know how helpless we become when we are to place or find a German *ü*, a Danish *φ*, or an Icelandic *ð* in its proper sequence. Indeed, the seemingly convenient tool of the alphabet is the enemy of all classification. From the point of view of Scottish place-names this means that, apart from first elements in complex or compound names — and even then only to be treated with caution — it cuts across all kinds of classifications which one might be tempted to apply: linguistic, historical, geographical, social, morphological, semantic, and so on. Since happily such an alphabetical straight-jacket may be ignored, it is possible, then, to proceed unshackled and with expectation to whatever system seems to be appropriate for this presentation. 'System' there will have to be, however personal or idiosyncratic it may turn out to be in the end.

It may help us to isolate the 'system' by which we intend to think our way through this book by indicating at this early stage another purpose which this volume will not fulfil at all, or only accidentally and *en passant.* I am referring to the aspect of meaning. The question 'What does this name mean?' has over the centuries dominated name studies, both in the field of place-names and with regard to personal names. This is true of amateur investigations, as well as of scholarly pursuits in the realm of onomastics.* During my 14 years in charge of the Scottish Place-name Survey, there was not a single week during which not at least one enquiry reached me concerning the meaning of a certain name, and usually there were several. Let us assume that the enquiry was about the name *Hawick* in Roxburghshire. If I was able to say that Hawick is first recorded as *Hawic* between 1165 and 1169 in the Liber Sancte Marie de Melros, and probably goes back to an Old English *haga wīc* 'hedge (or enclosure) farm', then the enquirer was, in the majority of instances, well satisfied. He had received an answer to his question, and perhaps even more information than he had expected; he now knew to which language the name Hawick belongs and what it 'means', or rather 'meant' when it was coined. It was the end of his enquiry.

What had been the beginning of it? Why had he wanted to know what the name Hawick 'means'? Perhaps his initial interest was created because he was born in Hawick or lived there or, not at all an uncommon stimulus, because his ancestors came from there. So there was this place-name *Hawick* without any apparent meaning or at least with none upon which the few people, who had talked about it in print, had been able to agree. Our enquirer took it for granted that those who had given the name Hawick in the dim and distant past had had something 'meaningful' in mind and that it might be possible to recover this original 'meaning', so that, by the application of a certain know-how and the proper method, something which is now opaque might be made transparent again. In this respect, he was certainly in line with the accepted view, basic to all onomastic studies, i.e. the notion that, apart from certain, fairly late and sophisticated, types of names, names had meaning when first created although that meaning may now frequently be lost or obscured. Indeed, one might well say that without this maxim there would be no point in, and therefore no scholarly discipline of, the study of names. The onomastic sciences would never have been born.

Because of its earliest spelling *Hawic* and also because of its modern form, Hawick is likely to contain the two old English words *haga* 'hedge, enclosure' and *wīc* '(dependent) farm'; it must therefore have been a compound *word* as well as a compound *name*, containing two simple *words* as its first and second elements. What is being recovered, consequently, is primarily '*word* meaning'; or in another sense, the search for the meaning of a name is ultimately the reduction of the name in question to the word(s) which it once was. In this process it again

*I shall, in this study, use the internationally accepted term *onomastics*, and the adjective *onomastic* from which it is derived, to refer to the study of names in general or to anything pertaining to names. The word *toponymy* will be used as a synonym of 'place-nomenclature', and *toponymics* is the study of toponymy. *Hydronymy*, on the other hand, means 'water-names', i.e. the names of streams and lakes. In contrast, anything called *lexical* pertains to words, not names, a distinction which is of some consequence to the argument of this book. This terminology may strike some readers as new and strange at first, but since it allows for precision as well as flexibility, its employment should soon become helpful as well as familiar.

becomes a mere lexical item which might easily and unselfconsciously find a home in any appropriate dictionary but especially in one oriented towards ascertaining word etymologies. Here it might be placed somewhere near *haw, hawfinch,* and *hawthorn* with which it shares the first part *haw* (Middle English *hage, hawe,* from Old English *haga* 'hedge'), an element which has not survived into Modern English as an independent word in its original usage, applying to a hedge or enclosure. Just as Old English *haga* 'hedge' is obsolete in Modern English, so Old English *wīc* 'farm' (and a number of other, related, meanings) has dropped out of use as a word. It seems to have lost its usefulness even earlier than *haga* but whereas the latter was replaced by its cognate *hedge* (OE *hecg,* ME *hegge*), *wīc* had to make room, perhaps as early as the eighth or ninth century, for OE *tūn* (Mod E *town,* Mod Sc *toon*), and the like. Compounds such as *bailiwick* are faint reminders of a once very important word which could claim Latin *vicus* 'village' as a relative.

The name originally given to the farm from which the modern town *Hawick* descended was therefore something like *haga wīc* 'hedge farm' and it must have been descriptive of the place to which it applied; compound *name* and compound *word* were still the same, and their identity was easily recognisable. *Haga wīc* was called *haga wīc* because it was *haga wīc*! Certainly in a purely lexical and semantic sense this can no longer be said of *Hawick. Hawick* is not understood to be 'hedge farm' nor is it anything like a 'hedge farm' to look at. It no longer has a lexical slot, no longer has 'word meaning' but has taken on a new 'name meaning' or 'onomastic quality' which isolates it (there is an identical name in neighbouring English Northumberland) as a municipal burgh, town, and parish, of approximately 17,000 inhabitants in the Scottish county of Roxburgh, on the river Teviot, 40 miles south-east of Edinburgh, and 35 miles north of Carlisle, producing knitwear, hosiery, tweeds, woollen manufactures, and so on. It even has its own postal code now: TD9 9AA.

Hawick as a name, therefore, 'means' quite differently from the compound word OE *haga wīc,* and it is this, its onomastic meaning, which has permitted it to survive although it has become meaningless from a lexical point of view, because the two words which coined it have become obsolete in English. It is indeed its existence as a *name* which has given it a 'power of survival' which ordinary words do not have. Meaningless words die because the economy of language does not allow them to be carried as ballast when they no longer serve a meaningful function. Names, on the other hand, survive because they can be meaningful as *names* even if they have become meaningless as words.

As a result of this power of survival they form very important raw material in the investigation of the history of the language to which they can be ascribed, especially the earlier phases of the history of the vocabulary of that language. In consequence, practically all investigations of Scottish place-names, whether as units or as types or as groups, until the early fifties paid particular, and often exclusive, attention to this lexical aspect of the names in question, to their reducibility to words, to their primary linguistic nature. It is probably no exaggeration to say that names were regarded as special or peculiar *words*, and it is in harmony with such a view that the study of names remained basically, to all intents and purposes, a handmaiden of linguistics, and no more. Very delicate and intricate procedures were developed by language historians to ascertain the original form and meaning of a given name, and modern onomastics has benefited immeasurably from such techniques of investigation and the reliability of their results. It would indeed be churlish to deny the indebtedness of onomastic studies to the pursuit of lexical etymology, for *names* are, as we have seen, after all first and foremost *words*; and the establishment of a name in its lexical and semantic context will have to remain the basic requirement of all name research. What has changed such research in the last couple of decades or so, is the realisation that the answer to the question 'What does this name mean?' is no longer the end of onomastic enquiry but the beginning. We have begun to treat names as names and not just as words with rather strange qualities. The study of names has grown up.

With regard to the name *Hawick*, we would now no longer be totally satisfied with the answer that its earliest recorded form is a twelfth-century *Hawic* and that on this basis we are entitled to believe that it is an old English name *haga wīc* 'hedge farm'. As part of an onomastic approach, we shall want to know, for instance, whether hedged in, or enclosed, farms were common in those days or perhaps, as the name appears to imply, somewhat rare because otherwise it would have been rather difficult to distinguish this 'hedge farm' from all the others in the vicinity. We shall want to find out whether, since *wīc* is an element replaced at an early stage by OE *tūn* and the like, its geographical distribution will give us a clue as to what may be an early phase of Anglian settlement in Scotland; we must therefore examine how Hawick relates to Berwick NTB, North Berwick ELO, Birswick DMF, Borthwick ROX, MLO, BWK, SLK, Darnick ROX, Dawick PEB, Fenwick ROX, AYR, Fishwick BWK, Handwick ANG, Hedderwick ELO, BWK, ANG, Heatherwick ABD, Prestwick AYR, Previck AYR, Sunwick BWK, as well as such similar looking but geographically more remote names as Lerwick SHE and Wick CAI. Once it has been firmly established which of these, and possibly other, names contain OE *wīc* as a second element and which do not, one will want to look into the relationship between this Scottish name-type and its English counterpart, as represented by Alnwick NTB, Keswick NFK, and Warwick WAR, but also by Dalwich SUR, Norwich NFK, and Woolwich KNT, etc. We shall also want to ask whether, given the Scottish terrain and the peculiar history and pattern of settlement, *wīc* referred to the same kind of inhabited place in Scotland as in England. Was the cultural and material background of necessity different in Scotland or could it have been the same in at least some instances? Do places referred to as *wīc* usually occupy similar sites with regard to soil, slope value, access to rivers, etc.? How does *wīc* relate to *tūn*, *hām*, and others in the context of a 'semantic field'? Does it show symptoms of onomastic fashionableness? Where altogether in the distribution in space and time, and on the social scale, does *wīc*, and therefore Hawick, belong? All these questions — and there are others which one might have posed — take the name Hawick, and all names containing OE *wīc*, out of their isolation and place them chiefly into a historio-geographical context, into the legitimate range of enquiry by the settlement historian; this means that they go far beyond the question asked by our original enquirer: 'What does the name Hawick mean?' They are onomastic questions, not linguistic-etymological ones. They are therefore also proper questions to ask within the context of this narrative account of Scottish place-names, especially in the light of the next argument which we wish to advance.

In order to take the next step in this preliminary, scenesetting evaluation of names as names, we shall have to abandon the single name *Hawick* which has taught us so much, and imagine another enquirer who, for reasons of his own, has decided to seek information about the name *Melrose*, in the same county but not on the same river as Hawick. In brief, the answer he would receive, would be: 'The first reference to the name goes back to the early eighth century when it is mentioned by Bede who calls it *Mailros*. It is a pre-English Cumbric name *Moelros* "the bare moor", equivalent to Gaelic *maol ros*.' This simple statement makes reference to a fact not mentioned so far in our discourse: Whereas the name Hawick survived the demise of the two words which coined it, within the same linguistic medium which created it, *Melrose* not only survived the obsoleteness of the equivalent two lexical elements but also the death, in this part of Scotland, of the very language which coined it. Without wishing to speculate on the extent to which the name may have been understood by the incoming Angles and may have continued to live on as a meaningful compound word in an at least partially bilingual society, we must conclude that the name *Melrose* soon became a lexically opaque linguistic fossil in a new linguistic stratum: a Celtic name in an English-speaking community. This clearly enhances its value as linguistic raw material even further since other evidence of the kind of Celtic spoken in the Tweed Valley before the arrival of the Angles is very scanty indeed. It also re-emphasises our earlier contention that names do not have to be meaningful as words (although they may be) in order to be adequately useful as names. There is, in fact, no reason to believe that once the original word meaning of a name has been recovered, it will therefore function better as a name. Both our Hawick and our Melrose enquirers may get an antiquarian 'kick' out of knowing what their respective objects of enquiry 'mean', it may even give them some personal satisfaction; they will, however, one suspects not be able to handle these names better as names unless they proceed beyond their etymological quests to some onomastic questioning. Making the meaningless meaningful may be a strong folk-etymological motivation observable in all languages at all times; however, it does not improve the name's ability to function, or increase its usefulness. Be that as it may, while Hawick-type names enable us to trace earlier phases of a language still spoken in the area in which they occur, the name Melrose is representative of the type which gives us the possibility to establish linguistic sequences and stratifications among different languages. Both types naturally allow corresponding implications concerning the settlement history of the people speaking these languages. Before we proceed to utilise Scottish place-names in the pursuit of such extra-linguistic enquiries, treating them in groups, categories and strata rather than as isolated instances, it may be helpful to demonstrate more fully on a further individual name how the investigation of a proper name history works which alone can provide reliable answers to our fundamental questions of linguistic origin and meaning, answers which subsequently permit us to put individual names into all kinds of contexts. When, a few pages earlier, we gave reasons for postponing the publication of a so-badly needed authentic *Dictionary of Scottish Place-names*, we already alluded to the fact that, regrettably, the situation with regard to the study of individual Scottish place-names is such that often even names of larger inhabited places, such as towns and cities, at present lack the kind of near-comprehensive documentation which allows a detailed analysis. Glasgow, Dundee, Paisley, Kilmarnock, Lanark, Peebles, Kirkcaldy, Banff, Nairn and many others fall within this category. This does not always mean that the etymology of such names is not known; in fact, we can fairly confidently etymologise all the names just listed! However, the gradual development of the name, both in form and application, and the ultimate emergence of the modern spelling cannot normally be followed from any discussion of these names now available in print, and in each case it is necessary to amass one's own list of extant spellings by laboriously searching through the relevant records. Without such a list one would, of course, be omitting an essential basic step in the investigation of a name and therefore seriously endanger the conclusions one might come to with regard to its origin, meaning, and significance, quite apart from its value as evidence in such broader issues as historical stratification and geographical distribution.

One particularly fascinating name which might with justification have been added to the enumeration of major Scottish settlement-names above, is *Falkirk*. It is an especially useful name for our purposes since, concerning it, we are more fortunate than with most individual Scottish names in so far as there does exist at least one quite detailed although not totally successful attempt at an account of the derivation and meaning of the name. This account, published in 1893, elucidates much of what we have to know about the historical background of the place called Falkirk, beyond the purely linguistic data necessary to establish a reliable etymology. Admittedly, *Falkirk* has had a more chequered history than most Scottish place-names and is also exceptionally well documented but because of its very complexity the study of its development as a name also demands special care. The various significant spellings as they occur from the twelfth century onwards may be grouped in the following way, without attempting comprehensiveness in the later stages, or overall chronological sequence:

(a)   *egglesbreth*
(b)   *Egelilbrich*
(c)   *Varia Capella*
(d)   *la Veire Chapelle*

(*e*)   *la Faukirk*
(*f*)   *Falkirk*

Since this is the only opportunity we have in this book to elaborate on the importance of a full analysis of documentary source material and of the role which surviving spellings play in onomastic case histories, we shall allow ourselves the luxury of examining in much greater detail than would normally be justified the unusually great variety of forms and spellings associated with the name *Falkirk,* as well as the nature and reliability of the written sources and the state of the scholarship devoted to the name. Of necessity the starting-point of this discussion will have to be some comment on the identification with Falkirk of the forms listed under (a) and of their relationship to each other.

(*a*)   *egglesbreth c.*1120 (1165-70) Symeon of Durham
                        *c.*1150 *Historia post Bedam*
          Eglesbreth ? 12th cent. (16th cent.) John Leland, *Collec-
                        tanea* 1, 384
          eaglesuret 1185-98 *Chronicle of Melrose*
          Eglesbryth 1268 *Holyrood Liber*
(*b*)   *Egelilbrich* 1164 *Holyrood Liber*
          Eiglesbrec 1166 *Holyrood Liber; Egglesbrec* Stevenson, *Illu-
                        strations of Scottish History*
          Egelbrech 1190-1200 Roger de Hoveden
          Eglesbrich 1247 *Holyrood Liber*
          An Eaglais Bhreac Modern Gaelic
(*c*)   *Varia Capella* 1166, 1240, 1247, 1319 *Holyrood Liber*
                        1242 *Pontifical of St Andrews*
          Varie Capelle (gen.) 1319 *Holyrood Liber*; 1531 (1534),
                        1537 *Register of the Great Seal*
(*d*)   *la Veire Chapelle* 1301 Bain, *Calendar of Documents*
          la Vaire Chapele 1303-4 Bain, *Calendar of Documents*
          la Veyre Chapele 1304 Bain, *Calendar of Documents*
          la Veire Chapele 1305 Bain, *Calendar of Documents*
(*e*)   *la Faukirk* 1298 Bain, *Calendar of Documents*
          Faukirk s.a. 1298 *Chronicon de Lanercost*; 1391, 1468
                        Exchequer Rolls; 1511 *Register of the Great Seal;*
                        c. 1564 Nowell *Map of Scotland*
          Fawkirk 1391, 1392, 1537, 1632, 1634 *Register of the
                        Great Seal*
          Fawkirc 1391, 1392 *Register of the Great Seal*
          Fawkyrk 1531 (1534) *Register of the Great Seal* (twice)
          Fauskyrk 1564, Mercator. *Map of British Isles*
          Fauskirk 1570 Ortelius, *Map of British Isles*
(*f*)   *Falkirk* 1458, 1557 (1580), 1580, 1581, 1587, etc.
                        Register of the Great Seal;
                        1546 *Holyrood Liber*; 1551, 1591-2 *Exchequer
                        Rolls;*
                        1594 *Brechin Registrum*

The four spelling variants under (*a*), as well as Hoveden's *Egelbrech* under (*b*), occur as part of an annal for 1080 which in more or less identical terms states that '*Quo anno idem rex Willelmus autumnali tempore Rodbertum filium suum Scotiam contra Malcholmum misit. Sed cum pervenisset ad Egglesbreth, nullo confecto negotio reversus, Castellum Novum super flumen Tyne condidit.*' From this entry it is, of course, by no means clear where in Scotland *Egglesbreth* lies, and it is only natural that at first it should have been looked for in the most southern parts of the country. In 1776, Sir David Dalrymple, for instance, equated it with Bridekirk near Annan, regarding *Eggles-* as standing for *Ecclesia* and the whole name for Latin *Ecclesia Bridgidae;* and in his index to the works of Symeon of Durham in 1885, Arnold thinks of a possible identification with Eccles in Berwickshire. Whereas Egglesbre*th* led Sir David Dalrymple to Bri*d*ekirk, the reading Egglesbre*ch* suggested '*Eglesbrec*, the old name of *Falkirk*' to Chalmers who in 1807 argued that 'if Robert had penetrated to *Annan*, he must have entered Scotland, from Cumberland, on the west: but, as his irruption was bounded by Falkirk, he must have come down to this well-known town, the scene of so many conflicts, through Northumberland, whither he certainly returned', to found Newcastle. Chalmers' view has become the generally accepted one, but although we are in agreement with it too, it was necessary to point out the, at least partly, extra-linguistic nature of the argument.

Although a detailed account of the history of the chronicles involved cannot be part of this discussion, it is, however, essential to give a brief survey of the relationship of the spellings to each other in order to assess their value and standing as the earliest, and therefore extremely important, forms of our name. The main question which arises in this respect is whether these spellings have come down to us independent of each other or have some kind of connection. The fact that they all occur in practically identical annals referring to the same year (1080) rules out the first alternative or at last makes it very unlikely; what we must determine therefore is the nature of the connection which exists between these five spellings. This in turn depends on the nature of the relationship of the sources. As far as Hoveden is concerned, both the *Historia Regum* ascribed to Symeon of Durham and the so-called *Historia post Bedam* are considered to be among his sources, a supposition supported by the presence of the phrase *autumnali tempore* which only occurs in these three versions. For the *Chronicle of Melrose*, the existing version of Symeon, and the *Historia post Bedam*, Anderson claims that the relationship is collateral and that for their northern English and Scottish material they all go back to a Northumbrian source of which no surviving text is known and which probably included a chronicle that ended before the annal for 1130. This would mean that the *egglesbreth* which occurs in that part of the *Historia Regum* for which Symeon himself is thought to have been responsible, the *egglesbreth* of the *Historia post Bedam*, and the *eaglesuret* of the *Melrose Chronicle* derive from the same original spelling, whereas Hoveden's *Egelbrech* derives from the *egglesbreth* of Symeon and the *Historia post Bedam*. Little appears to be known about the exact source of Leland's *Eglesbreth* which is said to have been extracted '*ex libro incerti autoris de episcopis Lindisfarnensibus*'. It is the same annal but without the Symeon/*Historia post Bedam* addition and is undoubtedly derived from the same source as the Melrose and Symeon passages, although perhaps closer to the first. The genealogy is therefore to be taken to be something like this

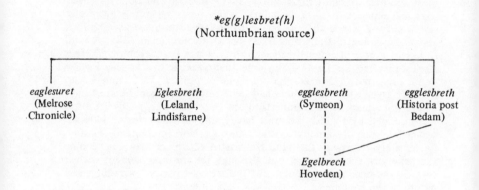

Consequently, all these entries have to be taken as *one* which is rather important when it comes to the assessment of the final consonant. This is clearly -*t* in the Melrose Chronicle and -*th* in Symeon and the *Historia post Bedam*. For the -*th* of the Lindisfarne spelling we have to take Leland's word, for the time being. On the basis of these four independently derived forms it appears reasonable to assume that the Northumbrian source also had -*t(h)*. Curious in this respect is Hoveden's -*ch* but if -*t* and -*c* were similar in the Symeon and *Historia post Bedam* MSS — and our extant manuscripts seem to confirm this — then a -*ch* could easily have been misread for a -*th*. In this connection, it is interesting that Leland, according to the 1770 edition of his works, read the Symeon spelling as *Egglesbirch* and copied the Hoveden form as *Egelbereth* which is at least a measure of the difficulty by which readers of the respective manuscripts were confronted when trying to distinguish between *c* and *t,* or other letters for that matter, since the *eaglesuret* of the Melrose Chronicle, if found in isolation, would hardly have allowed even the most daring scholar to amend it to **egglesbret(h)*. With this background in mind, we have to take our starting-point to have been a spelling ending in -*bret(h)*. Seeming confirmation of such a form comes from a much later and completely independent source, a charter in 1268 by Gamline, Bishop of St Andrews, to the Church of Holyrood, listing amongst other possessions '*Ecclesiam de Eglesbryth que hodie varia capella nuncupatur*'. This is in confirmation of an earlier charter of 1240 in which unfortunately the name becomes illegible after *Egl-*. Thus it is not possible to judge whether the -*th* is a misreading for -*ch* or an accurate copy. It is tempting, under the circumstances, to decide in favour of the former, as a singular -*th*

appears to be somewhat out of place in a series of charters and bulls which otherwise only show -*ch*, but certainly its existence must be taken into account in any evaluation of the -*th* spellings for the annal of 1080.

With or without support from the Holyrood charter, however, these spellings and their hypothetic source are there for us to interpret and should not be pushed aside lightly by emendation, as everybody before Watson used to do, who, in his discussion of our name, offered the suggestion that Symeon's *Egglesbreth* might be a British form, a proposal which prompted Johnston to add to his earlier derivation as Gaelic *eaglais breac,* the alternative 'or W[elsh] *eglwys brith*', 'speckled church', in the third edition of his dictionary. How serious and acceptable is the notion that a spelling occurring in a late eleventh- or early twelfth-century Northumbrian (monastic) annal might represent a genuine *p*-Celtic British (=Cumbric) place-name in Central Scotland? First of all, as *eglwys* < Latin *ec(c)lesia* is feminine in Welsh, the adjective would be *braith* < *breith* and not *brith* and also should show soft mutation after a feminine noun, i.e. *fraith.* Presumably a late eleventh-century form would have been something like **egluis breith.* However, as the corresponding mutation is never shown in the Gaelic form of the name (where one would have expected at least the occasional anglicised **vrech,* or the like), it is perhaps not necessary to take the apparent non-lenition of the initial consonant too seriously in this context. Perhaps more difficult to accept is the representation of -*ei*- by -*e*- in -*breth* for -*breith* although this would seem to have a parallel in *Eden-* < *Eidyn* in the twelfth-century forms of the name Edinburgh; nor is it easy to understand why the alleged Cumbric name should have contained an adjective etymologically less closely related (*brith* < **brikt-*) to Gaelic *breac,* rather than the cognate *brych* (feminine *brech*) < **brikk-.*

In addition to these two arguments, even bearing in mind the great power of survival inherent in place-names, it is not at all plausible that, unless a Strathclyde source with a Strathclyde version of the name was involved, a Northumbrian chronicler of the late eleventh century would retain a pre-Gaelic Cumbric form of the name at a time when Gaelic must have been spoken in the Falkirk area for at least 300 years, at the most conservative estimate. In our opinion, the Northumbrian source which provided the Chronicle of Melrose, Symeon of Durham, the *Historia post Bedam,* and the Lindisfarne chronicle quoted by Leland with the spelling **eg(g)lesbreth* was probably a fair copy of either a whole chronicle or, which is more likely, a number of draft annals, including the one for 1080, in which a copyist unfamiliar with the place-name misread a -*c*- in the draft version for -*t*-. We would therefore put a draft annal, perhaps not written much after the year 1080, before the fair annal in the Northumbrian source which all three (or four) chroniclers used, and assume that **eg(g)lesbreth* was a misreading for **eg(g)lesbrech.* This would, of course, not turn it into a Gaelic name but would at least allow us not to attach too much importance to the Northumbrian spelling as an indication of the survival, and therefore previous existence, of a Cumbric name for Falkirk. The isolated *Eglesbryth* in the Holyrood Charters could be explained in a similar fashion. This does not mean that we are ruling out the possibility of a pre-Gaelic Cumbric name altogether but we are not compelled by the spellings ending in *-t* or *-th* to presume Cumbric origin. Although in 1887 Skene considered our name in conjunction with the personal name *Brychan*, making the church of Falkirk 'the chief church' in *Manau Guotodin*, there is no indication in any of the primary sources to substantiate such a claim or to show that the church at Falkirk did exist in the time of the Cumbric-speaking Gododdin, i.e. *circa* AD 600.

Concerning the apparently Gaelic forms of the name, the spelling in the confirmation charter of 1166, by Bishop Richard of St Andrews to the Canons at Holyrood, is the most straightforward for it presents us with an unequivocal *-brec* as the second element. The fact that the editor of the Holyrood charters read *Eigles-* whereas Stevenson has *Eggles-*, has no influence on the etymology and only illustrates the difficulties even nineteenth-century and earlier experts encountered when transcribing these charters. Undoubtedly *Eiglesbrec (Egglesbrec)* stands for something like **Eaglais B(h)rec* which must have been the twelfth-century Gaelic form of our name. The charter spelling is vital when it comes to the interpretation of the respective references to Falkirk in the Bulls of Pope Alexander III in 1164 *(Egelilbrich)* and Pope Innocent IV in 1247 *(Eglesbrich)* as both of these, on the surface, show Brythonic rather than Gaelic forms of the adjective 'speckled'. The final *-ch* does not seem to have presented a problem to any other scholar discussing this name but is in need of some explanation. Everything hinges, of course, on the question as to whether it represents an unvoiced spirant [x] or the homorganic stop [k] in pronunciation. Unfortunately there is nothing in these two Bulls to indicate what *ch* normally stands for but as the names were presumably not taken down from oral dictation but copied from documents which had reached Rome from Scotland previously, it is perhaps not the orthographic habits of the scribes at the Holy See which matter here, but rather the significance of these spellings within a Scottish context. It should, however, be noted that Heriot appears in both Bulls as *Herth* which undoubtedly means a voiceless dental stop [t] (perhaps with strong post-aspiration), and that Bathgate is given as *bathcat* and *Bathketh*, respectively, where both spellings must have the same phonetic value. It is reasonable to assume that like *-th* and *-t-*, Anglo-Norman *-ch* and *-c-* might also be interchangeable in final position, or at least that *-ch* does not indicate a spirant. Then there are, if our previous arguments are acceptable, those two other spellings in *-ch* in addition to those occurring in the Bulls, i.e. the **egglesbrech* of the Northumbrian annal and the emended **Eglesbrych* of the charter of 1268 (and its predecessor of 1240). As far as the latter is concerned, the same situation appears to have existed as in the Bulls, i.e. both charters have *Herth* and *Bathketh* for Heriot and Bathgate, respectively.

The *Eglesbryth* for *Eglesbrych* (=*Eglesbryc*) sequence gains support from the spellings which are found in the same chartulary for the name

Kirkcudbright which, after being mentioned properly as *Kyrkecuthbert* in the twelfth century, is shown as *Kyrcudbryth* and *Kircudbrich* in the fourteenth and finally as *Kyrkcuthbryt* in the sixteenth. For Symeon's version *egglesbreth = egglesbrech*, it is significant that in the same annal he has *Malcholmum* which is rendered by Hoveden and the Melrose Chronicle as *Malcolmum*, and that elsewhere he has *Uchthredum* against Hoveden's *Uchtredum*. It is therefore not unlikely that his source had *-brec* and not *-brech*, and that the ending *-et* in the *eaglesuret* of the Melrose Chronicle is a copy of an earlier *-ec*. There seems consequently little doubt that the spellings in question are various versions and developments of an original final *-c*, or rather a velar voiceless stop [k], which points to a Gaelic *-brec* as the second element in our name.

This leaves the presence of the vowel *-i-* (or *-y-*) in the spellings found in the two Bulls and in the charter of 1268, and presumably also that of 1240. It is difficult to think of this as a mere spelling variation, as the full stress would be on this syllable, and one can only assume that this might be a reflection of a dative used as a locative, although Modern Gaelic appears to have standardised the nominative in this particular name.

The Latin versions of Falkirk are invariably *Varia Capella* in the nominative and *Varie Capelle* in the genitive. They all occur in Latin texts, and *Varia Capella* is usually translated as meaning 'the Spotted or Speckled Church'. Fortunately, the existing documentary evidence provides us with a very good insight into the exact usage and meaning of this strange description.

One important pointer in this respect is the observation that, from the very first, *Varia Capella* almost exclusively occurs in the phrase *Eiglesbrec que Varia Capella dicitur* (1166). Sometimes the word *nuncupatur* is used instead of *dicitur* and the charters of 1240 and 1268 even add the word *hodie* 'today' before the Latin name. Only in the charter of 1319, the Pontifical of St Andrews (1242), and in the reference in the Register of the Great Seal of 1531 does the term appear alone; and only in one instance, the last, is it linked with Fawkirk (1537 RMS: *apud ecclesiam Varie Capelle* alias *Fawkirk*).

Obviously the phrase '*Eiglesbrec* which is (now) called *Varia Capella*' implies that a change of name has taken place. It does not mean, as has been alleged, that medieval records use the Latin synonym. As *Varia Capella* in this phrase fills the exact slot normally allotted to the vernacular term in Latin documents of this kind, the conclusion is not that the Gaelic name has been translated into Latin but that *Varia Capella* is the Latin version of the new English translation of the Gaelic name, *Faw Kirk*. It is therefore evidence of the fact that by 1166 English was already so widely spoken in the area that, in a bilingual situation, the Gaelic place-name could be translated into the incoming language, whereas there was probably very little, if any, English influence in the Falkirk region in 1080. On the evidence of the 1080 annal, the district of Falkirk was still largely monoglot Gaelic in that year or a little later. The peculiar function of the phrase *que* (*hodie*)

Varia Capella dicitur also evidently rules out the theoretical possibility that *Fawkirk,* although not recorded until the medieval period, is really some centuries older and goes back to the time when the Falkirk region was part of English-speaking Northumbria, before the Scots crossed the Forth to the South. After 1268, nobody seems to have used the Gaelic name anymore, and by 1319 *Varia Capella* is probably accepted scribal and ecclesiastic usage for *Faw Kirk.* That this is likely to have been the case is supported by the Norman French form *la Veire Chapelle* which, with variations, appears in Norman writs of the first decade of the fourteenth century. The Latin term bows out in 1537 when *Fawkirk* is acknowledged to be the (vernacular) alternative.

Without the Latinised evidence we would not have known of the existence of the English name until 1298 when significantly it first appeared with the (French) definite article; and another century goes by before it is quite frequently found in official documents. The first element in *Faukirk, Fawkirk* is Middle English *fawe, faȝe* 'variegated, of various colours' which is not unknown in Scottish place-nomenclature, one of the chief examples being a compound with *side,* as in Fallside LAN, Falside ELO, FIF (2), ROX and WLO, Fawside BWK and Fawside KCD. Various forms of the English name are used right into the seventeenth century, including the curious *Fauskyrk, Fauskirk* which only occurs on maps and clearly shows that the adjective *faw(e)* is no longer understood so that on the analogy of other names, it seems to have been taken to be a personal, perhaps a saint's, name.

The last important phase of the history of our name starts in 1458 with the first isolated instance of the spelling *Falkirk* which from the second half of the sixteenth century onwards dominates the scene, although as late as 1634 it shares the references to the place with *Fawkirk* in one and the same charter. This new spelling must be understood as a result of false analogy, because the first element of our name was obviously considered to be in the same category as Scots *ba'* < *ball, wa'* < *wall, fa'* < *fall,* etc. An unhistorical *-l-* was therefore introduced into the 'standard', non-dialect spelling and has remained there ever since. In its turn it has produced the modern pronunciation-spelling [ˈfɔlkɛrk] which is now used by everybody except the inhabitants of the town itself who still call it Fawkirk [ˈfɔː kɛrk]. How long they will be immune to the influence of the spelling is another question.

The name *Falkirk* can therefore demonstrably be shown to have started out as a Gaelic **Eaglais B(h)rec* before 1080 (with a reasonable possibility of an earlier Cumbric name) and to have been translated into English by 1166 although there is initially only indirect evidence for this in the Latin *Varia Capella* and the Norman French *la Veire Chapelle.* This new English name is *Faw Kirk* which like the Gaelic and the Latin names means '(the) speckled church', a meaning which must have been derived from the peculiar aspect of the church, perhaps through the use of two kinds of stone occurring in the same quarry, unless a painted wooden church or one built in wood and stone can be

TABLE I

Early Forms of the Name *Falkirk*

Century	Gaelic	Latin	Norman French	English	
				Faw-, Fau-	*Fal-*
11	**egglesbreth* *(=egglesbrec)* *(1080)*				
12	*egglesbreth* *(?)Eglesbreth* *Egglesbrec* *Egelilbrich* *Eglesbrich* *eaglesuret*	*Varia Capella* *(1166)*			
13	*Eglesbryth* *(1268)*	*Varia Capella*		*(la) Faukirk* *(1298)*	
14		*Varia Capella* *Varie Capelle*	*la Veire* *Chapelle* etc. *(1301-1305)*	*Faukirk* *Fawkirk* *Fawkirc* *(1391)*	
15				*Faukirk*	*Falkirk* *(1458)*
16		*Varie Capelle* *(1531,1537)*		*Faukirk* *Fawkirk* *Fawkyrk* *Fauskirk* *Fauskyrk*	*Falkirk* *(1546, etc.)*
17				*Fawkirk* *(1622,1634)*	*Falkirk*
18					*Falkirk*

envisaged. By false analogy, a new spelling *Falkirk* is produced from the middle of the fifteenth century onwards which in turn has given rise to a new pronunciation [ˈfɔlkɛrk] although this is seldom used in Falkirk itself. The Gaelic name has survived as *An Eaglais Bhreac* but because of the modern English spelling and pronunciation, the connection between *Breac* and *Fal-* is now obscured and no longer immediately discernible.

In summary, the table on p. 15 may help us to understand the chronological sequence of the documentary evidence reflecting the development just described.

Falkirk is an exceptional name, and its chronological depth and linguistic variety are not paralleled by many other names on the Scottish map. For this reason it is both a good and bad example of the kind of detective story involved in the full documentation and analysis of early written evidence; good, because it does demonstrate the potential complexity stemming from an operation in the face of a large variety of spellings involving a number of languages — bad, because for most Scottish place-names the documentary evidence is so much more limited, both chronologically and linguistically. These limitations sometimes facilitate the investigation of a name with regard to its linguistic origin and meaning, especially when the elements in question are fairly straightforward, but more often than not they lead to a frustrating experience in this respect because the paucity of suitable spellings will not permit anything like a fully documented historical outline. Nevertheless, whether complex or simple, whether straightforward or obscure, the most comprehensive list of early spellings possible under the circumstances must be compiled before even a tentative pronouncement can be made concerning the etymology of a name. Such a list can also have a second function which, as in the case of *Falkirk*, can allow us at least to speculate on the type of language spoken in a given area at a given time, while also permitting us to establish a relative, if not an absolute, linguistic stratification; and that is, after all, one of the chief aims of this book.

2
The Written Evidence

As the detailed treatment of the name *Falkirk* has undoubtedly already demonstrated, the modern spelling of a name allows only extremely limited access to its onomastic properties, preserving intact, as it does in this case, only one half of a compound name in only one of four linguistic strata involved. It is therefore a basic, though elaborate, requirement of modern place-name research that, in addition to the recording of the local pronunciation of each name, all early spellings in written documents, both printed and manuscript, should be collected and used as a basis for an analysis of its sound development, formation and meaning. The shortcut from the modern map-form via the dictionary to a proposed etymology is no longer permissible.

In this respect, it has always been silently understood that, compared with England, Scotland is indeed much poorer as far as early spellings are concerned and that the proportion of names which will at the end of the day remain unexplained or at least difficult to interpret will therefore be higher than in England. The question arises whether this tacit assumption has a basis in fact or whether one is allowed to be more optimistic. In fact, we are really confronted with two questions: Firstly, is the general documentation of Scottish place-names really so very much later than its English equivalent? Secondly, how seriously does — real or hypothetical — lateness impair the satisfactory interpretation of names? Following up this second question one has perhaps to probe even more deeply and ask what qualifications such as 'early' and 'late' mean in terms of place-name documentation, when both epithets are obviously relative in any given context and not absolute chronological descriptions.

For an example of some of these problems and of their possible effect on Scottish place-name research, appropriate and accessible raw material is contained in three PhD theses produced in the University of Edinburgh: Angus Macdonald, *The Place-names of West Lothian* (1937); May Gordon Williamson, *The Non-Celtic Place-names of the Scottish Border Counties* (1942); and Norman Dixon, *The Place-names of Midlothian* (1947). From these three titles it is at once apparent that geographically the selection of names is limited to areas in the Scottish south-east, with a strong preponderance of English names and only little Gaelic influence, although West Lothian does at least convey some of the flavour of Gaelic place-nomenclature. What might at first look like a drawback may, however, suitably be turned into an advantage when it is remembered that our primary concern is to compare the English and Scottish situation from the point of view of early place-name spellings. In this respect, the three dissertations supply excellent basic material, quite apart from the fact that there are not many Scottish county surveys which have collected and set out the early forms in such reliable and systematic fashion (more or less adopting the methods of the publications of the English Place-name Society).

If there is still any doubt as to the general applicability, to Scotland, of the notion that early spellings help us to arrive at a proper etymology for a name when the modern form would have been quite misleading, a small number of examples will suffice to settle this point: Oxton in Berwickshire is, by such forms as *Hulfkeliston* and *Ullfkeliston* 1206 (*c*. 1320) *Kelso Liber* and *Ulkilstoun c*. 1220 (16th) *Dryburgh Liber*, shown to contain the Scandinavian personal name *Ulfkell* and not the word *ox*. Leadburn in Midlothian is not a compound of *lead* and *burn*, as the modern name might suggest, but turns out to contain Gaelic *leac* 'stone' and the personal name *Bernard*, because of such early spellings as *Legbernard c*. 1128 *Holyrood Liber*, *Lekbernarde* 1459 *Register of the Great Seal* (RMS), *Leckbernard* 1653 *Retours*, etc. Similarly Moorfoot MLO is shown to be Old Norse *mor þveit* 'moor place' rather than Old English *mōr fōt*, by a number of spellings contained in *Newbattle Registrum*, like *Morthwait* 1140-53, *Morthwayt* pre-1153, *Morthweth* 1174, *Mortwait* and *Mortwath* 1361, and others. There is therefore no doubt about it that there are many Scottish place-names which, mostly due to a process of full or partial re-interpretation, are superficially misleading when no attention is paid to their historical spellings.

Not quite so common are names which have no meaning whatsoever when only their modern form is taken into account but become meaningful when their earlier spellings are consulted. Again, only a few representative instances can be given in this context: Pinkie MLO makes little sense as it stands but early spellings like *Pontekyn* and *Pontekin*, both pre-1198 *Dunfermline Registrum*, point towards a compound of Welsh *pant* 'valley' and *cyn* 'wedge'. Hiltly WLO allows one or two guesses but only *Hildecliue* 1296 *Instrumenta Publica*, *Hildeclive* 1296 Stevenson, *Documents*, *Hildeclyve* 1226 and *Hildeclife* 1336-7 Bain, *Calendar of Documents* (CDS) permit a satisfactory etymology, such as 'at Hild's cliff'. Heriot MLO may serve as a third example, for only the spelling *Hereget* of 1198 CDS reveals it to be derived from OE *here-geat* which refers to a gap (in the hills) through which an army might pass, although OE *here-geatu* 'wergeld' has also been suggested.

Sometimes an earlier name for the same settlement or geographical feature is revealed. This is perhaps not so much a question of an earlier spelling being more useful than later ones but rather a complete name change which is not apparent from modern evidence alone. The name

Temple MLO, which came into existence when the place to which it was applied became the property of the Knights Templar must have existed side by side with, and later replaced, a Gaelic name *Baile nan Trodach* 'settlement of the warriors' which is evidenced from the *Ballentrodoch* of 1237 *Newbattle Registrum* right into the eighteenth century. In the same county, the parish-name Colinton, recorded as a name since the fourteenth century (*Colbanestoun* 1319 RMS), superseded an earlier *Hala c.* 1150-3 *Dunfermline Registrum*, *Halis* 1329 *Exchequer Rolls* (ER), *Haillis* 1561 *Dunfermline Registrum*, etc. which derives from the plural of OE *halh*, dative *hale* 'nook, haugh'. In Foxhall WLO we have an interesting instance of mis-translation from dialect into Standard English. The earlier forms are *Toddishauch, Todhauch* both 1539 *St Andrews Rentale*, *i.e.* a compound name containing Northern English *tod* 'fox' and Old English *halh* 'corner, angle, flat land beside a river', unless the first element is the personal name *Todd*. *Tod* was replaced by Standard English *fox* and *haugh* was confused with *hall*, roughly from the middle of the eighteenth century onwards.

These three categories of names — and there are other groups — the re-interpreted modern form, the meaningless modern spelling, and the replaced name prove without any shadow of a doubt the value of the collection and examination of early spellings in the Scottish place-names of the region covered by the three theses in question and — we may safely say — of the rest of the country as well. In all these cases, the modern spelling (and frequently also the pronunciation) would have been misleading, to say the least, but in all nine instances there were sufficiently early recorded forms to eke out the evidence. Does this mean that, as in England, records start early enough to be of assistance in the solving of etymological problems? How early are, in fact, the earliest Scottish sources?

Scotland has nothing to compare with England's *Domesday Book* of 1086, that invaluable source of English place-name spellings. There is also nothing to rival the Anglo-Saxon Charters and Rolls of pre-Norman date which on the first page of Ekwall's *Dictionary* produce such early dates as 972 for Abberton, *c.* 730, 811, 931 and 961 for Abington and 855 and 899 for Ablington. On the same page, eight other names (Abberley, Abberton, Abbotsham, Abdon, Abinger, Abney, Abthorpe and Aby) are first recorded in *Domesday Book*, five names (Abbotsbury, Abbotstone and three Abingtons) have early spellings going back to eleventh-century sources other than *Domesday Book*, seven names (Abberwick, Abbotsley, Aberford, Abergavenny, Abinghall, Abram and Abson) are first found in the twelfth century, and two names (Abbotston and Abridge) have their earliest spellings surviving from thirteenth-century sources. This may not be typical of the whole of Ekwall's *Dictionary* but it nevertheless underlines the fact that the earliest recorded Scottish tradition is centuries later than its English equivalent, for neither state documents nor monastic chartularies and registers begin much before the twelfth or, more often, thirteenth centuries, and fourteenth- and fifteenth-century spellings are quite frequently our earliest evidence. This will become clear in the main body of our examples and can therefore be stated here in advance in this summary form.

If the absolute beginning of our written place-name tradition is so much later than in England, does it follow that there is little hope of getting near the truth as far as the derivation of the majority of Scottish place-names is concerned? How early does a spelling have to be to be of value in the elucidation of the morphological and semantic origin of these names?

Again looking for parallel information on that much quoted first page in Ekwall's *Dictionary*, it becomes clear that of the spellings listed only two pre-Domesday ones, three Domesday ones, and two other eleventh-century ones are vital to the proper etymologisation of the names concerned, whereas otherwise four twelfth-century spellings, twelve thirteenth-century ones and one fourteenth-century one suffice to provide an acceptable etymology. In these latter cases, where earlier spellings exist, these are a welcome addition to our knowledge, very often confirming later spellings, but they are not essential. Does this give us new heart for the investigation of the place-names of Scotland where the documentary evidence begins just about the time when these English forms prove so decisive? Two groups of names more closely within the chosen geographical area — those ending in OE *hām* and those in OE *tūn* should provide a more factual picture. The first category is amongst the earliest English names found in Scotland and should therefore help us to throw some light on what might be termed the Scottish equivalent of the English pre-Domesday group of names which according to Cameron is quite numerous. Those ending in *-tūn* cover a much longer period, as some of them might be almost as old as the names in *-hām*, whereas others may have been created as late as the seventeenth century. They should therefore be good material for an assessment of the relativity of the term 'early spelling'.

All the names in *-hām* are in the so-called Border Counties: Berwickshire, Dumfriesshire and Roxburghshire (but not in Selkirkshire). They also occur in East Lothian for which we do not possess any sufficiently detailed study; two of the three oldest English names in Scotland can therefore not be included — Tynninghame and Whittinghame, but the third — Coldingham BWK — is well documented. If the documentation for this name were to go back no further than the thirteenth century, it would still be apparent from the spelling *Goldingeham* in *Scalachronica* that a vowel has dropped out between the particle *-ing-* and our word *hām*. The preceding century would indicate that this vowel was *-a-* for *c.* 1125 the name is recorded as *Coldingaham* in CDS. Coldingham is therefore undoubtedly an *-ingaham-* name, containing the genitive *-inga-* of the plural suffix *-ingas* 'the followers of, etc.'. In the same century, about five years earlier than this entry, MS E of the *Anglo-Saxon Chronicle* mentions for the year 679 the name *Coludesburh*, a parallel formation to our own name. This reference completes the story by furnishing the clue to the authentic form of the first element, which must have been *Colud*, and to the original form of our name **Coludingahām*, 'village of the settlers near *Colud'.* Admittedly the Anglo-Saxon Chronicle draws on earlier material, but nevertheless the written tradition does not have to go any further back than the early twelfth century to provide all the phonological and morphological evidence necessary for an authoritative etymology. It is in fact an unnecessary luxury that previously Coldingham is also mentioned as *Collingaham* at the end of the eleventh century (Lawrie, *Early Scottish Charters*) and in its parallel tradition even goes back to Bede's *Coludi urbem* and *Coludanae urbs* (*c.* 730). These supply confirmatory evidence, no more; otherwise the relevant twelfth-century records are quite sufficient for a satisfactory morphological and semantic solution.

If Coldingham can be assigned to the second or third quarter of the seventh century, the names in simple *-hām*, without the *-ıngā-* particle, were probably not much later. Most of them undoubtedly existed before the eighth century was over. Not one of them, however, is recorded until at least three hundred years later. This group of names is therefore particularly good testing ground for the worth of Scottish place-name documentation. There are ten of them altogether. The first of these, Birgham BWK, for which the modern pronunciation ['bɛːrdʒəm] is attested, is revealed as late as *c.* 1300 *Coldingham Correspondence* through the spelling *Briggeham* as having undergone methathesis (which by the way appears to have started to develop by the middle of the twelfth century, as the spelling *Birgham(e)* 1165 (1434) *Coldstream Chartulary* indicates). The palatalisation of the last consonants of the first element, still preserved in the modern pronunciation, is also apparent — if the spelling means anything — in the form *Bricgham* of 1095-1100 (15th) Lawrie, *Early Scottish Charters* [ESC]: in spite of its interest for the phonological evolution of the name, it is hardly necessary for the establishment of the etymology of the name which must be OE *Brycg-hām*. 'bridge settlement'. Two other forms recorded before the *Briggeham* of the *Coldingham Correspondence* are also not required to establish this etymology although they are fortunately available. Similarly, the late twelfth-century spelling *Hedenham* 1165-1224 (*c.* 1320) *Kelso Liber*, although misleading in its initial consonant, shows Ednam ROX both to be a *-hām*-name and to have been disyllabic in its first element at the time (*Eden-*). A little earlier, *Ednahim* 1165-77 (*c.* 1500) *Melrose Liber* provides a reflex of the inflexional ending of the first element which is clearly the name of the river Eden on which Ednam is situated. This is *Edene* 1178-09 (*c.* 1320) *Kelso Liber*, a spelling which fills a gap in the history of our settlement name, for in the compound of the river-name with *hām* the former never appears in its trisyllabic form but always with either the vowel of the second or the third syllable missing. During the second half of the twelfth century the form the name took must therefore have been something like **Edene-ham*. The written documentation begins at the beginning of the same century and does not really help any further. As far as the etymology and meaning of the name are concerned, no doubt is left by the spellings which have survived. Scottish documentation is in this respect quite satisfactory although no pre-twelfth-century spelling has come down to us. Only if the sound development of the river-name is to be followed up in order to establish the exact form which Ednam may have had when first created in, let us say, the eighth century, a look across the Scottish border to Cumberland and Westmorland becomes necessary where the identical river-name Eden, also recorded as *Edene* in the twelfth century, was fortunately included in Ptolemy's second-century account of Britain as *Itouna* which according to Ekwall 'became **Iduna*, whence OE **Idune* and with *u*-mutation *Iodune, Eodune* and later *Edene*'. It can be assumed with some certainty that the original form of Ednam ROX must have been **Eodune-hām* or **Eodene-hām* but not altogether on the strength of the native Scottish documentation. Semantically close to Ednam is Edrom BWK, for it contains the river-name Adder as its first element, as the thirteenth-century spelling *Hederham*, 1262 *Melrose Chronicle* shows, at the same time establishing *-om* as a reduction of *-ham*. Spellings like *Edirham* and *Ederham* which are available as far back as the last decade of the eleventh century are not helpful any more. Again, one might investigate the history of the pronunciation of the first element further but the derivation of the whole name is clear.

For Kimmerghame (House) BWK, there is the modern pronunciation [ˈkimərdʒəm] which alerts those who know the history of Birgham in the same county. Fourteenth-century documentation in 1332 ER helps to retrace the unassimilated *-b-* in the spelling *Kymbirgame*; two years earlier in the same source the form *Kymbridgeham* preserved the middle element perfectly, and in 1296 CDS the spelling *Kynbriggeham* restores the *-n* of the first syllable. However, only the *Cynebritham* of 1095-1100 ESC provides good enough grounds for postulating an OE *cȳna-brycg-hām* 'village at the cows' bridge' as the original form of the name. If the singular *-britham* of this spelling has any significance, one might, of course, have to look for a completely different origin for the part preceding *-hām*. A hypothetical OE **Cyneberhtinga-hām* 'village of the followers of *Cyneberht*' has been proposed but this seems to be difficult to prove. Kimmerghame is definitely a name for which one would like to have pre-eleventh century evidence to clear up any doubts which might still exist with regard to the proposed etymology. Nevertheless the spellings we have get us very close to the truth, one would imagine. Leitholm BWK only requires the thirteenth-century spellings *Lethame c.* 1230 and *Letham c.* 1200 (1434) *Coldstream Chartulary* and the knowledge that it is situated on the Leet Water to add it to the category of *-hām*-names and to suggest a straightforward meaning 'village on the Leet(Water)'. A spelling identical with the last also occurs in 1165-1214 *Melrose Liber* but does not add anything to our knowledge. For Midlem ROX the fifteenth-century *Myddilham* of 1429 *Historical Mss Commission* (Drumlanrig) is sufficient to indicate the identity of both elements, although earlier forms are available back to *c.* 1120 (*c.* 1320) *Kelso Liber (Middelham)*. The name quite obviously means 'the middle village'. Similarly, the etymology of Oxnam ROX is solved by the *Oxenham* of 1354 *Kelso Liber*. That it is OE *Oxena-hām* 'village of the oxen' is confirmed by the two spellings *Oxeneham* and

Oxanaham of 1152-3 (15th) in the *Whitby Cartulary*. Both Smailholm
ROX and Smallholm DMF share with Leitholm the re-interpretation of
the last element as -*holm*, as the spellings *Smailhame* 1465 *Dryburgh
Liber* for the former and, *Smalehame* 1429-30 RMS for the latter,
demonstrate. For the Roxburghshire name, the *Smalham* of *c.* 1300
Coldingham Correspondence and for the Dumfriesshire one the *Smalham*
of 1374-5 CDS remove all doubt about the first element, and both
names must be interpreted as OE *Smælhām* 'small village'. Any further
proof from earlier spellings is not required. Lastly (Town and Kirk)
Yetholm ROX is exposed as another -*holm* < -*ham* candidate by the
spelling *Yetham* of 1335-6 CDS. This is paralleled in earlier records.
The forms *Yatheam* 1214-43 *Melrose Liber* and *Gatha'n c.* 1050 (12th)
Historia Sancti Cuthberti help to identify the first part as OE *gæt, geat,*
probably in the meaning 'pass' rather than 'gate', but they are not
strictly needed.

As far as our ten names in -*hām* are concerned, it can be claimed with
confidence that the early Scottish spellings which have survived are
quite sufficient to establish convincing etymologies. Although only
Birgham and Kimmerghame preserve the generic element in a clearly
recognisable form, the -*holm* of Leitholm, Smailholm, Smallholm, and
Yetholm, the -*am* of Ednam and Oxnam, the -*em* of Midlem, and the
-*om* of Edrom are quite clearly shown to be of the same origin. With
regard to the specific elements, only Kimmerghame leaves room for
doubt; in the case of Ednam even the trisyllabic form of the river-name
can be reconstructed, and for Oxnam, and probably Kimmerghame,
reflexes of the OE genitive plurals *oxena* and *cȳna* have survived. This
is also true of the *Colinga-* in Coldingham which has the additional
good fortune of having the component preceding -*ing* established as
Colud-, by a parallel tradition. For this early group of English
settlement names in Scotland one can therefore state that the early
Scottish spellings, although in many respects later than those for their
English counterparts, are early enough to permit the establishment of a
satisfactory meaning and an acceptable etymology for each name. It is
undeniable that, mainly for the phonological aspects of the history of
the names, one would like to have even earlier spellings available, but
otherwise a certain amount of optimism is permissible with regard to
the worth of the relevant place-name documentation.

The second category of Scottish place-names to be examined, those
compounded with the basic element -*tūn*, is so numerous that it would
be impossible to deal with all of them in the same detailed fashion as
those in -*hām*. Only selected examples can be investigated but these, it
is hoped, will be adequately representative of the whole group of names
involved. As indicated above, names in -*tūn* (-*ton*) more or less span the
whole period of English-speaking Scotland, some of them being as early
as -*hām*-names, some as late as the seventeenth century; most of them
appear to have been created some time in between these two limits.
The relativity of terms like 'early' and 'late' is therefore more obvious
here than in the previous category because for names coined in the
seventeenth century contemporary seventeenth-century spellings are

naturally *early* enough (as, for example, for these three Dumfriesshire names: McCheynston which is *Makchymstoun* and *Makchynestone* in 1618, indicating the 'farm of the MacCheyne family'; McCubbington, first recorded as *Makcubbeintoun* in 1645 and owned by a family named MacCubbin at the period; and McMurdostown, first mentioned as *Macmurdiestoun* in 1625 when the farm was owned by John MacMurdie; all spellings are from the index to the *Register of Sasines for Dumfries*, etc.), whereas they must be considered almost too late to be valuable for names given in the Early Middle Ages.

Amongst the earliest names in *-tūn* are those containing the element *-ing-*. At least some of them are likely to have existed when *-hām-* names were still being created, and the problems are consequently not dissimilar. Carrington MLO, although recorded in a number of slightly varying spellings (*Caringtoun, Caryntoun, Karingtoun, Keringtone, Keryngtoun*, etc) right back to the early thirteenth, and possibly the late twelfth, century, remains obscure as to the proper form of its first element. A personal name *Cēnhere* has been suggested on the strength of Keresley WAR and Kearsley NTB but their recorded spellings, too, do not begin until approximately the same time as the ones for the Midlothian name and do not allow any convincing conclusion as to the first part which is possibly, but not necessarily, a personal name. An original form *Cēnheringatūn* is therefore strictly hypothetical; the written tradition is simply not good enough. The name Duddingston occurs in both Midlothian and West Lothian. Their chronological sequences of early spellings are almost identical; both have parallel traditions of *-ing-* forms (MLO: *Duddings-, Dudings-, Duddyngs-, Dudyngs-, Dodyngs-, Dodings-* back to 1214-49 *Holyrood Liber*; WLO: *Duddings-, Dudings-, Dodyngs-* back to 1219 *Inchcolm Charters*) and *-in-* forms (MLO: *Duddins-, Dudins-, Duddyns-, Dodyns-, Dodines-* back to 1153-65 *Kelso Liber*; WLO: *Dudins-, Dodins-* back to *c.* 1370-6 *Inchcolm Charters*), as well as a late development of spellings — and pronunciations — without the *-ng-* (MLO: *Duddis-, Dudis-* and *Dedis*, in the sixteenth and seventeenth centuries: WLO: *Duddis-, Dudis-, Diddis-* and *Didis-* in the second half of the sixteenth and in the seventeenth century). In the case of the Midlothian name, the *Du-* spellings go back to 1328 *Holyrood Liber*, whereas *Do-* is found from 1412 back to 1153-65 *Kelso Liber*: similarly the West Lothian name has *Du-* spellings as far back as 1432 *Laing Charters* and *Do-* forms from *c.* 1390 to 1219 *Inchcolm Charters*. The only two twelfth-century spellings available — *villa dodin* 1166-1214 *Holyrood Liber and Dodinestun* 1153-65 *Kelso Liber*, both for the Midlothian name — must weight the evidence heavily in favour of an original *Dodin(g)stūn*, probably without the *-g-*, as the very man who gave his name to Duddingston is mentioned in connection with the last entry as *Dodin de Dodinestun* and also appears in the Latinised genitive *Dodini* in the phrase *villam de Trauerlen* (the old name of Duddingston) *et terram Dodini in Berewyco* 1165-74 *Kelso Liber*. If these early spellings might be overrated in their implication that the *-ing-* forms are secondary in our two names, they appear to establish the *Do-* > *Du-*-sequence with some certainty. Similarly, if the *g*-lessness of the earliest spellings for Edington BWK (*Hadynton* 1095 (15th) ESC, *Edintun* 1165-82 *Melrose Liber*) is ignored, these simply confirm the name as containing a first element *Ead(d)a* or the like which occurs as a personal name in such English identical equivalents as Addington in Berkshire, Kent, Northamptonshire and Surrey. The eleventh- and twelfth-century spellings for these four names are exclusively *g*-less, as in the case of the Scottish name under discussion. For this no early spellings are really required although if they did not exist, the interpretation of its first element might be less certain.

A clear example of an early name in -*ingtun* is Edrington BWK which must be compared with the other Berwickshire name Edrom, analysed above, for both contain the river-name *Adder* as their first element, and are situated on the river of that name. The spelling *Ederington* of 1330 ER establishes the -*e*- of the second syllable of the river-name, and the much earlier *Hadryngton* 1095 ESC provides a glimpse of the sound development of the stem-syllable. The spellings are easily early enough to show Edrington to be 'the *tūn* of the settlers on the river Adder', if such proof were necessary. For Hassington BWK, the sixteenth-century *Hawsintoun* 1516-17 RMS draws attention to the earlier vowel quality of the first syllable, and the fifteenth-century *Halsyngton* 1406 RMS proves -*aw*- to have developed — as expected — from -*al*-. Earlier forms, which do exist, are not any more helpful and rather misleading. The question must therefore be left unanswered whether Hassington contains Old Northumbrian **hals* 'neck' (here probably in its topographic meaning of 'a small valley') or the tribal name *Haelsing(as)*; if the latter, Hassington would, of course, be an extremely important name from a historical point of view, but the evidence is not good enough to confirm this importance. Livingston WLO only needs a correction from -*i*- to -*e*- in the vowel of the first syllable to reveal its etymology. The form *Levingston* occurs as late as 1688 in the *Livingston Kirk Session Records* and from there right back to the Latinised *Uilla Leuing* of 1124-52 *Holyrood Liber*. The Leving in question appears in several charters of the reign of David I; the written tradition therefore goes back to his own lifetime. Mersington BWK is an instance of a name which has practically never changed its spelling since first recorded, and the *Mersington* of 1291 *Instrumenta Publica* does not further the quest for an etymology. The first element may be the same as a conjectured name **Mærsa* for Mersham in Kent (*Merasham* 858, 863; *Meresham* 1086), but although the spelling tradition is so consistent, it does not begin early enough to allow definite proof. A name in the same category is Upsettlington BWK, for a variety of spellings dating back to the last decade of the eleventh century is totally unhelpful, and a possible original form OE **Upp(e) -Setling-tūn* '(upper) farm near the ledge', which none of them completely confirm but also none of them contradict, might as well be based on the modern map form. In contrast, the spelling tradition for Shearington DMF begins so late (*Sherington* 1570 *Calendar of State Papers*) that any equation with Sherington BRK 'the *tūn* of Scīra's people' must remain speculative although well within the realms of possibility. Even more doubtful is

Thirlington BWK for which there seem to be no early forms, and it is questionable whether it contains as its first element the Old English adjective *pyrel* seen in Thirlwall NTB, Thurlbear SOM, Thurlestone DEV and possibly Thirlmere CMB, and forming, of course, also the first part of the Scottish name Thirlestane BWK, SLK 'stone with a hole through it'.

In this group, the percentage of names which cannot be satisfactorily explained on the basis of the evidence we possess or which do not have any early form, is perhaps rather high. With regard to some names, it is not even quite certain whether they are compounded with -*ing*-, although it is very likely that they contain this particle. Much longer, however, is the list of those names which at one time or another appear in spellings containing -*ing*- but seem to have attracted this element by analogy, rather than as part of an organic phonological development. Names of this kind can be grouped under two main sub-headings: (*a*) those which in their present form contain -*ing*-, and (*b*) those which occasionally in their written tradition have -*ing*-forms but do not possess them now. In both cases, the question as to whether they are likely to be original -*ingtūn*- names can undoubtedly only be answered from their early spellings. In a way, these names are one of the best hunting grounds for those who want to demonstrate the necessity for the scrutiny and proper analysis of early name forms, for since -*ing*- has fulfilled so many morphological uses and grammatical functions at all stages in the general history of the English language, and because of the many genuine names in -*ing*, -*ingas*, -*ingatūn*, -*ingahām*, and the like, the forces of analogy have always been particularly strong with regard to the substitution of this particular particle for similar sounding elements. In addition, the dialectal and colloquial change from a velar to an alveolar nasal, [ŋ] > [n] , which produced an opposition of -*in* in non-standard English against the -*ing* in cases of the standard pronunciation, also led to the incorrect restitution of -*ing* in cases where -*in* had not developed from -*ing* in this way. These three factors together produced quite a number of 'false' -*ington*-formations.

The most instructive of these is probably Symington MLO which as late as 1593 RMS reveals its true origin as *Symonstoun* and appears as *Symontoun* from 1584 *Register Privy Council* to 1664 RMS. If it seems surprising that such a well known personal name as *Symon* should have lost its identity and succumbed to the -*ingtoun*-analogy, it is instructive to note that both the Symingtons in Lanarkshire and Ayrshire have exactly the same origin and have shared the same fate of hypercorrect substitution. For all three there are sufficiently early spellings to tell the story. Not dissimilar appears to be Davington DMF but its earliest form *Davitoun* 1652 *Blaeu* is too late to allow the definite conclusion that this is 'Davie's farm'; it is also too late, on the other hand, to permit the claim that the name is identical with Davington KNT which in its twelfth- and thirteenth-century forms is *Dauinton*, *Davynton* and *Davinton*, and on the strength of these is, rightly or wrongly, interpreted as 'the *tūn* of *Dafa's* people', *i.e.* a genuine -*ing*- name. A personal name of Scandinavian origin is involved in Dolphington WLO which has this spelling and the closely related *Dolfing-* of the first element in an uninterrupted tradition back to 1490 *Acts of Council*; a spelling *Dolphingstoun* 1653 *Retours* shows a possessive *-s-*. The disappearance of the *-l-* in pronunciation is signified by *Dauphington* and *Daufingtoun*, both in 1692 in the *Kirk Session Records of Dalmeny*, and the *Doffyntoun* of 1540 *Protocol Book Johnsoun* indicates in addition that the *-ing*-form was not necessarily representative of the local pronunciation, as the source for *Doffyn-* was probably closer to local usage and less indebted to official scribal tradition. The West Lothian name is parallelled by Dolphinston ROX and others. The Roxburghshire example has a *Dolphingston* for 1475 *Historical Mss Commission* (Roxburghe) and a *Dolphington* for 1434 in the same source; the modern name has, however, reverted – as far as its official spelling is concerned – to a more original form, as demonstrated by the *Dolfynston* of 1354 *Kelso Liber* and *Dolfinestoné* 1296 CDS. The personal name involved is quite clearly ME *Dolfin* from ON *Dolgfinnr*, and the *-ing*-forms of both names are spurious.

Another group of names with Scandinavian associations is represented by the two Bonningtons of Midlothian and Bonnytoun of West Lothian. None of them is recorded before the fourteenth century, and although spellings with *-ing-* abound, there are many others in *-y, -i, -ie* and *-yn*, quite apart from *-yngs* and *-igis*, and in the case of the West Lothian name the *-y*-form has, of course, won the day (no doubt at least partly by association or confusion with the Scottish adjective *bonnie*). For the latter name and for one of the Midlothian examples the spellings are early enough to show that *-nn-* derives by assimilation from *-nd-* (*Bondyng-* and *Bonding-* from 1586 *Dunfermline Registrum* back to 1315 *Ms Royal Charters*, and *Bonding-, Bondyng-, Bending-, Bounding-*, all in the fourteenth century, RMS and CDS, respectively). However, whereas the identity of the personal name involved is clear (ON *Bóndi*), the written tradition seems to be too confused to allow a definite decision as to whether this is an *-ingtun*-name, or not.

Other names in this category must be dealt with more briefly: *Clerkington* MLO, although displaying this particular spelling as early as 1444 *Midlothian Charters*, is proved by the earlier series of *Clerkin-, Clerkyn-*, and *Klerkyn-* from 1563-1338 *Newbattle Registrum* to derive from a ME *clerkene tūn* 'farm of the clerics'. It belonged to the monks of Newbattle. *Lemington* ·BWK must have joined the ranks of the *-ington* names at a fairly late stage for in Blaeu's Atlas of 1652 it is still *Lemminden*, and earlier forms like *Lemonkton* 1306 *Melrose Liber*, *Lemontoun c.* 1304 (*c.* 1320) *Kelso Liber*, and *Lematon* 1296 *Instrumenta Publica* show it to have been OE *hleomoc-tūn* 'farm where speedwell grows' (compare Lemington in Northumberland). *Milsington* ROX is *Milsintoun* in 1652 *Blaeu*. The fact that this is apparently the earliest recorded form of the name is not too much of a drawback, as it points to the ON personal name *Mylsan* (from Old Irish **Maelsuithan?*) as a first element which is probably also found in the Yorkshire name Melsonby. The reference in *Blaeu*, of course, is too late to be absolutely conclusive, but it at least establishes Milsington as a non -*ing*-name. For Mordington BWK even a thirteenth-century reference would not have been sufficient to permit a satisfactory interpretation, for in *c.* 1276 *Historical Mss Commission* (Wedderburn) the name is still spelt *Mordingtoun*. Fortunately the last decade of the eleventh century produced at least three different spellings (all in ESC) – *Morthyngton*, *Morthintun*, *Morttringtonan* – and a combination of these makes OE *morð-hring* 'murder ring' (possibly applied to a stone circle) the most likely basis of the first element. As a final example of false -*ington*-formations may serve Morrington DMF which, according to the *Register of Sasines*, was *Morringtoune* in 1671 but *Morreintoun* in 1628. The latter presupposes an owner of the name of *Morin*, a common surname in Galloway. The place-name itself is probably not very much older than its first written record.

There are a few more names like Dolphinston ROX which survived a period of false -*ing*-formation some of these only show a fleeting attraction to this prolific element. Colinton MLO is frequently spelt *Colingtoun* and *Collingtoun* in the sixteenth and seventeenth centuries. The modern form is found as *Colintoun* as far back as 1488 *Acts of Council* and continued to be used in a parallel scribal tradition when the two -*ing*-formations were introduced. The sequence *Colinstoun* 1531 *Register of the Privy Seal* – *Colbyntone* 1506 RMS – *Colbantoun* 1479 *Acts of Lords Auditors* – *Colbanystone* 1406 RMS – *Colbanestoun* 1319 RMS proves the personal name *Colban* to have been the first element; it also illustrates very well the strong points of the better type of written tradition in Scotland. The Dumfriesshire name Dalswinton establishes itself in unbroken tradition back to 1290 CDS, when it is *Dalswynton*, as one of the most interesting names in the Scottish south because the later addition of Gaelic *dail* 'river-meadow' to OE *Swīn-tūn* 'pig-farm' is evidence of an early English and largely pre-Gaelic element in the population of that area. However, even this interesting and etymologically straightforward name is at least even once recorded as *Dalswingtoun* in 1309 Robertson, *Index*. Rowieston (Lodge) BWK makes a seventeenth-century appearance as *Rowingstoune* in 1654 in the *Commissariot Record of Lauder*, but is otherwise *Rowenstoun* in 1652 *Blaeu* and *Rowiston* in 1567 *Kelso Liber*. It is just possible that a family name *Rowan* is involved here but our evidence is not conclusive on this point. The only name which seems to go against this trend and to contradict our argument is Renton BWK. It is *Rennyngton* in 1296 CDS and *Regninton* in *c.* 1100 ESC. If these two forms are taken together, a hypothetical starting-point **Regningatūn* 'the *tūn* of Regna's people' may be assumed which is also suggested for Rainton DRH (*Reiningtone c.* 1170, 1228), Rainton YON (*Reineton, Domesday Book, Rennington* 1202, *Reynington* 1231), and Rennington NTB (*Reiningtun* 1104-8, *Renninton* 1176, *Renigton* 1242). In the last name **Regna* is short for somebody also on record as *Reingualdus* but this does not mean that this also applies to the other three names because other names in *Regn-* are also possible, like *Regengār, Regnhēah, Regnhere*, which are potential first elements in Rainford LNC and Rainham ESX. There is no indication in the early spellings for any of these names, which longer name is represented by *Regna* but this is not too worrying as it is practically certain that only the short form was used in the naming of the places concerned. Apart from Rennington N TB, all the place-names listed seem to have moved away from the -*ing*-form at an early stage, and the usefulness of early spellings is well demonstrated here. It is in a way gratifying to see that the form *Regninton* of 1100 for the Scottish Renton preserves the original shape of the personal name best.

Despite certain disappointments, then, the Scottish written tradition seems to be not at all unsatisfactory in the elucidation of the specific problems arising out of place-names in -*ingtūn*. How does it fare, however, with regard to another question that is continually troubling investigators of names in -*tūn*: the ambiguity of the last element when preceded by an -*s*-? This problem becomes acute whenever the first part is a personal name in the possessive case, and there are at least eighty examples of the combination personal name + *s* + *tūn* in the area covered by the three theses which form the basis of this investigation. Of these, eight (or 10 per cent) have a final -*stone* in their modern spelling and are only revealed as -*tūn*-names by a series of earlier spellings: Alderstone M LO is shown by spellings like *Awdenstoun* 1535 RMS and *Awdinstoun* 1586 *Proceedings Calder Baronial Court* to belong to the -*tūn*-category. Edmonstone M LO is well documented and from the seventeenth to the thirteenth century has spellings which prove that the last element is *tūn*: *Edmiestoun* 1557-85 *Dunfermline Registrum, Eadmundstona* 1338 *Newbattle Registrum,* and *Edmundistune* 1253 *Dunfermline Registrum* are three of these. Groundistone R O X is *Groundestoun* in 1535 *Register of the Privy Seal*; Howatstone M LO is *Howitstoun* in the *Kirk Session Records* for the parish of Midcalder for 1698; Johnstone D MF is *Jonistune* 1194-1214 *Historical Mss Commission* (Drumlanrig), and Malcomstone M LO is *Malcolmstoun* 1538 RMS. In all these cases there are − often numerous − other spellings to corroborate the evidence of the samples quoted. For Philpingstone W LO the *Philpenstoun* of 1643 RMS is sufficient evidence to dispel any doubts about the last element, and Watherstone M LO and Waterstone W LO are clarified as to their etymology by such spellings as *Watterstoun* 1643 RMS and *Waterstoune* 1670 *Kirk Session Records* (Ecclesmachan) respectively. Both are, of course, 'Walter's farm'.

Brotherstone B W K and Brotherstone M LO, on the other hand, can easily be shown to be straightforward -*stone*-names, because both of them have early spellings in Scots -*stanes, -stanis, -stanys,* and -*stane* throughout. Similarly, Loanstone M LO is Lonestane in 1614 RMS, but Flotterstone in the same county is unrecorded and, although a minor name, leaves at least a doubt in one's mind.

Names in modern -*stane* are usually unambiguous, like Bore Stane M LO, Caiystane M LO, Ericstane D MF, and Kellerstain M LO. Sometimes the fact that they are names of stones rather than of settlements is important corroborative evidence. Even in this group, however, there are exceptions, and if it were not for the earlier written evidence, names like Brunstane and Rowlestane would certainly be interpreted incorrectly. Brunstane MLO, a transplanted name, is *Brunstoun* in 1654 *Laing Charters*, and the other Brunstane in the same county is *Brunstoun* about the same time in 1655 RMS. For Rowlestane BWK the spelling Rollandstoune of 1451-2 RMS gives a clue as to the nature of both the first and the second elements. For several other names their earlier forms reveal that the confusion with *stone* (or *stane*) did take place at one time or another but did not lead to a complete replacement of elements. Some of these may serve as illustrative examples: Usually confusion may arise with the standard form *stone* as in *Dolfinestone* 1296 CDS for Dolphinston ROX, *Hawcarstone* 1453 *Laing Charters* for Halkerston MLO, and *Levingstone* 1301-2 CDS for Livingston WLO. However, two examples of *-stane* for *-stoun* occur. One is not surprisingly a third Brunston in Midlothian which is *Brunstane* in the eighteenth-century *Memoirs of Sir John Clerk of Penicuik.* The other is Edgerston in Roxburghshire which occurs in Blaeu's Atlas (1652) as *Egyrstain.*

If early spellings are of notable assistance in resolving such ambiguous alternatives, as to whether a name contains the element *-ing* or not, or whether the generic element is OE *tūn* or *stān*, they are, of course, of even greater importance in the interpretation of specific elements, especially of the proper forms of the personal names involved; these are some of the more striking examples: For Arniston MLO, the *Arnetstoun* of 1609 RMS establishes the dental consonant in the second syllable, *Arnaldstoun* 1507 *Laing Charters* reveals an earlier *-ld-*, and *Arnoldstoun* 1449 *Midlothian Charters* shows us that this *-ld-* was originally preceded by an *-o-* and that the name means 'Arnold's farm'. Dingleton ROX is still *Danyeltone* in 1682 *Melrose Regality Records* and produces the possessive *-s-* in the *Danyellyston* of 1359 ER and similar forms. It is, of course, 'Daniel's farm'. Although the *-s-* of the first syllable is not preserved, the *Ileffeston* of 1329-71 *Melrose Liber* and other spellings for Elliston ROX get us quite close to the personal name *Isleifr* involved. This may, of course, have developed into **Ill-leif* by this time so that a preserved *-s-* would have been anachronistic. Curious, in this respect, is the juxtaposition 'Johannes filius Yliff de Ylistoun' which is recorded c. 1220 *Dryburgh Liber.* Identical with Elliston is Illieston WLO which also has its *-f-* preserved in such spellings as *Illefston* 1335-6 CDS and *Ilvestune c.* 1200 *Historical Mss Commission.* For Hermiston ROX, the *Hirdmanstone* of 1305 CDS is sufficient to point to OE *hiordemann* 'herdsman' as the first element. Other earlier forms are simply confirmatory. Similarly Hermiston MLO has a number of spellings *Hirdmanstoun* and *Hirdmanestoun* from 1488 *Acts of Council* back to 1214-26 *Morton Registrum* to uncover its identical origin. The *Hirdmastoun* of 1494 *Acts of Council* demonstrates that the *-n-* of the second syllable disappeared before the *-d-* of the first. The Berwickshire Lyleston has a sufficiently good thirteenth-century tradition to enable us to establish the original bi-syllabic nature of *Lyle-* in the *Liolleston* of 1296 *Instrumenta Publica*, while the fact that *-oll-* derives from *-olf-* becomes apparent in the spelling *Liolftoun* of *c.* 1222 *Dryburgh Liber.* The personal name involved is presumably ON **Ligulfr*, a name which appears in twelfth-century charters as *Ligulf, Lyulf,* and *Liulfo.* Our place-name evidence is very close to that tradition. Oxton BWK has already been referred to; it is not at all unlike Falkirk in so far as it is probably the most spectacularly convincing of all examples one can quote from the area for the necessity to take full account of early spellings when attempting to interpret and etymologise place-names. The very misleading modern form Oxton is exposed by the *Uxtoun* of 1652 *Blaeu.* Two hundred years earlier, the first part had still consisted of two syllables as shown by the spelling *Ugistoun* of 1463-4 RMS. That the first syllable of this element that contained an -*l*- becomes clear from the *Ulkestoun* of 1273 *Dryburgh Liber,* and the same source shows that an -*l*- had also been part of the second syllable because it has *Ulkilstoun* about 1220, in a sixteenth-century copy. The true nature of the first element is finally brought to light by the spellings *Hulfkeliston* and *Ullfkeliston* of 1206 (*c.* 1320) *Kelso Liber*; it must have been the Scandinavian personal name *Ulfkell.* It is not often, of course, that one gets such an unbroken recorded sequence like this (*Ox-<Ux-<Ugis-<Ulkes-<Ulkils-< Ullfkelis-*), but when it does occur it is very satisfying. Compared with Oxton, the documentary evidence for Ulston ROX is probably rather tame but it is nevertheless also very reassuring to know that the twelfth-century forms *Ulvestona* 1165-1214 *National Mss of Scotland* and *Ulvestoun* 1147-52 ESC confirm the personal name involved to have been ME *Ulf*<ON *Ulfr*, a conclusion which otherwise one could only have reached by the consideration of analogical material elsewhere.

What conclusions can be reached on the basis of the material presented (and represented)? Is it possible to dispel the doubts raised at the outset about the value and competence of the available written tradition of Scottish place-names or does the evidence reinforce the opinion sometimes voiced that most of it is too 'late' to be really useful in search for etymologies and meanings? A thorough study of the problem appears to permit the following claims. Although Scotland lacks such sources as the Anglo-Saxon Charters and Rolls of pre-Norman days, as well as the extensive eleventh-century coverage provided by *Domesday Book,* otherwise the onset of the written tradition does not differ greatly in England and Scotland. Judging by the English evidence, however, pre-Norman documentation does not add greatly to the materials required for a satisfactory explanation of the semantic origin of the name. It is, however, of great value in tracing the detailed sound development from the times a name was coined to the present day. This, of course, only applies to pre-Norman names because for later periods — at least as far as the area covered by the three theses is concerned — early spellings are just as plentiful in Scotland as in England. Difficulties about the etymology arise only when a name dating back to pre-Norman times does not have any twelfth- or at least thirteenth-century documentation although even this is superfluous or merely confirmatory in quite a number of instances. Obviously the written tradition is much better in the region under discussion than in other parts of Scotland where an obscuring process involving the anglicisation of Gaelic names is parallelled by rather poor document- ation, quite apart from the complex linguistic mixture of the nomencl- ature owing to the fairly rapid succession of languages, as for example in counties like Fife, Angus and Kincardineshire. Similarly, the gaelicised versions of Norse names in the Hebrides and elsewhere have hardly any early documentary backing whatsoever, but just as England has in the course of our argument, from time to time furnished guidance with regard to early English names in Scotland, so Norway, and sometimes also Iceland, provides excellent comparative material to make up for the lack of early spellings.

As regards the relative value of terms like 'early' and 'late' when applied to toponymic documentation, a spelling may be called 'early' when it is close to the date at which a name is likely to have originated. 'Lateness', on the other hand, is implied when no documentation is available within centuries after the creation of the name. This does not mean that 'early' spellings are necessarily better than 'later' ones, but as a general rule chronological 'lateness' also means deterioration in the absolute value of a spelling. This point is proved particularly by names for which early spellings exist which are contemporary with the creation of a name.

It would, of course, have been more persuasive to see this investigation based on a wider geographical area than the one covered by the three theses but, apart from Aberdeenshire, no comparable evidence is readily available from any other part of Scotland. It might also have been more preferable to use a more systematic approach linked with tabular summ- aries and statistics rather than the impressionistic results obtained from the presentation of selected evidence. Nevertheless, the name material under discussion has doubtlessly shown that, when handled with adequate knowledge and caution, Scottish place-name documentation can supply the answers to the majority of etymological quests, even if pre-Norman spellings are largely lacking. When treated in combination with the modern pronunciation and the relevant comparative material from outside Scotland, this documentation is assigned its rightful place in the study of Scottish place-names; and, when all has been said and done, the dictum, with which this chapter began, still stands that in the interpretation of a Scottish place-name 'all early spellings in written documents, both printed and manuscript, should be collected and used as a basis for an analysis of its sound development, formation and meaning'.

The practical application of this essential realisation for our immediate purposes is twofold: (1) Wherever possible, relevant early spellings will be provided in the remainder of this volume, so that the reader may form his own opinion as to the validity of the etymological argument advanced; and (2) when such evidence is not mentioned, as in the frequently very extensive lists of names connected with some of the denser distribution maps, it can be assumed that the necessary research in this respect has been done to the best of this writer's ability. At no point will material be used or introduced without the basic desideratum of reliable etymological investigation, central to the establishment of lexical meaning. That there are degrees of success in such an undertaking, is understandable, with corresponding distortions occurring here and there, but in no instance will there be deliberate or careless falsification of the evidence through neglect of our own basic rules.

3
Distribution in Time and Space

The reader who has survived the first two, admittedly rather closely argued, chapters will, or at least should, be aware of one overriding and all-important fact: place-names do not exist in isolation. Individual names can therefore hardly ever be interpreted successfully on their own and for their own sake. Located where they are, they have horizontal links with other place-names — identical, similar or different — and created at a particular point in time, they have vertical links as part of a continuously changing linguistic evolution in that part of the country in which they have their being. Sometimes such development is locally restricted, often it affects larger regions and, in some cases, the whole of the country. Because they have, thus, distribution in both space and time, i.e., geographical scatter plus linguistic stratification, place-names have come to be recognised as valuable raw material for the study of settlement history or, as one should perhaps rather say, of the settlement history of speakers of various languages. The name Hawick has served as a good example of a name which has survived from an earlier phase of the language still spoken in Scotland today, and the name Melrose as an illustration of an onomastic survival from a now extinct pre-English Celtic stratum, whereas the name Falkirk was proof of various linguistic influences at different times — Cumbric (=British), Gaelic and English. These examples are obvious and unambiguous, serving their purpose well. The chronological sequence of their documentation and the fact that Cumbric is known to have been extinct in both the Melrose and Falkirk areas for many centuries, while there are no longer any local native speakers of Gaelic left around Falkirk, makes the outlining of sequential strata fairly easy, i.e. in addition to the toponymic evidence extra-onomastic factors provide us with information the names themselves cannot furnish; for, if there is one drawback, it is that they hardly ever provide reliable absolute dating evidence. Apart from a few exceptions, the absolute historical or pre-historical framework, in which place-name evidence may be usefully placed, has to come from elsewhere, especially from documentary history and prehistoric archaeology. This is a fact which must be borne in mind when the interpretation or significance of particular place-name distributions is considered, for it is obviously of

the utmost importance to give names more than just the vaguest
relative position in a distributional pattern, whether in time or space.
In this respect it is almost always less difficult to handle the sequence
of two different languages rather than chronological strata within the
same language, since it is easier to distinguish two completely different
linguistic systems than structural differences within the same language.
Many of the latter are so slight as to be almost undiscernible, especially
when they only concern, for instance, first elements in compound
names.

A good example of this kind of problem is furnished by the group of
southern Scottish names already alluded to in the last chapter, i.e.
names ending in OE *tūn* 'an enclosure, a farmyard, an estate, a village',
but in this case without the connecting particle *-ing-*. This is a generic
element which refuses to be ascribed to a particular period because it
remained productive toponymically from soon after the earliest settlements (overlapping with the later phase of the *hām*-names presumably)
till at least the seventeenth century, and it is, of course, still alive,
as an appellative, in certain Scottish dialects as *toon* in the sense of
'farm', as well as in Standard English *town*. Due to this long period of
productivity it is, in the southern part of the country, the most common
place-name element in Anglian and later English settlement names,
especially of individually owned farms and estates, as the large number
of personal names as explanatory elements shows.

Because of their proliferation it is, of course, important to fit
tūn-names into the chronological picture, even though the element
itself simply does not allow any such conclusion, and we have to rely
on other criteria. It appears, however, that there are four, or maybe
five, ways in which such an analysis might be approached. The first
three of these are non-linguistic and concern (*a*) the date when a
particular name was first recorded, (*b*) the geographical situation, and
(*c*) the present status of the place to which a given name applies. The
fourth, and this is undoubtedly the most important and the most
promising, examines the first element, and the fifth is really a
combination of the first and fourth because it asks whether any of the
personal names used as first elements can be identified with known
persons.

It has already been established that written documentation before
the twelfth century is extremely rare, and even then the flow of
information is very slow and very sporadic indeed. Many of the names
in question are, in fact, not mentioned before the thirteenth, fourteenth,
fifteenth or even sixteenth centuries, and in the absence of any other
historical documentation, this is a severe handicap, especially as the
fact that Saughton MLO is on record as *Salectuna* about 1128, that
Plumdon DMF is *Plunton* in 1210-12, that Rowlestane BWK first
occurs as *Rollandston* in 1390, that Middleton MLO is not recorded
till 1449 (as *Middiltoun*) and that the Dumfriesshire Fenton is *Fentoun*
in 1583-84, does by no means indicate in itself that the names concerned
were created in the twelfth, thirteenth, fourteenth, fifteenth and
sixteenth centuries, respectively. They may have been but it is not

likely, and the most these dates can furnish are valuable *termini ante quem* – how much *ante* is another question, and one that says nothing about the especially intriguing and interesting Dark Age period between the arrival of the Angles in the seventh century and that of the Normans in the twelfth. In 1128, *Salectuna* 'willow farm' may have been just founded, may have been ten, or 100 or even 200, 300 or 400 years old. Nevertheless the date of the earliest documentation is, of course, important and not as arbitary and irrelevant as may seem at a first glance.

As far as the geographical situation of named places is concerned, it is quite obvious in the case of earlier names ending in *-ingahām*, *-hām*, *-ingtūn*, *-worð*, and *-bōtl* that these early Anglian settlements occupy some of the best sites in an area which itself was well within what one would normally expect to be that part of Scotland where Anglian settlers pushing northwards from Northumberland would first settle. It is therefore natural to assume that names in *-tūn* which are found in the same area as these early elements, on similarly advantageous sites, are possible candidates for the earliest phase of *tūn*-names whereas names on poorer sites and outside this area – or both – are probably later.

Here the third criterion, the relative status of the modern place name might also help to say something about its age, although one cannot lay down any hard and fast rules. A parish name is certainly more important than a village name, and the latter has a higher status than a mere farm name, and even this may be regarded as superior to a name which has been 'lost' altogether. However, status is by no means a sure criterion and must be used with caution.

Of prime importance in this context is the nature of the first element; this is the only valid *linguistic* criterion although onomastics is not mere linguistics but much more. If, in fact, it is possible to establish a relative chronological order of the first elements, the delineation of strata within a given stratum is comparatively easy. In Scotland, as in England, this is especially fruitful in those instances in which the first part of the compound is a personal name, for it seems to be reasonable to assume that monothematic names like the strong form **Pæc(c)* of an Old English personal name *Pac(c)a*, as in Paxton BWK (*Paxtun* 1095-1100), or *Sprow*, as in Sprouston ROX (*Sprostona* c. 1120), are earlier than dithematic names like *Eadred* in *Adderston ROX (*Edristona* 1271), *Ecghere* in Edgerston ROX (*Edgerstoun* 1541), *Regenwald* in Rennieston ROX (*Rainaldeston* 1296), *Aldwine* in Addiston BWK (*Auldenestun* 1165-77) and Alderstone MLO (*Aldins toun* 1452), or *Eadmund* in Edmonstone MLO (*Edmundston* 1248). The two groups of place-names in *-tūn* containing these respective personal names should therefore also be placed in chronological order (always allowing for a certain overlap, of course). Pre-English Celtic personal names may also point to a certain antiquity of the names concerned, especially if the place-names in which they occur are found at some distance from the Cumbric kingdom of Strathclyde which must have survived for a number of centuries after the Angles first reached

Scotland. Putton BWK may be a case in point. It is *Pewtoun* in 1496 and *Putoun* in 1547 and may contain Celtic *Pŭh*. Pumpherston MLO (*Poumfrayston* in 1421) is 'Pumphrey's farm' from the Middle Welsh *ap Hwmfre* 'son of Humphrey', and Merchiston in the same county (*Merchinston* 1264-66) has the Old Welsh personal name *Merchiaun/ Merchion* as its first element.

Gaelic personal names in *tūn*-names are most likely to be associated with a temporary Gaelic overlordship over the area, roughly from the second half of the tenth to the twelfth century, with names like Makerstoun ROX (*Malcarvastun* 1159) containing a Gaelic *Maelcarf* < **Maglo-carvas*, Maxton in the same county (*Mackistun* 1187-9), *Mackustun c.* 1226) pointing to a personal name *Maccus*, Comiston in the Edinburgh area (*Colmanstone* 1336-37) with *Colman* <Gaelic *Colmán* < *Columba*, and Gilmerton, not far away, showing in its early form *Gillemuristona* 1166-1214 that it contains the name *Gille Moire* 'Mary's servant'.

Scandinavian personal names also occur with our element, such as *Dolgfinnr* in the four different Dolphinston (ROX: *Dolfinestone* 1296), *Isleifr* in Elliston ROX (*Ylistoun c.* 1220, *Ilivestun* 1214-49), *Ulfr* in Ulston ROX (*Ulvestoun 1147-52*), and *Sveinn* in Swanston MLO (*Swaynystoun* 1214-40). Most of these are probably not much older than their first recorded form. As these are to be discussed in detail separately below, it is only necessary to point out at this stage that these and others not listed here are not indicative of any large-scale Scandinavian settlement in the region, but only imply individual ownership by people with Scandinavian names. The persons concerned may not even have been Scandinavians themselves because most of the personal names in this category appear to have been fashionable among non-Scandinavians in northern England also. If this is borne in mind, they are nevertheless valuable pointers to a relative chronology of our *tūn*-names in southern Scotland.

Even later must be names in which *tūn* is compounded with names of Norman owners, and it is significant, although by no means surprising, that the very first name in this group is not mentioned till the second half of the twelfth century (*Gocelynton* MLO, now 'lost') and that most of them do not appear on record till centuries later. Names of this kind would not have been possible in Scotland before the first half of the twelfth century and even then they would be rare. Dingleton ROX (*Danyelstona* 1343), Samieston in the same county (*Semanstoun* 1452, *Simalstoun* 1471, *Sammelstoun* 1489) 'Samuel's farm', and Watherstone MLO (Walterstoun 1593) are cases in point.

Fairly near the end of the line must be such Dumfriesshire names as Demperston(*Dempstertoun* 1652), McCheynston (*Makchymstoun* 1618), McCubbington (*Makcubbeintoun* 1645), and McMurdostoun (*Macmurdiestoun* 1625) all of which are associated with, or even owned by families or individuals bearing the names concerned at this particular period, the seventeenth century.

When it comes to non-anthroponymic first elements, however, the story is much less clear. It is presumably permissible to say that names like Hutton BWK (*Hotun* 1095-1100) < OE *hōh-tūn* 'hill-farm' (also Hutton DMF, *Hotune* 1210-12), Merton BWK (*Myrtona* 1221, *Mertun* thirteenth century) and Morton MLO (*Mertun* 1264-66) < OE *mere-tūn* 'lake-farm', and Straiton MLO (*Stratun* twelfth century) 'farm on the (Roman) road' are comparatively early, although this cannot be argued with the same confidence as the relative antiquity of names like Sprouston and Paxton. And what about Fulton ROX (*Fougheltone, Foultone* 1296) < OE *fugol-tūn* 'bird-farm', Reston BWK (*Ristun* 1095-1100) < OE *hrīs-tūn* 'farm by the brushwood', Milton DMF (*Mylnton* 1550) < OE *mylentūn* 'mill-farm', and Cranston MLO (*Cranestoun* 1153-65) 'crane's farm'? Unless we know that a word involved became obsolete as an appellative in the living language at a certain stage — a very difficult thing to establish as frequently the place-name may be the only evidence that the word was still alive when the name was coined — only extra-linguistic criteria can help here, like the date of the first record, the geographical situation, the present status, etc.; there is, unfortunately, a very large group of these names which would depend on such assistance from external sources of information.

In contrast to these stands that class of names for which the combination of the first and fourth criteria make a cast-iron and irrefutable argument, that group in which the person whose name forms the first element, can be identified as a historical person. In connection with Elliston ROX we know that 'Johannes filius Yliff de Ylistoun' granted land to Dryburgh in 1220; in Berwickshire, Swein, son of Ulfkill, was witness to a charter in which King Edgar granted Swinton to the monks of St Cuthbert about 1100; and between 1153 and 1159 Wicius of Wiceston, now Wiston LAN, gave the church of the place to the monks of Kelso. There are others, although these are just about the earliest who can be definitely identified.

This last category stands, of course, by itself, and normally we have to rely on one or more of the other criteria, mainly the linguistic one but by no means neglecting the other three. At the beginning of the scale would probably be a name like Sprouston to which all criteria ascribe relative earliness: it is mentioned at the beginning of the twelfth century (which is, as we know, early for Scotland), has a good situation in the Tweed valley not far from Kelso, is not only a village but also a parish name today, and, last but not least, contains a monothematic Old English personal name. In comparison, Roberton, although in the same county and also a parish name today, has a much less favourable situation on a tributary (Borthwick Water) of a tributary (River Teviot) of the Tweed and furthermore has as its first element an Anglo-Norman personal name. The Robertons in Lanarkshire and Ayrshire would be subject to the same chronological limitation by the personal name and lie outside the probable early settlement area of the Angles. For most names, however, our information is much more limited.

Fortunately, the stratification of *tūn*-names is probably one of the most intractable problems we are likely to come across in this respect and the degree of difficulty and of delicacy of division encountered with regard to this generic should not discourage anybody. It should, on the other hand, also be remembered that even at this advanced stage of onomastic research in Scotland we do not yet have the means, and perhaps not the evidence either, of solving all problems to our complete satisfaction, not within the rigorous methodological limits of systematic research, anyhow. Here are challenges galore for future generations of name scholars.

If *tūn*-names are representative of settlement names in which the generic term remains constant while the qualifying first element undergoes a number of interpretable changes, a much more usual approach to the isolation of strata within the stratum would be the separation of name-types containing different generic elements. English (or Anglian) names ending in *-ingahām, -hām, -ingtūn, -worð,* and *bōtl* have already been claimed to be on the whole earlier than names in *-tūn.* Similarly, in other linguistic strata of Scottish toponymy — Scandinavian, Gaelic, Cumbric, and perhaps even Pictish — internal sequences can be worked out on the basis of the ascription of different generic terms to different periods, with considerable times of overlap, of course. The breaking up of continuous linguistic change is awkward at best, well-nigh impossible at worst, but must nevertheless be attempted, especially when chronological stratification and geographical distribution are always so closely linked in the case of place-names. Scotland as a whole may have fairly well-defined boundaries mainly indicated by its coastline but even these do not exclude from our consideration everything that lies beyond the seas. For the elucidation of Scandinavian names in Scotland, Norway or Iceland may have something to offer, the interpretation of Gaelic names may benefit from the Irish evidence, for material of value in the examination of Pictish names we may even cross the English Channel to the Continent, and English and Cumbric names are likely to have their counterparts south of a border which, after all, did not exist when many of these names were coined. In a country like Scotland, with a long history of linguistic immigration, it is not only what the immigrants brought with them that is important but also what they left behind at their point of departure or what they dropped on the way.

Of all the many possible examples from these languages, one generic will at this stage have to suffice to make our point, Gaelic *sliabh,* 'a mountain'. This has been said to be common in Ireland but very rare in that sense in Scotland. If such a claim has substance, one wants to know, for instance, where this element *sliabh* occurs in Scottish place-names. Does it turn up sporadically all over those areas of Scotland in which other Gaelic place-names are to be found in plenty; or has it a limited distribution? Is there anything in its geographical distribution which allows us to assign it a definite place in the relative chronology of Gaelic place-names in Scotland? Which word, or words, have replaced it in the regions in which it does not occur, and what other meanings does it have, in addition to 'mountain'? Is it still alive in present-day Scottish dialects, and if so, where and in what meaning?

The question of geographical distribution and its implications for the related chronological problems is worth pursuing above all. Does *sliabh* occur in Galloway, for example, the most southwesterly part of Scotland separated from Ireland by a narrow stretch of water? Sir Herbert Maxwell's *Studies in the Topography of Galloway* (1887) and his later *Place Names of Galloway* (1930) contain a list of about three dozen names which apparently contain *sliabh* as a first element. In the great majority of them it takes the written form *Slew-*, and Maxwell's geographical references – with three possible exceptions, the names concerned are all said to be in the parishes of Kirkcolm, Leswalt, Portpatrick, Stoneykirk and Kirkmaiden – make it quite clear that their distribution is practically, although not totally, limited to the most westerly part of Galloway, the *Rinns* peninsula. Maxwell consistently translates *Slew-* (< *sliabh*) as 'moor' but does not give any other indication of the nature of the features to which the names in question apply. Relevant Ordnance Survey sources supply additional names as well as data with regard to the exact position, a description of the feature concerned, alternative spellings, etc.

Thus Ordnance Survey name-book descriptions of the geographical features, to which the names apply, show that, with two exceptions, all *Slew-* names are hill-names. Only *Slewgulie* and *Slew-whan* are points of rock on the coast. Whether they were named from hills nearby or whether some other etymology should be considered for the first element is difficult to say. As far as all the other names are concerned, they are descriptive of hills varying in height between 150 and 838 feet, mostly between 200 and 400 feet (other common words for the same type of feature in the Rinns are *Knock-* < Gaelic *cnoc*, and *Hill,* the latter frequently added pleonastically to names containing *Slew-* or *Knock-*). The shape of the hill does not seem to have determined whether it could be called a *Slew-* or not; more or less any elevation might have been referred to in this way. It is noteworthy that only two of the 'uncertain' examples bear the epithet 'heathy' whereas many of them are expressly stated to have *arable* soil.

There is therefore scarcely any doubt that *Slew-* means 'hill' rather than 'moor' in the Rinns of Galloway, although some of the features so designated may be moorland elevations. It is also hardly necessary to prove that *Slew-* does in fact represent *sliabh*, as implied above. The nearest modern relative in both spelling and pronunciation appears to be Manx *slieau* [Sl' u:] 'mountain' as in *Slieau Chiarn, Slieau Ruy, Slieau lhean, Slieau veg, Slieau Whallian, Slieau Doo, Slieau Freoaghane, Slieau Curn, Slieau Karrin, Slieau Managh, Slieau Ouyr, Slieau Volley.* At least Manx *Slieau lhean* and *Slieau Karrin* have identical equivalents in the Galloway names *Slewlan* and *Slewcairn.* Presumably the background to both sets of names is similar and in this connection it is of interest to note that the Manx Manorial Roll has *Slew whellin* for *Slieau Whallian, Slewvolly* for *Slieau Volley,* and *Slew oure* for *Slieau Ouyr* in 1703, as well as *Slewmanagh* for *Slieau Managh* in 1643. These are in all probability Anglicised spellings which occur at a time when the linguistic Anglicisation was also just about complete in Galloway.

Only in one of the three dozen or so Galloway instances do we seem to get a glimpse of a potentially earlier form, i.e. in the alternative spelling *Sleivemein* for *Slewmeen*. On the surface this is much closer to the Irish material than the rest of our examples, for *Slew-* is not at all evident on modern or recent Irish maps where *Slieve* is the normal Anglicised spelling. That this has not always been so, however, is shown by some sixteenth- and seventeenth-century documents. One only has to glance through the *Topographical Index of the Parishes and Townlands of Ireland in Sir William Petty's Mss Barony Maps* (*c.* 1655-9) and *Hiberniae Delineatio* (*c.* 1672) to become aware of this. Amongst the townlands in both these sources we find such spellings as *Slewbog, Slewcorka, Slew(c)ulter, Slewduffe, Slewena, Slewgole, Slewmon, Slewmore* and many others. In cases where the two sources differ, the Barony Maps have the *Slew-*form, the *Hiberniae Delineatio* something else, as in *Slewfellinie/Sleaufelline, Slewnaman/Sleaucanaman, Slewnamuck/Sleavenamuck, Slewvaneur/Sleiuanever, Slewroe/Sleroagh,* and *Slewgullen/Slugullin*. If one wants to determine the phonetic value of *Slew-* in these documents, a certain ambiguity must remain unresolved, for both *Sleave-* and *Slu-* (apart from some others) appear as alternative spellings. In cases for which we have diachronic documentation, *Slew-* seems to have persisted until the seventeenth century anyhow; cf. *Church Mountain* (Wicklow) which is *Slewecod* in 1590, *Slewcod* in 1596, *Slewgod* in 1610, *Slewcod* in 1613, but *Slievegad* in 1760. The complete disappearance of *Slew-* may, on the other hand, be at least partly due to the standardising influence of the Ordnance Survey in the past century. A more detailed discussion of the Irish material would be out of order here, but from the evidence collected by the Survey of Irish Dialects it would appear that, if the map-spellings *Slew-* and *Slieve-* have any significance at all, a form more appropriate to Munster and Connaught has replaced one more suitable for more northern Irish dialects. It would also suggest that the affinities of Galloway *Slew-* are not with the Isle of Man alone but also with parts of the Irish north. In any case, there is no doubt that our Galloway evidence is convincingly paralleled in Ireland in the records of the sixteenth and seventeenth centuries.

As far as Scottish Gaelic is concerned, the published studies cover the various dialects only sporadically. Some of them do not contain the word *sliabh* at all, either because the word is not known or because it (or its nominative singular) does not happen to have been part of the recorded texts. On the basis of whatever published accounts we do have and of the collections of the Gaelic section of the Linguistic Survey of Scotland, we might, however, conclude that, as far as the pronunciation of *-iabh* is concerned, the dialect association appears to be much closer with Man and the northern parts of Ireland than with the surviving dialects of the Scottish *Gaidhealtachd*. This may potentially imply an ancient connection, but it could also simply be the result of geographical proximity.

With regard to individual etymologies, the range is from the easily discernible to the utterly obscure. The three *Slewfads* obviously contain the Gaelic adjective *fada* 'long', and the four *Slewdowns* the colour adjective *donn* 'brown' (despite the 'Fort hill' on the Royal Engineers'

Map of 1819 which apparently equated -*down* with Gaelic *dun*). The second element in *Slewlea* is another colour adjective, Gaelic *liath* 'grey', and *Slewlan* is probably an anglicisation of *Sliabh Leathann* 'broad hill'; whereas *Slewmeen* is most likely *Sliabh Mìn* 'smooth, or level, hill'. If *Slewmuck* is *Sliabh (na) Muice* 'hill of (the) pig' or *Sliabh (nam) Muc* 'hill of (the) pigs' (cf. Irish *Slievenamuck*), then *Slewhabble* is almost certainly *Sliabh a' Chapuill* 'mare, or colt, hill'. The unidentified *Slewcairn* must contain a form of Gaelic *carn* 'cairn', possibly the genitive plural, and for the second element of *Slamonia* one might think of *mòine* 'moss, bog' or its derivative *mòineach* 'mossy, boggy' (cf. *Slewmon* in Ireland). *Slewdonan* will have to be linked with *Kildonan* = Gaelic *Cill Donnain* 'Donnan's church', whereas *Slewbarn* probably derives from Gaelic *bearn* 'breach, gap'. *Slewcreen* could be *Sliabh Crion* 'dry hill' or perhaps rather *Sliabh Cruinn* 'round hill'. In other cases etymologies are much less certain, for the difficulty in any definitive interpretation lies in the complete absence of early documentation for these minor names. Although speculation as to the derivation of some of these less definite examples would be an interesting exercise, there is no need for it in this context. What is much more important for the present discussion is that a number of *Slew*- names in the Rinns of Galloway has identical equivalents in Ireland, in addition to those in the Isle of Man. On the whole, this must be due to a common vocabulary of words likely to enter into Gaelic hill-nomen-clature but the mere fact that these words, and names, are shared by Irish and Rinns of Galloway Scottish Gaelic is nevertheless significant and speaks of a fairly close connection, not at all unexpected in view of the geographical proximity of this part of Galloway to Ireland and of the rather similar development in the pronunciation of our word in both areas.

Such a link might have existed from the very first years of Gaelic-speaking settlement in Galloway right to the time when Gaelic ceased to be the linguistic medium of daily communication in south-west Scotland. Some of the easier etymologies of *Slew*- names would indicate a later date, some of the more obscure an earlier one. The crucial question remaining to be examined is whether our group of names does not merely represent a localised usage of *sliabh* in a peninsula with a long coastline facing Ireland and it is therefore necessary to look at place-names containing this element in Scotland as a whole. The first result of a search in the Ordnance Survey Name Books for names of this kind bears out the general impression of how rare — in any meaning — this word is in Scottish place-names, for there are hardly as many examples in the rest of Scotland as there are in the Rinns of Galloway alone. The second conclusion is that these few names, when plotted, occupy a very limited area (see Map 1) with Islay and Jura particularly well covered. There are also examples in Colonsay and Lismore, Kintyre, Mid Argyll and in Arran, the remainder of a very thin dis-tribution mainly taken up by mainland Inverness-shire and two outliers in the Island of Canna. The example south of the Forth is *Slamannan* which, as it appears as *Slefmanyn* in 1275 is usually interpreted as 'hill

1   Gaelic *sliabh*

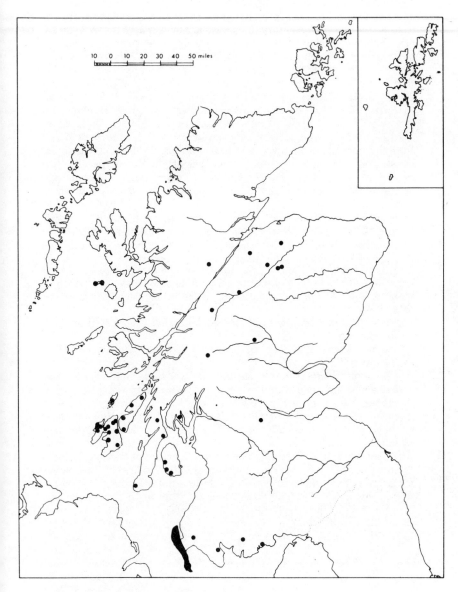

● Name containing *sliabh*

Area of greater density of names

or moor of Manu', and it has been suggested that in this name Gaelic *sliabh* is probably a translation of Welsh *mynydd*. A very large part of the distribution pattern is therefore astonishingly identical with that of the early Dalriadic settlement of Gaelic speakers in Scotland from the middle of the fifth century onwards, although *sliabh* was obviously still a creative place-name element when the Gaelic settlement movement spread further north-east. That it did not remain productive for very long is shown by its absence in the major part of what once was, and partly still is, Gaelic speaking Scotland (and that includes those areas on which the present-day pronunciation of *-iabh* most closely approximates that which must be underlying Galloway *[Sl] ew-*). In these areas it was of course — at least in the meaning of 'mountain' — replaced by Scottish Gaelic *beinn,* and there is consequently no instance of *sliabh* meaning 'mountain' amongst all the names shown, although it sometimes refers to hills of considerable height. In this respect, a few descriptive quotations from the Ordnance Survey Name Books demonstrate quite clearly what the range of the word *sliabh* was when these names were given:

Islay: *Sliabh a' Mheallaidh* 'a ridge', *Sliabh Mór* 'hill', *Sliabh na Sgáile* 'hill', *Sliabh nan Coiseachan* 'a large tract of moorland', *Sliabh nan Grainnseag* 'a piece of moorland', *Sliabh a' Chatha* 'a low moorland ridge', *Sliabh Bhirgeadain* 'tract of heathy ground'.

Jura: *Sliabh na Móine* 'large mossy declivity', *Sliabhan Riabhach* 'a plot of rough heathy pasture', *Sliabh Aird na Sgitheich* 'stretch of moorland', *Sliabh Allt an Tairbh,* 'piece of moorland', also *Sliabh a' Chlaidheimh.*

Arran: *Sliabh Fada* 'low flat strip of muirland', *Sliabh Meurain* 'low flat heath hill'.

Canna: *Sliabh Meodhanach* 'large hill', *Sliabh na Creige Airde* 'heathy hill'.

Mainland: *Sliabh Gaoil* (South Knapdale) 'large hill', *Sliabh nan Dearc* (Saddell and Skipness) 'hillside', *Sliabh Bán* (Laggan) 'small moor', *Sliabh Lorgach,* now *S. Loraich* (Kilmonivaig) 'extensive range of moorland', *Sliabh a' Chuir* (Duthil and Rothiemurchus) 'large plain or muir', *Sliabh an Ruighe Dhuibh* 'large, heathy clad hill'.

All these descriptive references apply to the nature of the geographical feature named, and are not translations into English of the names themselves. The other surveyors' descriptions not mentioned here come within this range of meanings which, apart from its Biblical usage, also reflects the semantic range of *sliabh* in Modern Scottish Gaelic, given in dictionaries as '1. Mountain of the first magnitude (Bible) 2. Extended heath, alpine plain, moorish ground. 3. Extensive tract of dry moorland. 4. Mountain grass, moor bent grass. 5. Face of a hill.' It has also been possible to confirm all these meanings, with regional variations, from native speakers of Scottish Gaelic. *Sliabh,* then, is still alive in some areas, although not as a very common geographical term, long after it ceased to be productive in place-names.

Returning to our original questions, at least some answers can now be suggested: Apart from a dense cluster in the Rinns of Galloway, and sporadic occurrence in the rest of Galloway, *sliabh* is found in a very limited area more or less identical with that of the known Dalriadic settlement and the first few centuries of expansion which followed it on the mainland. It is an early element which, although still alive in Scottish Gaelic in general, is no longer productive in naming and probably has not been toponymically creative for a number of centuries. Its survival in the Rinns and some adjacent parts of Galloway, if it is not a, for various reasons much less likely, later localised infiltration due to geographical proximity, therefore apparently bears witness of another early Irish colony outside the Scottish Dalriada (and the Isle of Man), and *Slew-* < *sliabh* may well be assignable to a pre-Norse stratum of Gaelic speakers in the area. If this is correct or even probable, it would be an important early item in the stratification of Gaelic names in Galloway. Whether, however, many or any of our *Slew-* names go back to the so-called 'Cruithnian' settlers, as has been claimed, is another question which the place-names themselves do not answer, and it must suffice at this stage to regard them simply as potential evidence of a pre-Norse Gaelic-speaking settlement in the Rinns of Galloway. It is, however, significant that on the basis of the evidence here presented it would follow that, although the rest of Galloway did share in this early stratum, it did not do so to any noticeable extent. Perhaps it should also be made clear that the vast majority of Gaelic place-names in the Rinns, as in the rest of Galloway, do not belong to this early phase but are centuries younger. A Gaelic generic which has a similar distribution and is considered to be of the same antiquity is *carraig* 'rock, cliff', as in Carrickadoyn, Carrickoflion, Carrickahawkie.

Here, then, is a fine example of toponymic evidence providing information which historical documents or other linguistic sources lack completely. However well-informed we may be about the Dalriadic settlement further north, the corresponding settling of the Scottish south-west by Gaelic speakers from Ireland seems to have gone on completely unrecorded. Whether this was because of a difference in the nature of the two settlements or for some other reason, we do not know. What is so impressive, however, is the fact that onomastic research in this case fulfils anything but a 'handmaiden' role, only supporting secondarily conclusions already established by another discipline. The investigation of names containing Gaelic *sliabh* has not only pointed to satisfactory methodological approaches in the isolation of a single stratum within an evolving and spreading language, it has also almost accidentally but nevertheless quite convincingly, laid bare important primary evidence for the beginnings of Irish Gaelic settlement in the most south-westerly portion of Scotland, and although it cannot be expected that there will ever be total identity in the conclusions based on archaeological and onomastic source material, archaeologists have regarded these findings as important enough from their point of view, to make the supporting statement that, in Charles Thomas's words 'isolated archaeological finds from Galloway, the spread of a type of early ecclesiastical site (the enclosed developed cemetery) which may be regarded as Irish-inspired, and several minor pointers in the same direction, are amounting to reliable evidence for a separate settlement in this south-western area'. If place-name research was able to take the lead here, there is no reason why it should only see itself in a supportive role elsewhere in the country and in other periods when extra-onomastic evidence is more plentiful. The study of Scottish place-names has its own independent course to chart, relying on its own methodology and taking account of the peculiar nature of toponymic raw material. Its investigations should go parallel to those of other disciplines and should avoid the inadvertent inclusion of non-onomastic, and certainly of non-linguistic factors in the development of an argument. Only when the onomastic argument has been finally formulated in its own right, is comparison with parallel extra-onomastic/extra-linguistic undertakings permissible, and can true complementation be achieved. If at that point there is a large measure of coincidence this is to be regarded as a happy and desirable circumstance. If, on the other hand, onomastic findings and those of neighbouring disciplines do not tally, this does not automatically invalidate the onomastic conclusions or cast doubt on the reliability of name evidence. After all, linguistic people with certain naming habits are not necessarily identical with archaeological people of certain burial or drinking habits, to choose a hypothetical but obvious example. Certainly the procedures employed in the isolation of an early Gaelic stratum in Scotland are primarily onomastic/linguistic and therefore lead to onomastic/linguistic conclusions.

4
The Youngest Names

The naming process is a continuum which has never been interrupted since it first began. In fact, naming is so intimately linked with the history of the human race, and its mastery over the world that surrounds it, that ultimately the history of naming may be the same as the history of the human spirit or, putting it in the proverbial nutshell, man always has been and still is a naming animal. While the acquisition of language, another exclusive human trait, has given him the tools with which to name, the building of an ever-increasing, ever-changing connotative vocabulary is not identical with the even more sophisticated analytical, isolating creation of denotative names, giving identity to this place or that, individualising you and me. That this is not simply a linguistic matter is demonstrated by the numerous and powerful name taboos observable and still practised in many world religions. Naming and knowing names are power and potentially salvation, being known places one in the unenviable Rumpelstiltskin position of the over-powered not likely to escape from exploitation or eventual destruction.

The implications of this general principle for the specific tasks set for the student of Scottish place-names are clear. He has to reckon with a situation in which the creation of names is both millennia old and still in progress. He must therefore look upon the Scottish map as a palimpsest of layer upon layer of toponymic writing, some of it very faint, half obscured or half erased, and all of it still being written upon by new generations of name-givers. In dealing with this somewhat complicated situation, he has fundamentally two main approaches open to him. He can either try to reconstruct toponymic history as it happened, starting from the earliest known stratum and working his way towards the present, or he can begin with the contemporary evidence and, removing layer after layer from the map palimpsest, i.e. the different linguistic strata and the intra-systemic strata within each stratum already mentioned, gradually move backwards through history into prehistory until he reaches the last layer of meaningful, interpretable name material. To this author the second alternative has always appeared to be the more practicable, since it is not only based on the sound principle of moving from the well known via the lesser known to the unknown, but also incorporates a way of looking at history which

most of us unconsciously adopt with regard to our own view of the
past and for which the term 'genealogical' is perhaps the most appropriate; the family tree, after all, provides the historical link of the present
generation with those who went before. Another applicable metaphor
might be that of the archaeological excavation in which layer after
layer of soil is removed from top to bottom in order to lay bare what
lies below, and yet below, and below again until there is nothing else
to find. Once the genealogist or the archaeologist has completed his
task, there is no reason why he should not — indeed there is every
reason why he should — then turn around to look forward or upward,
as the case may be, in order to reconstruct the reconstructable.

It is obvious from these remarks that the approach to stratification
to be chosen in this book will be the second of the two alternatives,
the 'genealogical' one. This will necessitate looking at the various
contributions immigrant languages have made to the naming of places
and geographical features in Scotland, bit by bit, and chapter by
chapter. The temptation may be to regard the glimpses afforded by
surviving place-names at earlier and earliest strata as more interesting
and more revealing than the information they provide about the more
recent past, so that the whole process of stratification becomes an
elaborate search for a past Golden Age of naming, the further back the
better. Here, this temptation will be avoided as far as possible, even if
a natural fascination with the distant past is understandable and not
completely inexcusable, for the main point is that each stratum matters
for its own sake and is not simply to be 'dug' through in order to reach
the lowest layer of names.

Within this basic framework our first concern has to be with the
youngest names on the available maps or, perhaps even more recent and
less tangible, with those names which have so far only existed in oral
tradition or family use and may or may not one day find their way
onto the printed map, making them accessible to all who can read. It is
not surprising in this respect that our generation does not get much of
an opportunity with regard to the naming of major features, unless one
looks upon the much extended use of existing names in the naming of
new towns and housing estates as instances of major naming, a practice
of which East Kilbride, Cumbernauld, and Livingston, on the one hand,
and Clermiston, Camperdown, and Easterhouse, on the other, would
be good examples. Here, however, it is not the name which has changed
but the feature named. Instances of another type of comparatively
recent 're-naming' might be the officially decreed changes which turned
the shires of Haddington, Edinburgh and Linlithgow into East, Mid-
and West Lothian, respectively, and similarly converted Forfarshire into
Angus. Both Lothian and Angus had centuries ago been names broadly
applicable to the areas to which they were thus re-introduced, apparently
on the principle already alluded to, that the earlier the name can be
said to be, the more desirable it is. The motive which changed another
county-name from Dumbartonshire to Dunbartonshire was not a special
love for antiquity but a desire, as it turns out misguided, for clarity,
because the county name would thus be clearly distinguished from the

name of the county town, Dumbarton. That this had, and has, never been necessary in the cases of Inverness and Inverness-shire, Peebles and Peeblesshire, Selkirk and Selkirkshire, and most closely related of all, Dumfries and Dumfriesshire, does not appear to have occurred to officialdom, and the linguistic process of assimilation which would turn *Dun-* into *Dum-* before a following *-b-*, and therefore make it easier to pronounce, seems to have eluded them, too. Lexical meaning does, of course, not enter into any of these changes.

Perhaps the greatest impact recent generations have had on geographical naming in Scotland, and elsewhere, has been in the area of street and house naming, the former an official function in most communities, the latter a private privilege for those who cannot identify with a mere house number (or like to confuse the postman). Both naming processes have produced their own peculiar additions to the lexical and morphological structure of Scottish place-nomenclature.

Street-names are, in fact, quite a good example of strata within a stratum. Although clearly belonging to the youngest stratum of Scottish place-names they have historical depth, have succumbed to fashions over the years, and are therefore not at all homogenenous semantically or chronologically. The street-names of the Scottish capital may here serve as appropriate illustrations.

Obviously the oldest names must be in the Old Town rather than in later extensions, and none are more instructive than the names of the many wynds and closes that branch off the Castlehill, the Lawnmarket (formerly Landmarket), the High Street, the Canongate and the Cowgate — themselves early examples of straightforward descriptive street-naming. The majority bear the names of former chief residents or owners, like Semple's Close, Paterson's Court, Brown's Close, Todrig's Wynd, Galloway's Entry and Hastie's Close. All of these, and many others, have identifiable personal associations. Some refer to the occupations of people who lived in the street or owned property there; examples are Skinner's Close, Baxter's Close, Writers' Court, Shoemakers' Close, Hammermen's Close, Taylors' Close, also Blackfriars Wynd, Bishop's Close and Advocate's Close. Buildings and markets in the vicinity are commemorated by Old Posthouse Close, Old Stamp Office Close, Old Bank Close, Castle Wynd, Old Assembly Close, Tolbooth Wynd, Bakehouse Close, College Wynd, Horse Wynd (royal stables), Fleshmarket Close, Old Fishmarket Close, and others. Named after inn signs were Anchor Close, Bull's Close, Whitehorse Close and the Cap and Feather Close which disappeared when the North Bridge was built in 1765. Geographical position is indicated by Netherbow, West Bow and World's End Close (at the very end of the High Street), and Leith Wynd led to Leith.

Whereas local history is the common factor in the above names, and many others in the Old Town, by the time the New Town was conceived 200 years ago, Edinburgh, like most other capitals and cities in Europe, was beginning to copy the Paris fashion of naming streets after royalty. Princes Street (which should have been St Giles Street, but at George III's request was named after the future George IV and the Duke of York), George Street, Queen Street, Frederick Street, Charlotte Street, and undoubtedly Hanover Street bear witness to this trend. In the decades that followed, Edinburgh further copied Paris by commemorating other persons of note in its street-names, as in Abercromby Place, Moray Place, Ainslie Place, Melville Street, Randolph Crescent, Palmerston Place etc. The fact that certain nobles bore names derived from place-names (Northumberland Street, York Place, Cumberland Street, etc.) probably helped to introduce place-names as first elements, as did the fact that many streets and roads were called after the places to and through which they led, like Dalry Road, Gorgie Road, Slateford Road, Morningside Road, Newington Road, Grange Road, Colinton Road, etc.

The most striking new feature with regard to street naming is a morphological one. A good example which comes to mind is the network of streets in the Edinburgh suburb of Fairmilehead called Swanston Avenue, Swanston Gardens, Swanston Place, Swanston View, Swanston Terrace, Swanston Drive, Swanston Grove, Swanston Crescent, Swanston Rise, Swanston Way, Swanston Loan, and Swanston Green. These are all named after the village of Swanston which they overlook, about half a mile away. Originally, of course, a Swanston Street, or the like, would be the street leading to Swanston, as the older name Swanston Road nearby confirms, but the absence of any directional implication is not the striking innovation here. What is new, and by no means peculiar to Fairmilehead or to Edinburgh, is the fact that the qualifying element, *Swanston,* remains constant while the generic element, *Avenue, Gardens, Place,* etc. varies. This is a complete reversal of earlier and, it seems, more effective morphological street-name patterns which provide for a very small number of generics and in which the qualifying element is the distinguishing one and therefore never repeated in any given community, in order to avoid confusion. It is also symptomatic for the attitude towards suburban street-naming that, within this long and impressive list, the name Swanston *Street* never occurs, the term *street* obviously ranking very lowly in the social hierarchy of street-name generics. Popular usage, by the way, calls this area very appropriately 'The Swanstons'.

Although a systematic survey of house-names has never been undertaken even within one town or a residential part of a larger community, a few comments are in order here, since house-names are probably the last bastion of private naming today and therefore might give us at least some indication as to how the present-day generation of potential name-givers might name places if there were more places for them to name. The impression one gets is that the descriptive category would still be fairly strong as is indicated by such names as *Seaview* or *Hillcrest.* A second group commemorates places which, for some reason or other, are of special, perhaps nostalgic, interest to the owners so that *Thurso* might commemorate a honeymoon or *Morven* a family holiday or former place of residence. In middle-class suburbia, all kinds of mysterious reasons frequently prompt non-Gaelic speaking residents to give their houses Gaelic names, perhaps because they seem to be more Scottish than Scottish-English names, and the misspellings and misunderstandings caused by this custom are numerous and often humorous. The story of the elderly lady who in her retirement insisted on calling her home *Tigh Beag* 'little house', failing to recognise that this ordinarily refers to a certain outhouse at the bottom of the garden, illustrates only one aspect of this phenomenon. Cryptic names provide another extensive category, sometimes making use of the first syllables of the inhabitant's names, like *Fradoba* for Francis, Doris and Barbara, and sometimes simply reversing the spelling, like *Nostaw* for Watson. Presumably, in their application of linguistic humour these names and others like them try to retain the name not as a means of communication but as a shield guarding private property like an onomastic hedge or wall. As the survival of names depends on their acceptance by a linguistic community, it is not at all certain that names such as these, if used in a wider context, would live beyond the lives of their creators.

Of necessity, this study will have to rely almost exclusively on names recorded in writing at one time or another. Room must be provided, therefore, for at least a footnote on those names which have never entered written tradition and are therefore, if they lived and died in the past, not accessible to any investigation. That such names have always existed in large numbers cannot be doubted, and we shall never really know how much poorer we are for not ever knowing them. The only way in which to get hold of them at all would be in current oral tradition. Two prominent examples in this category would be *The Highlandman's Umbrella* in Glasgow and *Holy Corner* in Edinburgh. Both are well known and widely used but no street-map has ever shown them. The former, the bridge carrying the rail tracks across Argyle Street and into Central Station, is, of course, the traditional gathering place of Highlanders resident in Glasgow, whereas the latter is formed by the junction of Morningside Road and Colinton Road on which or near which at least three churches are situated. It used to be the usual name bus conductors would call out when approaching this particular stop, although in recent years the less humorous and more pragmatic 'Napier College' seems to have replaced it, acknowledging the building of an institution of higher learning not far away.

There may be those who are inclined to think that names of this kind, with their colloquial, humorous overtones, should be relegated to the category of nicknames and the whole realm of folk-naming which tends to see and therefore label places differently from the formal name giver and user. Although there is no harm in such a suggestion as long as popular naming is not regarded as inferior to the accepted, 'official' version, it should nevertheless be remembered that before the days of officially created or sanctioned names – and that does not take us very far back – each naming process included a longer or shorter phase during which the name stayed in oral tradition until public agreement, i.e. usage beyond the owner, a family, or a restricted group of people, turned a private label into an accepted and acceptable name. It is good to know that, despite the dominance of the printed form and word, people are still acting as if they belonged to an at least partly pre-literate society in which the audible utterance has an important place — or might this be one of the first signs of an emerging post-literate society?

If we regard the youngest stratum of Scottish place-names as stretching roughly from the Middle Ages to the present — from the beginning of the decline of Gaelic onwards, let us say, or, historically speaking, from the time of David I — then it gives us so much material to work with that we have to be highly selective in the choices to be paraded in this chapter, since it is probably correct to say that most names in use today were coined during that period of an ever-increasing population and of proliferating new settlements, both large and small. Some additional special facet in the naming process will have to be the deciding factor for inclusion in our presentation.

One category which would qualify under such conditions is perhaps the domain of the local historian rather than the specialist in languages, for it consists of names which contain a personal name which is not identifiable by linguistic means but with the help of local historical documents.

We know that Fort William, for instance was so named by General Mackay in 1690, after William III. Similarly, Fort Augustus received its name in 1730 from General Wade, the famous road- and bridge-builder, who named it after William Augustus, Duke of Cumberland, a royal gentleman for whom Scottish popular tradition has another less flattering name. William and Augustus are quite easily identified, then; but what about the Helen in Helensburgh, the Betty in Bettyhill, the Campbel(l) in Campbeltown, and so on?

As far as Helensburgh is concerned, the local historian will tell us that in Janaury 1776 the land of Malig or Milrigs was first advertised for feuing by Sir James Colquhoun of Luss. When it had begun to be laid out as a residential district it was first still known as Mulig or simply as the New Town, but was later named by the superior in honour of his wife, Lady Helen, who was the daughter of William, Lord Strathnaver.

A younger relative of Lady Helen appears to have given her name to Bettyhill, although under less pleasant circumstances, for the place of this name, on the north coast of Sutherland, was 'founded' by Elizabeth, Countess of Sutherland, about 1820, to accommodate crofters evicted from Strathnaver. Elizabeth was born on 24 May, 1765, and was the only surviving daughter of William, eighteenth Earl of Sutherland.

In the same year as Sir James Colquhoun, at Helensburgh, Sir James Grant of Castle Grant also planned a new town in a different part of Scotland, a town which has become one of the most beautiful resorts — Grantown-on-Spey. Sir James lived from 1738-1811, was the seventh Baronet of Grant, chief of Clan Grant, MP for Elgin and Forres from 1761-68 and for Banff from 1790-95. No lack of biographical information here. A century earlier the Register of the Great Seal records under the date of 15 October, 1667, in a charter to Archibald, Earl of Argyle, Lord Kintyre, Campbell and Lorne, a grant: 'erecting the said town of Lochead into a free burgh of barony, to be called the burgh of Campbeltown.' There is no need to explain beyond this entry what (or who) the first element in this name is. In the same Register, a charter dated 2 November, 1546, gives us evidence of the fact that the town of Faithlie had also been erected into a free burgh of barony in the previous century. If you do not know where Faithlie is, later charters will give you the answer, because in 1592 we read that it is called, in Latin, *burgum et portum de Fraser*, and in 1601 the vernacular name Fraserburgh is first documented. The town was, in fact, given its present official name by Sir Alexander Fraser of Phillorth, although in the whole of Buchan you are more likely to hear it called *The Broch*.

There are other names of this kind, like Douglastown in Angus, which commemorates the fact that William Douglas of Brigton, about 1790, made his corn-mill buildings available for trials involving a new machine for spinning flax, etc. In all the places discussed, from the middle of the sixteenth to the beginning of the nineteenth century, an element of planning by an individual and official recognition of the efforts of that individual are involved. Where older names have been supplanted, they quite frequently survive in local oral tradition, like the Gaelic names *An Gearasdan* for Fort William, *Cill Chuimein* for Fort Augustus, *Ceannloch* (*Chille Chiarain*) for Campbeltown, and *Torr nan Clar* for the Ross-shire Janetown, but otherwise the new names, like the places to which they apply, have become firmly established on the Scottish map.

It may seem superfluous here to emphasise that, apart from the Hebrides and the adjacent mainland, every single new and meaningful place-name coined in Scotland today is linguistically of English origin, is created in the linguistic medium practically everybody uses as a means of communication, in one form or another. We can probably go even further and claim that, even in those parts just excepted, the majority of new names are likely to be English rather than Gaelic, although without accurate information this must be a matter for conjecture. In this respect the situation has been more or less stable for a century or two, with a gradually shrinking Gaelic-speaking area being exactly balanced by an increasing English-speaking dominance or, looking at it from a slightly different point of view, with English stepping in wherever Gaelic moves out, sometimes after a considerable period of bilingualism of the kind to be found in the Gaelic-speaking parts of Scotland today. Some of Scotland's youngest place-names have therefore been born in a setting in which two languages were in contact over a period of time. In this type of situation a number of basic relationships between the place-nomenclature of one language and that of the other develop, all of which can be documented on the current scene:

(a) The two names for the same place are completely unrelated to each other, illustrated by such doublets as the North Uist names Gaelic *Baile MhicPhail* 'Macphail's farm'/English *Newton,* and Gaelic *Port nan Long* 'Ships' Harbour'/English *Newtonferry.* Other unconnected names would be *Caithness* and *Gallaibh*, *Sutherland* and *Cataibh*, *Hebrides* and *Innse Gall*, *Scotland* and *Alba*, *Campbeltown* ARG and *Ceannloch*, *St Andrews* FIF and *Cill Rimhinn*, to list just some of the more prominent examples; others were mentioned on p.53 above, in another context. A peculiar case is the doublet English *Brodick*/Gaelic *Traigh a' Chaisteil* in the island of Arran, in which the English name is of Scandinavian origin, reflecting a Norse *Breið-vík* 'Broad Bay', which may have survived because of map influence. Each half of the doublet belongs strictly to the onomastic system of one language and cannot be used by the other so that even a bilingual individual will not normally interchange them.

(*b*) The name in one language is a translation or part-translation of the name in the other language; this appears to be the result of the closest contact between speakers of the two languages concerned, with the incoming language usually being required to do the translating, as in another North Uist name, Gaelic *Cearamh Meadhonach* = English *Middlequarter*, or the Ross-shire *An t-Eilean Dubh* which is the *Black Isle* in English. As we saw earlier (p.53) Campbeltown was called *Lochhead* in English, translating Gaelic *Ceannloch (Chille Chiarain)*, before being renamed in 1667. A part-translation may be *Boat of Garten* INV from *Coit Ghartain*, and in at least one case the translation may have gone in the other direction so that English *Peterhead* ABD was rendered in Gaelic as *Ceann Phadruig*. Full translations form a much smaller group than might be imagined, probably again a result of the onomastic nature of these names which does not call for transparent lexical meaning.

(*c*) The name in one language is a phonological adaptation of the name in the other language; by definition such a name becomes instantly meaningless in the receiving language (it may, of course, also have been without lexical meaning in the donor language). Phonological adaptation is the most common toponymic phenomenon in linguistic contact, and documentation for this kind of doublet therefore abounds as, for instance, in *Ben Lee* (Uist) for *Beinn Liath*, *Sleat* (Skye) for *Sleibhte*, *Rannoch* ARG/PER for *Raineach*, *Banff* BNF for *Banbh*, or *Drumnadrochit* INV for *Druim na Drochaid*. The Scottish map contains literally thousands of such anglicised names. Naturally, the limited number of written symbols available in ordinary English orthography is not always adequate to represent the phonological changes fully and unambiguously. *Sleat*, for example, stands for [sle:t] which is much closer to the original Gaelic than the non-local spelling pronunciation [sli:t] often heard nowadays. It is noteworthy that the systematic investigation of such adaptations, or more specifically anglicisations, which have, after all, been happening for hundreds of years, has never really been attempted for purposes of historical linguistic research in Scotland. Here is a field wide open for a person with the right kind of training.

(*d*) The name in one language is phonologically adapted by the other, as under (*c*), but a morphological 'translation' adds a plural marker in the receiving language because the name was in the plural in the donor language. This must be the origin of quite a number of Scottish place-names ending in an otherwise curious and inexplicable -*s*. The notion of 'more than one' was apparently dominant enough to be transferred even when the name had become semantically opaque. Usually, under these circumstances, the English -*s* is added to the phonologically (and orthographically) reshaped Gaelic singular, as in *The Trossachs* which stands for Gaelic *Na Trosaichean* 'the cross-hills'. Similarly, *Largs* A Y R can be explained only as an English plural of Gaelic *learg* 'slope'. *Leuchars* F I F represents an English plural of Gaelic *luachar* 'rush, rushes'. *Fetters* in the same parish (*Fotheris* 1536; *Fethers* 1588) must be based on Gaelic *fothair* 'slope', parallelled by *Foithear* (on Loch Ness-side) of which the English form *Foyers* shows a plural while the underlying Gaelic name does not. *Lawers*, on Loch Tay, together with *Ben Lawers*, reflects the fact that there are three divisions of this community: *Labhar Shios* 'East Lawers', *Labhar Shuas* 'West Lawers', and *Labhar na Craoibh* 'Lawers of the Tree'. In *Binns* W L O an English plural -*s* has been added to Gaelic *beinn,* dative-locative of *beann* 'peak'. Although frequently an echo of a Gaelic plural, these names are consequently not always parallelled by or derived from such forms. In a couple of instances, English spelling devices have obscured the presence of our final -*s*. *Lix* P E R, so often associated in the popular mind with a Roman milestone bearing the numerals LIX, is in reality the English plural of Gaelic *lic*, dative-locative of *leac* 'flagstone, hard slope'. There are Lower, Upper and Mid Lic. The rhyming *Stix,* in the same area, reflects Gaelic *Na Stuiceannan* 'the stocks or stumps'.

(*e*) As a consequence of (*c*), i.e. phonological adaptation and resulting lexical meaninglessness, the receiving language adds a generic of its own which tautologically repeats a generic already contained in the adopted name. Like (*a*) and (*c*), this is a process which can happen several times in succession when different languages come into contact with each other over a long stretch of time. There is therefore no shortage of illustrative material, like *Point of Ardnamurchan* in which the English word *point* pleonastically expresses the meaning of Gaelic *àrd* 'promontory'. In *Glenborrodale* (Ardnamurchan) and *Glen- cripesdale* (Morvern), Gaelic *gleann* 'valley' repeats Norse *dalr*, both of which appear on the map in the anglicised form, of course. Similar Gaelic-Norse tautologies are contained in *Eilean Shona*, at the entrance to Loch Moidart, and *Loch Moidart* and *Loch Sunart*. In the first, both Gaelic *eilean* and Norse *ey* mean island", and in the latter two, both Gaelic *loch* and Norse *fjorðr* signify 'an inlet, a sea-loch'. In the map-names *Lussa River* and *River Forsa* (both in Mull), there appears to be a gap in the sequence (compare Brodick Bay in Arran), since English *river* and Norse *a* (and in Arran, of course, English *bay* and Norse *vík*) mean the same thing, but undoubtedly *river* is in both cases a translation of Gaelic *abhainn*, as local oral tradition proves. A name in which three languages participate in a tautology is *Ardtornish Point* which applies to a peninsula jutting out from Morvern into the Sound of Mull; in this case, Norse *nes*, Gaelic *àrd*, and English *point*, in that chronological order, all refer to the same promontory. It should be stressed that these names are not to be considered as part-translations in which the translated element has not been replaced but has been allowed to remain. In fact, the element of translation is so conspicuously absent in such names, because of the reduction of what were originally compound names to simple ones, that the generics are no longer recognised. Whereas Fishnish Point (Mull) is an example of tautological duplication, the neighbouring Fishnish Bay shows that the onomastic item *Fishnish* is understood as a new, meaningless unit without lexical reference. Similarly, the settlement (!) names Glenmore and Kentra have produced the new combinations Glenmore River and Bay, and Kentra Bay and Moss, respectively, in which neither Gaelic *gleann* 'valley' nor *traigh* 'shore' figure as meaningful elements. It only remains to point out that all the names in this category have been abstracted from the, randomly chosen, sheet 45 of the one-inch Ordnance Survey maps of Scotland (Seventh Series).

(*f*) The name in the outgoing language is not in any way adapted, translated or replaced by the incoming language. This is often true of very minor names like those of fishing-rocks on the seashore or names of small features in now depopulated areas in which all linguistic continuity is lost. Such lack of correspondence results either in the more or less temporary retention of the name in the onomastic system of the outgoing language and/or in its complete loss, an atrition process which is, of course, not limited to bilingual situations. Potential examples would be, from Illeray, the northern part of Baleshare on the west side of North Uist, *Bruthach an t-Samsain* 'Samson's Brae' where, according to local tradition, a very strong man is supposed to have lived in the past; or *Cnoc a' Pheursa* 'Signal-pole Hillock' which is a reminder that the men of the community used to be called by the hoisting of a signal of some kind (*peursa*) on a pole, to gather there to arrange the distribution of seaweed. On the coast not far from the Butt of Lewis we find *Bodha Dhomhnuill Bhàin* 'the (submerged) rock of Fair Donald' and *Geodha nan seann duine* 'the old men's bay', and up in the hills of the parish of Barvas in the same island is *Allt nan Uan* 'the stream of the lambs'. These five names and thousands of others apply to very small features and are not recorded on any map, but can still be recovered from local oral tradition. Frequently, they are only known to one or two people at present, and the likelihood of their survival even within the dwindling Gaelic-speaking community is extremely small.

Sometimes several of the above processes (except *f*) are involved in producing a totally new name-type in the incoming language, a type which might never have been created spontaneously without this linguistic interaction. A particularly instructive case in point, of which one example (*Boat of Garten*) has already been mentioned, is that of English names containing the preposition *of*. Because of its special problems and its linguistic and historical ramifications, not because of the importance of the names in question, it merits detailed consideration, in this context of the youngest stratum of place-names in Scotland.

Anybody studying Scottish river-names will be struck, though not surprised, by the predominance of the generic *burn* in the naming of smaller water-courses. The Scottish one-inch Ordnance Survey maps show more than 2650 such names, by far the largest category among Scottish-English stream-names and one that is to be found all over Scotland. As is normal in English (and Germanic) compound names, the. generic *burn* is usually placed last and preceded by the qualifying element. There is, however, a peculiar, but sizeable, variant of this hydronymic type in which the defining element follows *burn* and is linked to it by the preposition *of*, a word order which results in the subtype '*Burn of X*', the *X* representing in the majority of cases the name of a place, hill, valley, or loch, or a primary river-name. Of the 261 names in this category, 165 or 63.2 per cent belong to this main group. By far the largest sub-section is formed by names containing the name of a human settlement, with 97 examples. Fifty-four names belong to the category of names describing the surrounding terrain through which the stream flows. Only three names – a mere 1.15 per cent – refer to characteristics of the water or the water-course themselves. This semantic distribution suggests that the group of names under discussion is a rather recent innovation in Scottish river-nomenclature, since names referring to some feature outside the stream named tend to be later than those describing some quality of the stream itself.

Some are named after the terrain through which they flow, like *Burn of Achlais* STL (Gaelic *achadh* 'a field'), *Burn of Drumcairn* ANG (Gaelic *druim* 'ridge'), *Burn of Swartaback* ORK (ON *bakki* 'hill, bank'), or *Burn of the Boitain* SHE (ON *botn* 'bottom, valley'). Others contain the names of human settlements (*Burn of Birse* ABD, *Burn of Houstry* CAI, *Burn of Oldtown* ANG), hill-names (*Burn of Hamarifield* SHE, *Burn of Melmannoch* KCD), valley-names (*Burn of Crockadale* SHE, *Burn of Glendui* ABD), or loch-names (*Burn of Ola's Loch* SHE, *Burn of Petta-water* SHE). Others again incorporate the primary stream-names which they have replaced (*Burn of Boyne* BNF, *Burn of Breitoe* SHE, *Burn of Turret* ANG).

The geographical distribution of these names reveals as the two main strongholds the north-east, on the one hand, and Orkney and Shetland, on the other. Central Scotland has a few scattered names which belong to this category, but only two isolated strays occur in Ayrshire and Wigtownshire, respectively, in an otherwise empty Scottish south. The north, the east, and the west are completely free from the *Burn of X* type.

The phrase-name *Burn of X* consists of two English words and represents an English genitival construction, used and understood both lexically and grammatically in modern Scottish English. Morphologically, the compound formation of these names also points to a late stratum of Scottish hydronymy, and we have already emphasised that the semantic aspect of this group of names – preponderance of 'names from names' and of defining elements describing the surroundings of the named watercourse – suggests that it is a fairly recent innovation. We may, then, initially define the type *Burn of X* as a fairly recent Anglo-Scottish creation.

Why is our name-type absent from the otherwise so thoroughly Scottish area south of the Forth-Clyde line, especially from its southern, south-eastern and eastern parts? The answer seems to be that, although *burn* is a most prolific hydronymic element in this area in names with the normal Germanic word-order in which it is preceded by the qualifying element, *Burn of X* names do not occur because they are later than the period in which the main body of Scottish names of Germanic origin was created in this part of Scotland, and because there has never been any name pattern of sufficiently dense distribution belonging to some other model language and stimulating imitation by, and borrowing into, Lowland Scots nomenclature. Both the time-factor and the absence of a suitable substratum have apparently contributed towards this lack of the type under discussion in southern Scotland.

As far as Fife and Kinross are concerned – and, in a way, Clackmannan whose only example *Burn of Sorrow* shows only superficial morphological connection with our type, but is otherwise semantically quite distinct – similar circumstances appear to account for the blanks in the distribution. It seems that names of the type *Burn of X* are not coined in the river-nomenclature of Scottish-English origin unless there is a given pattern of different linguistic provenance suggesting imitation; such a pattern must have been absent or not suggestive enough when Scots reached these three counties, or it may be just that the linguistic contact between substratum and superstratum was not close enough to make either translation or adaptation of earlier name models possible.

The absence of our names from the counties along the Scottish west coast from Sutherland to Bute, and their relative scarcity in central Scotland must be explained differently. These are the parts which are either still Gaelic-speaking or in which Gaelic was spoken comparatively recently. Here Gaelic was not superseded by Scots but by a regional variant of Standard English, and the *Burn of X* type has therefore never reached them.

This means that names belonging to our category are excluded from, or are almost completely lacking in, (*a*) areas which have been 'English' ever since the Angles arrived in Scotland, (*b*) districts which were anglicised at a very early stage, (*c*) the *Gaidhealtachd* (Highlands) proper, in the modern as well as in the historical sense, which has never been reached by Lowland Scots.

The mainland area in which our names occur in great number, is the Scottish north-east. There are 131 of them altogether, forming roughly one-half of the names of this type mentioned on the one-inch Ordnance Survey maps. In the great majority of cases the defining element is of Gaelic origin, and it is in the underlying Gaelic stratum that we shall have to look for the model. The most common type of Gaelic stream-name is the one in which *allt* 'burn' is followed by a common noun or a proper name in the genitive preceded by the definite article. There are literally hundreds of examples to choose from, represented here by *Allt a' Chaoruinn* ROS 'burn of the rowan-tree', *Allt an Lochain Duibh*

INV 'burn of the little black loch' (it flows out of *Loch Dubh), Allt an t-Sneachda* ABD 'burn of the snow'. *Allt an t-Sniomh* LEWIS 'burn of the twist', *Allt na h-Innse Buidhe* ARG 'burn of the yellow haugh', *Allt na Muic* SUT 'burn of the pig'. In the same category are names in which the defining element is qualified by another noun which results in the dropping of the definite article before the first noun, according to Gaelic grammatical rules, as in *Allt Bad nan Clach* SUT 'burn of the clump of the trees', *Allt Creag a' Chait* NAI 'burn of the craig of the cat', *Allt Uamha na Muice* ARG 'burn of the cave of the pig'.

The development from this original Gaelic pattern to our modern Scottish name-type happens almost in front of our eyes:

First stage: Gaelic *Allt an t-Sluic Leith* 'burn of the grey hollow'.

Second stage: (*a*) *Burn of Slock Lee* – where *Burn of* translates Gaelic *Allt (an)* and the Gaelic defining element is anglicised (in the nominative!). (*b*) The whole name is translated: *Burn of Blackpots* and *Burn of Oldtown* (both in Angus) are strongly suggestive of being full translations of Gaelic **Allt na(n) Linneacha(n) Dubh(a)* and **Allt and t-Sean(a)-bhaile*. They may, however, belong to stage four.

Third stage: *Burn of*, followed by any – usually anglicised – Gaelic element, if it has been part of an original stream-name in *allt* or not, as for instance, *Burn of Knock* KCD, *Burn of Corrhatnich* MOR, *Burn of Badenhilt* ABD.

Fourth stage: *Burn of*, followed by any defining element, regardless of its linguistic origin, *cf. Burn of Berryhill* ANG, *Burn of Cauldcots* KCD, *Burn of Davidston* ABD.

This is, of course, not the only way in which Gaelic names of the *Allt an*-type are adapted when *burn* infiltrates into Gaelic river-nomenclature. In names like *Ishag Burn* PER, *Lochbroom Burn* PER, *Strath Burn* CAI, *Strone Burn* PER, the defining elements precede *burn* in their anglicised forms, and the definite article has been dropped. This word-order is extremely common amongst hybrid names of this kind.

The Gaelic name-type does, however, reveal quite clearly the source of the category of name under review. The north-eastern names of the *Burn of X* class did not come into being by spontaneous genesis, but as the result of a bilingual contact situation between outgoing Gaelic and incoming Lowland Scots.

Concerning a *terminus post quem*, place-names of Anglo-Saxon origin first begin to appear in charters related to the north east round about 1220, and it can be assumed that the north-eastern *Burn of X* names are later than the thirteenth century; how much later can only be shown by more detailed research into every single name in old documents. Whatever such detailed study may turn up, they are without a doubt a fairly recent stratum in Scottish river-nomenclature. The creative impulse which brought them into being must have been linguistic contact, or, more precisely, favourable conditions for the type *Burn of X* were given whenever Scots came into contact with a substratum of Gaelic, from the late Middle Ages onwards.

Two major objections have been voiced to this explanation, and if they stand, the conclusions arrived at after careful examination of our *Burn of X* names may be partially or altogether invalidated. The first criticism has been that the evidence on which the argument is based is too slender because it consists exclusively of names of small and medium sized water-courses, showing only one generic term: *burn*. The second objection has been raised by way of an alternative explanation of the rather striking geographical scatter of these names, and it has been proposed that this may be due to the whimsies of a particular surveyor at the time when these names were first recorded by the Ordnance Survey.

With regard to the second of these objections it can be said that, if this type of name were entirely due to the person responsible for the recording of names when the areas in question were first covered by the Ordnance Survey, one would not expect to find it in any other source or in genuine oral tradition. A simple check shows us that *Burn of X* names do occur on earlier maps. Consultation of William Roy's unpublished Military Survey of 1747-55 furnishes, for instance, names like *Burn of Crombie* and *Burn of Bly* in the Glenlivet area of Banffshire, and *Burn of Bogendolich* and *Burn of Bulg* in Kincardineshire; these are on record at least a hundred years before the first Scottish Ordnance Survey maps proper, and although Roy's map contains fewer names of water-courses than the O.S. one-inch maps, the geographical distribution of name-type *Burn of X* does not seem to differ to any marked degree from the modern situation.

As to local, colloquial usage of *Burn of X* names, the position appears to be this: if the second element of the name is the original name of the water-course, the *Burn of* part is very often dropped. The map has *Burn of Tervie*, for instance, for a tributary of the River Livet in Banffshire but locally this is always called (the) *Tervie.*. If, however, the defining element of the name refers to some other geographical feature in the vicinity, either by name or by description, *Burn of* remains. with normal dialectal shortening of the preposition to *o '*. This widespread usage in the areas concerned cannot be ascribed to any map-maker, however great the influence of the map may have become even on local users of place-names, and we must regard the majority of instances of *Burn of X* on our maps as genuinely taken from oral tradition, at one time or another.

The other objection, the expression of concern because of the limited basis for the argument advanced, is best dealt with by an examination of other generic elements and of names not applying to streams but to other geographical features. The section of Roy's map which contains the two Kincardineshire stream-names mentioned above, shows that this name-type is by no means confined to the element *burn*; it also contains amongst others, *Mill of Blackymuir*, *Kirk of Pert*, *House of Fetterkarne*, *Cotts of Newton*, and even *River of North Esk*. The last two types of formation are not to be found on the one-inch map, with *Cotts of* in some instances having been replaced by *Cotton of*, but in respect of many other generic elements this formation is quite prolific even on the modern map, and it would be interesting to see how far the distribution of some of these coincides with that of the type *Burn of X.*

(a) Water of X

The generic in this type is one which in Scottish river-nomenclature is normally applied to water-courses larger than those designated as *burn. Water,* in this respect, seems to take an intermediate position between *burn* and *river,* although not every *burn* is smaller and not every *river* larger than a *water.* There are 47 names of the type *Water of X* on the O.S. one-inch map, amongst them *Water of Ailnack* INV, *Water of App* AYR, *Water of Buchat* ABD, *Water of Ken* KCB, *Water of Leith* MLO, *Water of Malzie* WIG, *Water of Tulla* ARG, and *Water of Unich* ANG.

Two aspects of the mainland distribution of *Water of X* show a strong resemblance to that of *Burn of X:* (1) A thick cluster of names in the northeast, and (2) the complete absence — with one or two exceptions — of this name-type from the Lothians, the Border Counties, and the Highlands and Islands. Strikingly different, on the other hand, are the frequency with which this type occurs in south-west Scotland, and its total lack in the Northern Isles. With regard to the first of these differences, there is no apparent reason why the type *Burn of X* should be so scantily represented in south-west Scotland, whereas *Water of X* names are fairly plentiful in the same area in which, after all, Gaelic was gradually ousted by Scots and where there must have been prolonged contact between these two languages. However, the type *Bishop Burn, Kildonan Burn, Palnure Burn* is dominant in the Scottish south-west; perhaps earlier Germanic influence — both Anglian and Scandinavian — on this part of Scotland has something to do with it. Nevertheless, the general picture provided by the distribution of *Water of X* on the mainland is completely in accordance with the conclusions reached on the basis of the scatter of *Burn of X:* The influence of a Gaelic substratum on a top-layer of Scots.

For the absence of *Water of X* in stream-names in the Northern Isles (the type does occur in at least two loch-names in Hoy (Orkney), the *Water of Hoy* and *Water of the Wicks*), the pattern may have been set by the Old Norse generic *vatn* which is probably behind both the *water-* and the *loch-* names in Orkney and Shetland.

(b) Mains of X

The distribution of *mains* 'originally, the home farm of a landed estate' is, like that of *burn* and *water,* not at all confined to the *Mains of X* areas when *mains* is preceded by a qualifying element. There are, for instance, plenty of names containing *mains* in the Lothians and in the Borders but in all these instances the generic follows the defining element, as in *Castle Mains* BWK, *Keith Mains* ELO, *Melville Mains* MLO, etc. *Mains of X* names, however, are only to be found in the two definable areas in the north-east and south-west with the vast majority of them concentrated in east and north-east

Scotland, from Fife to Ross and Cromarty. Here are some of them: *Mains of Auchindachy* BNF, *Mains of Balmanno* KCD, *Mains of Cairnbrock* WIG, *Mains of Callander* PER, *Mains of Dunmaglass* INV, *Mains of Keithfield* ABD, *Mains of Usan* ANG. Their total number is almost 300.

That the usage of these names may have been more widespread − in documentary evidence, anyhow − a few centuries ago, is indicated by a number of recorded forms of names in West Lothian, like *Mains of Kincavill* in 1569 (now lost), *North Mains of Torthraven* 1571 and *The South Mains of Trattrevin* 1473 (now simply North and South Mains). As the shortened form of Middle English *demeyne* seems to be first on record in the second half of the fifteenth century, this may also provide a clue as to the date when this name-type developed, which can hardly have been much before the time when it was first recorded in writing.

It is difficult to point to any underlying Gaelic model for the type *Mains of X*. It rather looks as if the type of name in which the preposition *of* links the generic and specific elements, had already been established in Scots as a pattern when the social and agricultural situation demanded that the concept and reality of the 'home farm' had to find linguistic expression, in order to distinguish it from the 'big house' itself or from the *Cotton* or *Newton* bearing the same name. The idea of the *Mains* belongs to the post-Gaelic, feudal pattern of life, rather than to the Gaelic period. The distribution of this category does, however, not clash with that of the two groups examined so far, groups that are obviously much more directly linked with Gaelic name patterns, at least on the mainland.

(c) Bridge of X

The geographical scatter of names of the type *Bridge of X* is rather surprising, compared with those examined so far, for although the stronghold of these names is again the north-east, their much greater penetration into Central Scotland as far as the Great Glen disturbs the pattern established. Names outside this pattern are, for instance, *Bridge of Allan* STL, *Bridge of Awe* ARG, *Bridge of Coe* ARG, *Bridge of Grudie* ROS, *Bridge of Nevis* INV, *Bridge of Oich* INV, *Bridge of Weir* RNF, etc., whereas most of the others are found in the more 'conventional' regions for this name-type. Conveniently, the Gaelic prototype for this category still exists, the most instructive instance being *Drochaid Chonoglais* right beside *Bridge of Orchy* ARG. Other examples are *Drochaid Coire Roill* ROS and *Drochaid Lusa* in Skye, supporting the assumption that the majority of these names on the Scottish mainland were probably created by direct translation from the original Gaelic.

Their more extensive distribution must, seemingly, be ascribed to their association with means of communication, especially in those cases which occur west of the 'normal' area of *of*-names. Bridges spanning water-courses, which were otherwise difficult if not impossible to cross, must have been vital points in the scanty system of roads in the Highlands, and Lowland drovers and other travellers must have been well acquainted with them so that they became known far beyond their immediate neighbourhood. This extra-linguistic factor appears to be the main reason for the distribution of this name-type.

Even when the somewhat deviating distribution pattern of this last group of names is taken into consideration, the cumulative evidence of the *Burn of, Water of, Mains of,* and *Bridge of X* names surely proves that the second objection to the basic explanation of this name type must be invalid, at least as far as the Scottish mainland is concerned. The Gaelic model and the sequence Gaelic → Scots account for all of them though many of the names quoted may have been coined long after the initial contact between these two languages, and some of them may indeed have come into existence in a later monolingual rather than in a bilingual environment.

Any interpretation of the situation in the Northern Isles and adjacent Caithness has to be particularly concerned with names containing *burn,* since the other generics do not occur in the north at all, or only in small numbers. Two significant differences have to be taken into account. There is, first of all, the time factor. According to what we know about the settlement of these parts from the Scottish Lowlands – Fife and Kinross in particular – Scots '*X of Y*' names cannot be earlier than the end of the fifteenth or the beginning of the sixteenth century. This would put the initial chronological limit of these names a few hundred years later than their north-eastern counterparts although it is more than probable that names in this category were still coined in the north-east when they were first introduced into Orkney and Shetland. The second point of difference is the absence, in the north, of a Gaelic name-type which might have served as a model. Excluding the remote possibility of spontaneous creation (which is, after all, not possible on the mainland), two alternative explanations remain: Either the '*X of Y*' names in the north were formed on a Scandinavian model or they were introduced by immigrants from the Scottish mainland. Despite claims to the contrary, there is no evidence which satisfactorily accounts for a Scandinavian origin of our '*X of Y*' pattern in the Northern Isles, especially since there is nothing in Scandinavian toponymy itself to suggest such a prototype.

Actual examples of *Burn of X* names are, from Orkney, *The Burn of Turbitail* (Rousay), which in its lower course is known as *The Burn of Gue* and *The Burn of Vacquoy,* and from Shetland *The Burn of Aith* (Fetlar), *The Burn of Setter* (Yell), *The Burn of Holsas* (Conningsburgh), and *The Burn of Laxobigging* (Delting). Sometimes more than one generic forms names with the same specific as in the Shetland names *Hill, Wick, Head* and *Burns of Gutcher* (Yell). Unst, on the other hand, provides a pointer towards the variety of elements involved in this kind of name pattern, frequently employing both generic and specific elements of Norse, not Lowland Scots, origin. There are, amongst others, *Wick of Collaster, Point of Coppister, Ness of Wadbister, Head of Mula, Taing of Noustigarth, Geo of Henken, Ward of Clugan, Keen of Hamar, Holm of Skaw, Lee of Saxavord, Breck of Newgarth,* many of these being coastal features. It cannot be doubted, therefore, that 'X of Y' is a well-established pattern in the Northern Isles. Its apparently Norse 'look', does not imply, however, that the pattern itself is consequently Norse, for there is nothing in the Norse background to these names which could have been responsible for their spontaneous creation all over the Northern Isles, and it is necessary to presuppose an ' X of Y' type in the incoming, receiving, adapting language — Lowland Scots.

As to the age of this type, there is evidence that the pattern 'X of Y' existed in Shetland at the beginning of the seventeenth century, for the Court Book of 1615 has *the mylne of Urafirthe, the . . . hill of Urafirth, the hous of Wasland* or *Vasland, the hill of Quarfe, the ile of Moussay, the ile of Rue*, and *the hill of (Conn)sburch*, whereas one year earlier *the loch of Coginsburch* and *the ile of Wais* are on record, always with the definite article and still hovering on the brink between appellative and onomastic usage. For Orkney, there are some hints in Storer Clouston's *Records of the Earldom of Orkney* which cover the years 1299-1614. In this collection, the first examples of the pattern, under discussion appear in the last decade of the fifteenth century, in 1492, when we have *Nethirtown of Grenyng* (Marwick), *Bordland of Swarthmale* and *Bull of Rapness* (Westray), *Bull of Kerston* (Stromness) and *Bull of Hove* (Hoy). In the last three cases, *Bull* represents Old Norse *bú* 'farmstead, estate, etc.', which was apparently used by the incoming Scots in the same way as their own term *mains*, although there exist really no data on which to determine exactly when the peculiar formula *'Bu of X'* first came into use. It is reasonable to assume that the farms so named had been settled before they were named in this fashion.

Of course, the *'Bu of X'* formula is part of a much larger and much more comprehensive invasion of this Scots name-type from those parts of Scotland where it had developed in linguistic contact with Gaelic. The pattern encountered in the Northern Isles is nothing but the exported result of this contact situation, and in this way the Gaelic original 'Allt a'—' or 'Loch a' - -' or 'Cnoc a'—' are ultimately, although indirectly, also responsible for that plethora of 'X of Y' names in Shetland, Orkney and the eastern ('Scandinavian') half of Caithness. Independent creation must be ruled out.

Obviously the northern Isles, in their initially bilingual and subsequently post-Scandinavian linguistic setting, additionally share with the Hebrides all the other categories of names brought about by such a situation. English names created in such a way belong by definition to the more recent newcomers to the Scottish toponymic scene.

Closely related to the imported name *pattern* is the imported *name*, i.e. a name introduced for some reason from another country and more often than not from a language never spoken in Scotland or in the British Isles. Since the motivation for such transfers, which might consequently be termed, in the broadest sense, cultural rather than linguistic, may be anything from a personal whim to fashionable conditions created by a general historical or economic situation, the

Scottish map is dotted with individual names or groups of names that betray their non-Scottish origins straightaway and arouse interest because of this their inherent quaintness. Perhaps the most widely distributed of these is the name *Waterloo* which occurs in at least ten different Scottish counties, from Shetland to the Borders. In each case, there is little doubt about the connection of the name with the military event in 1815 but it is not always easy to determine the particular relationship in each instance. In Ross-shire it was formerly the name of an inn named after the battle; in Skye it is said to have been so called from veteran soldiers resident therein at one time, and in Perthshire it is also explained as the name of a row of houses originally built for veterans returning from Waterloo. One suspects that a number of these names started out as nicknames rather than as part of an official naming policy, but more detailed investigation into both oral tradition and local historical documents should furnish some more satisfactory information. Another name which had indirect martial connections is *Portobello* near Edinburgh which ousted the older village name *Figgate*, after having first been given to a house built about 1750 by a sailor who claimed to have been present at the capture of Puerto Bello in Panama, by Admiral Vernon, in 1739. The same English admiral also figures in the Lanarkshire name *Mount Vernon*, in Old Monkland parish near Glasgow. Although nobody disputes that the Scottish name is ultimately derived from George Washington's estate in Virginia, the accounts as to how the transfer took place differ slightly. Almost all of them, however, attribute the introduction of the name to Scotland (replacing the estate name *Windyedge*) to George Buchanan, one of the so-called 'Virginia dons' because of his extensive tobacco trading with Virginia, who was also responsible for the building of 'the Virginia Mansion' in Glasgow and whose son Andrew started and is commemorated in, Glasgow's Buchanan Street. However, although it is usually stated that Glasgow's *Mount Florida* stems from the former Mount Florida House which was occupied by a family from Florida, USA, early nineteenth-century spellings such as Mount Floridon (1840) and Mount Floradale (1819) cast doubt on such an explanation without suggesting anything more conclusive in its place.

At least one of the several *Egypts* in Scotland also has military links. The name *Egypt* in the parish of Kirkpatrick Juxta in Dumfriesshire was 'given to houses by General Johnstone who was one of Abercrombie's officers, and who served in Egypt about 1800 during the time of Napoleon's invasion'. The same general and landowner, incidentally, is also responsible for the names *Grand Cairo, Rosetta*, and *Valenciennes* in the same parish. *Egypts* in other counties may refer to encampments of gypsies or 'Egyptians' or have to be interpreted in a Biblical context. The latter suggests itself for the lost Edinburgh name *Egypt* which is mentioned from 1652 to 1773 in the neighbourhood of *Canaan* and *Jordan (Burn)* in the Morningside-Braid district of the city, Biblical influence is also behind such names as *Joppa* (in Portobello) and *Goshen*, a common eighteenth- to nineteenth-century farm-name in several counties, standing as a kind of onomastic metaphor for 'land of plenty', 'land without plagues', after the Old Testament Goshen in Egypt where Joseph settled his father and brothers. Medieval monastic tradition has given us such well-disguised Edinburgh names as *Sciennes* which has such sixteenth-century spellings as *Shenis, Sheynis, Senis,* and *Cenis,* and (The) *Pleasance,* also on record from the sixteenth century onwards (*Pleasance, Plesance, Pleasans,* etc.). Whereas the former derives from the Dominican nunnery of St Catherine of *Sienna,* the latter is the name of the site of the nunnery of St Mary of *Placentia* — two Italian place-names in the middle of the Scottish capital. These are only a few examples of the type of name reaching Scotland through Biblical or Christian tradition, or both, but they clearly point to the strength of that tradition in the naming of, mostly minor, settlement names in Scotland, a strength which is perhaps only rivalled by the nostalgic naming of houses after faraway and exotic place-names by sailors returning to their native land after a lifetime on the oceans. Relevant, in this respect, and not at all quixotic, might be the Peebles-shire name *Lamancha* which owes its existence on the Scottish map to Admiral Sir A. Cochrane who apparently gave this name to the Grange of Romanno around 1736, because he had lived in the appropriate province of Spain.

Names like *Mount Vernon, Waterloo,* and *Egypt* are like communications from other linguistic and cultural worlds. In addition to this kind of transplantation of whole names from elsewhere onto Scottish soil, there is at least one instance in which only a generic element was imported from abroad. The circumstances under which this happened are somewhat bizarre, but fortunately we have enough evidence to tell almost the whole story. The name in question is *Friockheim* ANG. Tempted by the suggestive element *-heim,* at least one German scholar felt inclined to think that this might be evidence for the presence of Swabians in the area, since *-heim* is a very common generic element in many parts of Germany. Any comment on this seemingly far-fetched idea will have to include the admission that the *-heim* of *Friockheim* is indeed a German element, while rejecting the view that this might go back to German, particularly Swabian, settlers. In the Episcopal Register of Brechin, in a document of 1613, there is reference to a place called *Freok* which is mentioned with Pressock and Gardyne (spelt *Pressok* and *Gardin* respectively), and 50 years later, in 1663, the same place-name is spelt *Friock.* This is undoubtedly an Anglicisation of some form, probably a locative, of Gaelic *fraoch* 'heather', and likely to be quite descriptive of the place to which the name applied. For the later transition from *Friock* to Friockheim we have unusually exact printed evidence in the form of a slightly brownish handbill about five and a half inches by seven inches in size, printed by P. Cochran in Arbroath, and now in the Angus Folk Museum at Glamis. The bottom right-hand corner is a little torn, but fortunately the most important item, the date, is still legible. The full text of the bill reads:

FRIOCKHEIM

The Spinning Mill and Village of Friock, of which Mr. GARDYNE of Middleton is the Superior, and Mr. JOHN ANDSON, Proprietor holding in Feu, hitherto called *"Friock Feus"*, from this date henceforward is to be named *"FRIOCKHEIM"*, and of which change of designation, this, on the parts of Mr. Gardyne and Mr. Andson, is notice unto all whom it may concern.

FRIOCKHEIM, 22nd May, 1824.

Although there is no absolute certainty regarding the motives for this change, it is known that the John Andson in question was the son of the man of the same name who was Provost of Arbroath from 1811 to 1814, and that he is alleged to have lived long in Germany. It is more than a guess to infer from this information that nostalgia for his lengthy stay abroad probably induced him to introduce the place-name element *-heim* from Germany, thus creating one of the most curious hybrid names on the Scottish map.

5
Early English Names

Since there have been speakers of English in Scotland for well over 1300 years, the place-names created in the early phases of this linguistic stratum can hardly be classified as belonging to the 'youngest' names on the Scottish map. These early names, coined by the people we call Angles, and therefore to be termed Anglian rather than English, are not only illustrative of the considerable historical depth of the English contribution to Scottish nomenclature, but are also the only usable linguistic evidence available to afford us a glimpse of the earliest stages of English settlement in Scotland.

Our hope of finding Anglian place-names of a comparatively early nature in Scotland, especially in the Scottish south, does, of course, stem from our knowledge, derived from the meagre historical, literary and genealogical sources for the period, of a gradual northward movement of Anglian raiders and settlers, beginning – at least so Bede alleges – with the founding of the kingdom of Bernicia by King Ida in 547, probably consisting of no more than a small band of Anglian pirates on Bamburgh Rock. This small colony expanded rapidly and considerably during the reign of King Æthelfrith (*c.* 593-616), victor of Degsastan in 603 against the Scots of Dalriada, and creator of the Kingdom of Northumbria by gaining control over Deira to the south. Christianity came to the Northumbrian Angles under his successor Edwin of Deira (616-32), the date normally given for this decisive event being the year 627. During the rule of the next king, Oswald of Bernicia (633-41), the fortress of Edinburgh or Cumbric *Eidyn* was besieged and captured, allowing occupation and subsequent settling of the Lothians. Oswy who reigned after his brother Oswald from 642-71 had acquired the Cumbric kingdom of Rheged by marriage about 645, and under him the westward and north-westward movement along the shores of the Solway Firth to the west coast of Cumberland and to Galloway must have taken place, leaving Strathclyde the sole survivor of the three Brittonic kingdoms in existence at the beginning of the Anglian occupation. By the middle of the seventh century, then, the Firth of Forth was the northern boundary of the Northumbrian kingdom and about 680, in Ecgfrith's reign (670-85), Trumwin was installed as 'Bishop of the Picts' at Abercorn. In 685 Ecgfrith was killed in the battle of Nechtansmere or Dunnichen in Angus in an unsuccessful attempt to subdue the southern Picts; as a result of this event, the Anglian northward movement was halted, and even in Bede's time about 730, shortly after Whithorn (or *Candida Casa*) had become an English bishopric, the Forth was still the frontier between the Picts and the Angles. In 750 Eadbert appears to have added the Ayrshire district of Kyle to the Northumbrian possessions, and in the last decade of the same century the Vikings attacked the monasteries at Lindisfarne and Yarrow, as well as Iona.

How far does the place-nomenclature reflect this Anglian advance and the area and extent of early Anglian settlement?

Place-name research in England has demonstrated that the element OE -*ing* as a name-forming suffix is of the greatest significance in this respect, as it is known to belong in some formations to the earliest strata of Anglo-Saxon settlement. For a full understanding of its meaning and chronology, at least four main categories have to be distinguished: (1) Final singular -*ing*; (2) Final nominative plural -*ingas*; (3) Medial -*inga*-, which is the genitive plural of -*ingas* in compound place-names; and (4) Medial -*ing*- meaning 'associated with'. Recently it has also been shown that a variety of dative-locative forms and their compositional derivatives have to be reckoned with. A composite distribution map published by the English Place-name Society shows place-names in -*ingas* and -*ingaham* but not the 49 Old English names ending in singular -*ing*; these are most prevalent in Kent, Hampshire, Essex and Berkshire although they are also found further up the Thames valley and in East Anglia and the East Midlands. They do in fact belong to such an early phase of Anglo-Saxon settlement that they are of no interest to the settlement history of Southern Scotland. Names in -*ingas*, on the other hand, and those in -*ingaham* do occur in Northumbrian territory, and as they have also been claimed to be the earliest Anglian names in Scotland, the justification for such claims has to be examined in some detail.

First, the names in final -*ingas*. These were originally folk-names with the generalised meaning of 'an association of people dependent in some way or another upon the leader whose name forms the first theme'. They therefore first applied to communities of people, later referring also to districts or some place within the district. In their original meaning and function they quite clearly belong to the age of migration, but in the Old English period two main groups have to be distinguished, those expressing a personal and those expressing a geographical association. How far does this type which in England has a more easterly and southeasterly distribution particularly in areas of early Anglo-Saxon settlement, occur in Scotland? It has been suggested that five place-names contain this element: *Binning* WLO and *Binning Wood* ELO, *Crailing* ROX, *Simprim* BWK, and *Cunningham* AYR. The first, *Binning*, now *Binny*, has been shown to be an analogical development, with *Bennyn*, *Benyn*, *Bynin*, *Binin*, etc. representing the original ending; and as *Binning Wood* ELO is probably a transferred name based on this West Lothian *Binning*, these two will have to be rejected as candidates. Next, *Crailing* ROX, of which these are the medieval recorded forms:

Craling	1147-50 (17th) Lawrie, *Early Scottish Charters*
	1301 *Index British Museum*
Cralingis	(pl.) 1147-50 (17th) Lawrie, *Early Scottish Charters*
Creling	1147-52 (Morton) *ibid.*
	1295 *Instrumenta Publica*
Craaling	1165-1114 *National Mss of Scotland*
Treiling	(p) 1180 *Acts of Parliaments of Scotland*
Creglinge	1256 Bain, *Calendar of Documents*
Crelenge	1296 *ibid.*
Cralyng	1456 *Historical Mss Commission* (Roxburghe)

At first sight, this looks like a *ling*-formation from a Celtic river-name identical with the rivers *Crai* in Wales and *Cray* in Kent. The Old English form of this would have been something like **Craeg*, the water-course in question being the Oxnam Water on which Crailing is situated. However, a compound of OE **Crā*, cognate with ON *Kra*, 'nook, corner', and OE *hlync* 'ridge, slope' must be taken into consideration and is indeed more probable, as the geographical position suits this analysis. There is no trace of a plural -*s* anyhow, so that this name can at the very most be classed as doubtful.

Simprim in the Swinton parish of Berwickshire is the fourth name supposed to be a possible -*ingas*- formation. On record it appears thus:

Simprinc	1153-65 (*c.* 1320) *Kelso Liber*
Simprig	1159 *ibid.*
	1246 *Pontifical of St Andrews*
Semprinc	1251 (*c.* 1320) *Kelso Liber*
Sympring	*c.* 1280 *ibid.*
	1370 Bain, *Calendar of Documents*
Sempring	*c.* 1300 *Coldingham Correspondence*
Sympryng	*c.* 1415 *Kelso Liber*

It is tempting to think of the first element in the English name *Sempringham* LIN as an identical parallel, but as the oldest recorded spelling of the English name is *Sempingaham* in 852, the -*r*- appears to be intrusive. The Berwickshire name could, of course, quite independently be based on a potential personal name, such as a nickname belonging to the stem of the English verb to *simper*, for which Scandinavian parallels exist in Norwegian *semper*, Swedish *simper, semper* 'affected, prudish'. Although this might not be a particularly suitable name for a hero or leader, it is not impossible, and bearing in mind that again there is no indication of plurality, Simprim might still be a potential -*ingas* name, since final -*s* rarely appears in the Middle English sources of the Midlands and northern counties of England.

The last candidate is *Cunningham*:

Incuneningum (regio) *c.* 730 Bede, *Historia Ecclesiastica*
In (On) Cununingum (Cunigum) *c.* 890 *Old English Bede.*
Cunegan 1153 *Glasgow Registrum*
Cuninham 1180 *ibid.*

Undoubtedly, Bede's reference represents a genuine dative plural of an -*ingas*- name after the preposition *in*; this is supported by the fact that Cunningham is a regional name. There are therefore no linguistic difficulties. The doubt that arises stems from the geographical position of this district name; in fact, the question is whether the identification is right and whether Bede is indeed referring to Cunningham in North Ayrshire. The full quotation from his *Historia Ecclesiastica* (Book V, Chapter XII) is: *'Erat ergo pater familias in regione Nordan hymbrorum, quae uocatur Incuneningum'*, and we also hear that the worthy man's name was *Drycthelm*. Now, even someone as single-minded as Bede would not have claimed that Cunningham was a district of Northumbria at about 700 when Drycthelm was apparently there, nor even at the time when the *Historia* was written. The district of Kyle, which lies to the south of Cunningham, and therefore nearer to Bernician territory in Galloway and Carrick, was not annexed until 750, and it is difficult to understand what a man with the good patriotic Anglian name of *Dryhthelm* 'helmet (or protector) of the people' was doing in North Ayrshire half a century earlier, even if one were willing to stretch a point as far as the *regio Nordanhymbrorum* is concerned. Personally, I am not convinced that Cunningham is in fact meant, and I find the temptation great to revive the theory which identified Bede's *in Cuneningum* with the area around *Chester-le-Street* in Durham which is first on record as *Cunca-* or *Cunceceastre* about 1050. Chester-le-Street lies in the heart of Northumbria, but even if this identification has its own problems, this does not strengthen the case for Cunningham, since both the *-ing-* and the *hām* appear to be late adaptations (the former indeed later than the latter).

With respect to the presence of folk- or settlement-names in *-ingas* in Scotland, then, there are three doubtful candidates, two for linguistic, one for extra-linguistic reasons. Of these, *Simprim* is perhaps the strongest claimant, but even it is too uncertain to provide convincing evidence. The safe conclusion therefore has to be that names in *-ingas*, just like those in singular *-ing* are totally lacking in Scotland. In this connection it is also of interest that there is no trace whatever in Scottish place-names of words such as *alh, hearg, wīg*, all denoting 'temples', or *bel* 'funeral pyre' with its compounds *bēl-stede* 'place of the funeral pyre' and *bel-haga* 'funeral pyre enclosure', or names of pagan divinities such as *Woden, Thunor* or *Tīw*, in fact the whole vocabulary of Anglo-Saxon heathen worship. The absence both of this terminology and of names in singular *-ing* and plural *-ingas* taken together surely implies that the Angles cannot have occupied much ground in the Border Counties before their official conversion to Christianity in 627, and if non-linguistic conclusions from this place-name evidence are permitted, the inference might well be that the chances of finding an extensive pagan Anglian cemetery in Scotland are probably very slender — but then this is just the kind of conclusion a name scholar should not come to.

What, then, are the earliest Anglo-Saxon *ing-* formations in our area? These belong to the *-ingahām* type or the like, i.e. names ending in OE *hām* 'village, homestead' (itself an early word) in which the first part is the genitive plural of a folk-name in *-ingas*. Of these there are three definite examples and one doubtful one: The definite ones are

Whittingehame and *Tynninghame* ELO, and *Coldingham* BWK, the doubtful one is *Edingham* KCB. Names like *Penninghame* WIG (*Penygham* 1644, *Pennygham* 1652, *Pennegem* 1756) and *Fotheringham* ANG (*ffodryngay* 1261, *Fodringeye* 1291, after the English *Fotheringhay*) are non-genuine examples similar to *Cunningham,* and therefore practically irrelevant, in the same way in which *Stirling* STL and *Bowling* DNB and names containing words like *bigging* or *shieling* had to be excluded from the discussion of the first two groups of *-ing-* names because they are not early material. Of the three genuine *-ingahām* names, *Whittinghame* [ˈhwitindʒ əm]] (*Whitingham* 1254, *Whityngham 1336)* is identical *with* Whittingham NTB (*Hwitincham c.* 1050), and *Whicham* CMB (*Witingham* 1086), which also presuppose as their basis an Old English personal name *Hwīta.* Etymologically it is therefore an OE *Hwītingahām 'settlement˙ of *Hwīta's* people', or more likely *Hwītingiahām or *Hwītindʒe-hām 'the settlement at Hwīting (=at the place called after *Hwīta*)', as every single one of these names shows assibilation of the velar *g* in *-ing-*; this is most clearly seen in *Whicham* but is, of course, also implicit in the modern pronunciation of the East Lothian name, [ˈhwitindʒəm]. In this respect, *Whittingehame* fits in well with the evidence from neighbouring Northumberland. Whittingham LNC (*Witingheham* 1086), otherwise alike in its compositional elements, does not share the assibilation. For *Tynninghame* the genitive plural form *-inga-* is beautifully preserved in the early spellings:

In Tininghami 756 *Annals of Lindisfarne* (first hand)
Tinningaham c. 1050 (*c.* 1180) *Historia Sancti Cuthberti*
Tiningaham 1140–8 *Symeon of Durham* (s.a. 757)

The meaning is evidently 'village of those dwelling by the River Tyne' in which *Tīningas is a formation similar to that of *Avening* GLO 'dwellers on the Avon'.

Coldingham also contains an earlier geographical name, but the old forms pertaining to it must be divided into two streams:

(a)	*Coludesburh*	679 (*c.* 1120) *Anglo-Saxon Chronicle* (E)
		c. 890 (*c.* 1000) *Old English Bede*
	Colodesbyrig	699-709 (late 9th-early 10th) *Anonymous Life of St Cuthbert*
	Colodaesburg	*c.* 710 (11th) *Life Bishop Wilfrid*
	Coludi urbem	*c.* 730 Bede *Historia Ecclesiastica*
	Coludanae urbs	*ibid.*
(b)	*Collingaham*	1095-1100 Lawrie, *Early Scottish Charters*
	Coldingham	1097-1107 *National Mss of Scotland*
		1100 Lawrie, *Early Scottish Charters*
		c. 1255 Bain, *Calendar of Documents*
	Coldingeham	*c.* 1100 Lawrie, *Early Scottish Charters*
	Goldingeham	1126 *ibid.*
		early 13th *Scalacronica*
	Coldingham	1176 *Melrose Chronicle*

Of these, the series in *-burh* or *byrig* 'a fortified place' is probably the older, perhaps part-translating a Brittonic (Cumbric) *Caer Golud* or the like with reference to a fortress on St Abb's Head. Coldingham might then be interpreted either as *Coludingaham* 'village of the people at Colud', or as an elliptical form based on the name *Coludesburh* and so meaning 'village of the people of Coludesburh' (cf. *Happisburgh* NFK which may be present in *Happing Hundred* as 'the folk belonging to Happisburgh', rather than 'the folk of a man called *Haepp'*).

Edingham north of Dalbeattie in the Stewartry KCB is recorded too late (*Edinghame* 1554 RMS) to provide a sound basis for such a thorny problem as the earliest Anglian names in Scotland, unless it can be equated with the *Edyngaheym* of *c.* 1124 ESC; but this seems to apply rather to a 'lost' name *Ednemland* near Annan DMF.

From a map prepared by the English Place-name Society it becomes clear that the distribution of *-ingahām* is rather more northerly and easterly than that of *-ing* and *-ingas*. Without wanting to revive the old theory which saw tribal associations in German place-names ending in *-ingen*, *-ingheim* or *-heim*, the *-ingahām* names are certainly more characteristic of Anglian territory than, for instance, of Saxon, and the three Scottish names near the coast (Map 2) are probably the northern-most appendix of this Anglian *-ingahām* area; their formation must have been just possible and no more, in the early phases of the Anglian settlement of Votadinic territory.

In the same way in which *-inga-* appears to be only attached to *-hām* in Scottish place-names and not to other words like *burna, feld, ford, halh*, etc., as in England, the connective particle *-ing-* is found only with *tūn*; and just as *tūn* is slightly later in Scotland than *hām*, so names ending in *-ingtūn* belong to a later period than those in *-ingas* and *-ingahām*. Once the numerous non-genuine late adaptations like *Abington* LAN (*Albintoune* 1459), *Newington* (Edinburgh), *Symington* (several) from a personal name *Symon*, and others, have been eliminated, there remains a genuine residue of early material in such Berwickshire names as *Edington* (*Hadynton* 1095 [15th], *Hoedentum* 1095-1100 [15th], *Edingtonam* 1095 [15th]) 'farm associated with *Ead(d)a'*; *Edrington* (*Hadryngton* 1095 [15th]) 'farm associated with the river Adder'; *Mersington* (so 1291) 'farm associated with *Mērsa* or *Mērsige'*; Renton (*Regninton* 1095 [15th], *Reningtona* 1235) 'farm associated with Regna or Regenwald'; *Thirlington*, perhaps from an Old English personal name *þyrla*, although OE *pyrel* 'hollow' is a possibility as in *Thirlmere* CMB, and *Upsettlington* (*Upsetintun* 1095-1100 [15th], *Hupsetligtun* [p] 1153-65 [*c.* 1320]; *Upsedilington c.* 1240), from OE *Setling-tūn* 'farm by the shelf, ledge', and probably also *Carrington* MLO, *Haddington* ELO, *Hassington* BWK, and *Shearington* DMF, the old forms of which leave some doubt as to whether they are genuine *-ingtūn-* names or not. The distribution of those which can be identified as genuine (Map 2), links nicely with the rest of the Northumbrian evidence and appears to point to a slightly more advanced stage of Anglian occupation, probably in Oswy's time. The absence of names of this type along the northern shores of the Solway Firth (apart from one possible exception) should be noted.

Another place-name element, which is likely to be a good indicator as to where the Angles first began to carve their kingdom out of the

2   Anglian names containing *-ingtun, ingham, bōtl, bōðl-tun*

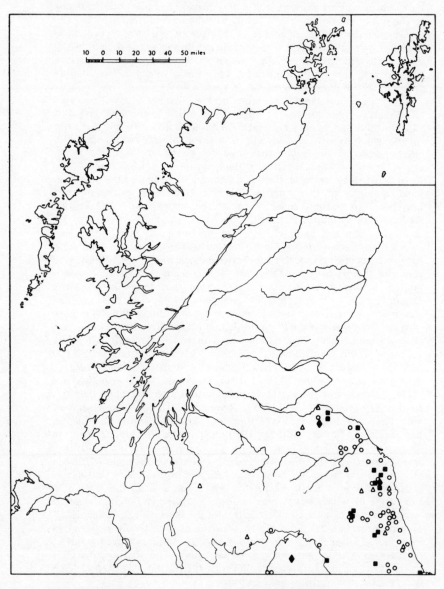

10   0   10   20   30   40   50 miles

○ Name containing *ingtun*   △ Name containing *bōtl*

■ Name containing *ingham*   ◆ Name containing *bōthl₊tun*

3   Anglian names containing -*wīc*, -*hām*, and -*worth*

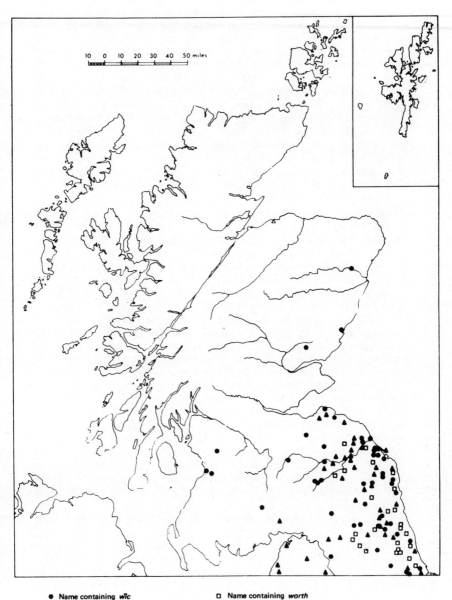

● Name containing *wīc*   □ Name containing *worth*
▲ Name containing *hām*

Cumbric territory in the south of Scotland, is *hām*. In contrast to *tūn*, which originally meant 'enclosure', *hām* always meant the 'homestead' or 'group of homesteads' itself. The English distribution suggests that it was becoming obsolete in place-name usage as the settlement advanced towards the west. Its Scottish distribution (Map 3), from which obviously later types of name like the several *Cauldhame*, and also the very curious *Letham* with its strange scatter and heterogeneous origin, have to be excluded, is therefore bound to be of significance. The names which can be used as sound evidence are all situated in Roxburghshire, Berwickshire, and East Lothian, with one outlier in Dumfriesshire, *Smallholm* (*Smalham* 1304), which has an identical equivalent in *Smailholm* ROX (*Smalham c.* 1160 [16th]), both deriving from OE *Smael hām* 'small village'; the tendency to substitute -*holm* for -*hām* is also evidenced in *Leitholm* BWK (*Letham* 1165-1214) 'village on the Leet Water', and *Yetholm* in *Town* and *Kirk Yetholm* ROX (*Gatha'n c.* 1050 [12th] ; *Yetham* [p] 1165-1214) from OE *gaet hām* 'village near the gate or pass'. Others are *Ednam* (*Ædnaham c.* 1105, *Ednaham* 1107-17) 'village on the river Eden', *Oxnam* (*Oxenham* 1165-1244), from OE *Oxenahām* 'village of the oxen', *Midlem Middleham c.* 1120 [*c.* 1320] 'the middle village', all in Roxburghshire *Birgham* [ˈbɛːrdʒəm] (*Brygham* 1095 [15th]) from OE *brycg* 'bridge', *Edrom* (*Edrem* 1095 [15th], *Ederham* 1095) 'village on the river Adder', and *Kimmerhame* [ˈkimərdʒəm] (*Chynbrygham* 1095 [15th]) possibly based on an Old English personal name *Cyneberht*, all in Berwickshire; and in East Lothian there are finally *Morham* which in the thirteenth century is also called *Morton* '*hām* or *tūn* by the moor', **Aldhām* 'old village' in *Oldhamstocks* (*Aldhamstoc* 1127), and one of the *Lethams* which should perhaps rather be marked as doubtful. *Twynholm* KCB may or may not contain an element *hām* (*Twyneme* 1605), and the same applies to *Penninghame* WIG (*Penygham* 1644, *Pennygham* 1652, *Pennegem* 1756). Puzzling is *Eaglesham* RNF which appears to contain Welsh *eglwys* or Gaelic *eaglais* 'church'. If the second part is indeed *hām*, the name may stem from a possible period of temporary Anglian overlordship over Strathclyde in Ecgfrith's reign. Otherwise the geographical scatter is again well in keeping with what has already been indicated by other generics. In a way, names in *hām* cover the same area as those in *inghām* and *ingtūn* combined, that is the coastal strip from the English border to East Lothian and the main river valleys of Roxburghshire and Berwickshire, linking up without a break with Northumberland. The Tweed appears to be rather a magnet or link than a divide.

The elements -*ingahām*, -*ingtūn*, and *hām* nicely establish a basic area of Anglian settlement, but there is a certain amount of additional material which completes the English evidence already gathered and mapped for Northumbria. There is, for example an OE *worð* meaning, like *tūn*, 'an enclosure'; it is known from documents as early as the seventh century and can further be proved to be early because it forms compounds with *hām* and folk-names in -*ingas*. Although it is obsolescent or obsolete in the literary period, it continued to be used in place-names, and the reason why it is of such importance in toponymic evidence is that it — like some other elements — appears to have been very productive in Northumbria and especially Bernicia, as the names in Northumberland and Durham testify. In Scotland three names contain or contained this element, all of them in the most 'Northumbrian' counties of Berwickshire and Roxburghshire, two of them in fact south of the Tweed (Map 3). There is *Polwarth* BWK (*Paulewrhe* [p] 1182-1214, *Paulewurth* [p] [13th]) probably compounded with a personal name *Paul.* This is the only one which has preserved its original generic, for in *Cessford* ROX (*Cesseworth* 1296) 'Cessa's enclosure', *worð* has been replaced by *ford,* and in *Jedburgh* ROX (*Gedwearde c.* 1050 [12th], *Gedwirth* 1177 [16th]) 'enclosed village on the river Jed', *burh* has taken its place. This shows that *worð* must have gone out of use at an early date when a better-known element was substituted. This process of substitution is closely paralleled in the neighbouring county of Northumberland where in at least five cases *wood* has replaced *worð,* which both north and south of the present border lends, as another early generic element, its weight to our argument.

Another element appears to belong to a slightly later period. It means 'a dwelling, or dwelling-place, house' and in English takes the forms *bōðl, bōtl,* and *bold.* Of these three, only the first two interest us here, the first both as a generic and in the compound *boðl-tūn* (= Bolton) which is clearly Northumbrian, the second, also chiefly northern, in its later form *bottle* or, unrounded about the seventeenth century, *battle.* *Bōðl* alone, of which there are four instances in the rest of Northumbria, occurs in Scotland in the name *Maybole* AYR which appears as *Maybothel* (*Maybothil*) in 1189-1250, and as *Maibothel* in 1204-30. Other references to *Maybole* are *Meibothelbeg* and *Meibothelmor* 1185-96 which are interesting because of the later (!) additions of Gaelic *beag* 'small' and *mór* 'big' to this Anglian name. The first element is most likely the same as in *Mawbray* CMB which is *Mayburg'* in 1175, *Mayburch* in 1262, etc. If so, it would be from OE *mǣge* 'a kinswoman, a maiden', with the whole name meaning 'the kinswomen's (or the maidens') dwelling', but other explanations are, of course, also possible. To the English *Boltons* can be added one example from East Lothian (*Bothel-, Bowel-, Boeltun c.* 1200); and for *bōtl* there is the simplex *Buittle* KCB (*Botel* 1296; *Butil* 1456, 1471), which practically coincides in its earlier forms with the *Bootles* of Lancashire and Cumberland, as well as the compound names *Morebattle* ROX (*Mereboda c.* 1124 [12th], *Merbotil* 1174-99 [1500]) from OE *mere-bōtl* 'dwelling by the lake', *Eldbotle* ELO (*Elbotle* 1128; *Ellebotle* 1160-2) and *Newbattle* MLO (*Neubotle* 1140) which, when founded as a Cistercian monastery by David I in 1140, is supposed to have been called thus to distinguish it from *Eldbotle,* the 'old building'. In the distribution of this element (Map 2) the examples from the Stewartry and from West Ayrshire are noteworthy but even they, in their isolation, only confirm the impression of a thin ruling class of Anglians after Oswy's marriage, rather than of a thorough settlement. The situation is similar with regard to one further Old English generic element, already alluded to above (p. 5) as part of the discussion of the name *Hawick* ROX, the term *wīc* which, because of its extensive distribution in England, must be regarded as a truly Anglo-Saxon, rather than a purely Anglian, place-name generic, although it is obviously still of Anglian provenance, as far as Scotland is concerned (Map 3).

When attempting to isolate names containing *wīc* on the Scottish side of the border, there is, of course, always the initial possibility of confusing it with ON *vík* 'bay' as in *Wick* CAI or *Lerwick* SHE, but both the early forms and the geographical location of the names in question fortunately help to overcome this little difficulty. Due to the minor type of settlement to which *wīc* originally applied (see p. 81 below), several names containing this generic appear to have been 'lost' or have not been identified.

Of the numerous Scottish names in -*wīc*, the best known now applies to a place outside Scotland, Berwick-on-Tweed NTB (*Berwic* 1095, *Berewic* 1130-33, *Berwich* 1136); it is included here since the county-name derived from it, Berwickshire, applies to a Scottish county and since the settlement, to which the name was first given, was for a long time in Scottish territory. Of identical origin is North Berwick ELO (*Berewic* 1165-72, *Norh' berwic* 1160-85, *Northberewich* 1215-26, *North Berrick* 1690, etc.). Both names derive from an OE *berewīc* 'barley farm', referring to a grange or an outlying part of an estate; there are many English parallels, from Cornwall to Northumberland. The term *berewīc* also occurs as a common noun in charters. In contrast to North Berwick, Berwick-on-Tweed is called *Suthberwyche* 'South Berwick' in 1287, and is similarly designated from the end of the thirteenth to the fifteenth century. Berwick ABD (earlier *Berrek*) is almost surely an imported name.

Birswick DMF., for which there is no early evidence, may be from OE *bȳres-wīc* 'byre farm'. The two surviving examples of Borthwick are in Roxburghshire (*Bordewich* 1165-69, *Borthewyk* 1335-36) and Midlothian (*Borthwyk* 1361, *Borthic* 1473), whereas Borthwick BWK (*Borthwic* 1501, *Borthwick* 1692) and Borthwick SLK (*Borthwic* 1410, *Borthuik* 1538) are now 'lost'. OE *bord wīc* 'home farm' (or, 'the farm which supplied the board or table of the lord of the district'), is the usually accepted explanation because of the numerous Borelands or Bordlands in the formerly Gaelic-speaking territories of Scotland. However, the same word OE *bord* may imply 'board = plank = wood', as has been assumed for some English wood-names like Bordley YOW and Borthwood IOW. Borthwick may therefore mean 'wood farm' rather than 'home farm', especially in view of the fact that the *Bordland* of Scotland does not appear to have any exact counterpart in English settlement names. It is more than probable, by the way, that all four names go back to the Roxburghshire original.

For Darnick ROX (*Dernewic c.* 1136, *Darnyke(e)* 1565) there is no identical equivalent in England. It is an OE *derne wīc* 'hidden farm', perhaps because it was situated in woodland or overgrown with vegetation. Nearest geographically is the hybrid name Darncrook NTB in which *derne* is combined with ON *krókr* 'nook, bend'. Since Dawick

PEB (*Dawik* 1501-2, *Dayik, Daik* 1580) is apparently not recorded before the sixteenth century, the quest for an etymology is highly speculative, the Old English words *dā* 'doe' and *dawe* 'crow-like bird, jackdaw' being the most likely candidates for the first element, although *dawe* does not seem to be recorded in English place-names. Whereas Fenwick ROX (*ffenwic* [p] *c.* 1280, *Fennyk* 1511) is most likely OE *fenn wīc* 'mud farm' or 'marshland farm', and therefore identical with Fenwick NTB and YOW, the Ayrshire Fenwick (*Fynnickhill* 1620, *Finwick* 1687, *Fennick* 1775) is not as straightforward, as it is not certain whether the medial -w- is generic or not. A cluster of names from Lennox DNB (*Fynwik* 1545, *Fynwikblair* and *Finwikmalice* 1548, *Fynwik-Drummond* 1565) may be indicative of Gaelic origin, but the proximity of Prestwick may make Fenwick AYR an early English name.

Fishwick BWK (*Fyschewike* 1095, *Fiscwic c.* 1100, *Fischik* 1548) and Fishwick LNC are the same in origin. Both must have been 'dwellings where fish were cured or sold', or there may have been fishponds there. The Angus name Handwick (*Handwik* 1487) apparently contains -*wīc* as a generic, but an etymology of the specific element is difficult to provide because of the, not unexpectedly, late evidence. Perhaps it is OE *hana* 'a cock', in which case Handforth CHE (*Haneford* 1158-81) would afford a parallel in the development of a *d* after *n*. Of the four developments of OE *hǣddre wīc* 'heather farm', two are in the area in which early English names are common, and two are in the north-east like Berwick ABD and Handwick ANG. These first two are Hedderwick ELO (*Hatheruuich* 1093-4, *Hathervic* 1165-1214) and Hedderwick BWK ('lost', in Lauder: *Hatherwik* 1509, *Hedderwick* 1696), whereas the north-eastern instances are Hedderwick ANG (*Hathyrwich* 1267-81, *Hathirwyk* 1296-1320) and Heatherwick ABD (*Haddirweik* 1600). They are paralleled by Heatherwick NTB. Hawick ROX (*Hawic* 1165-69, *Hawyc* 1264-66), from OE *haga wīc* 'hedge (or enclosure) farm', has already had detailed treatment (p. 3); it is again paralleled by an identical name in neighbouring Northumberland.

Like Hawick, Prestwick AYR (*Prestwic* 1165-73, *Prestwyc* [p] *c.* 1272, *Prestik* 1556) is a parish name which argues for a certain status in historical times, too. The same as Prestwick NTB and BRK and Prestwich LNC, it is derived from OE *prēost wīc* 'priest's dwelling', or *prēosta wīc* 'priests' dwelling', probably the same as Prestwick NTB and BRK and Prestwich LNC. In the general context of names in -*wīc*, a name so far west is perhaps rather surprising at first sight but if one adds Fenwick (see above), possibly Previck ('lost', near Annbank AYR: *Previck* 1429, with uncertain etymology), Maybole in the same county further south (see p. 77), the curious Eaglesham in nearby Renfrewshire (see p. 76) and, even if the ultimate origin of the name may be different and non-English, the district name Cunningham (see p. 70), one has an intriguing group of names containing 'early' English elements like *wīc, bōtl* and *hām*, in this corner of Scotland. (The obviously Norse Busby RNF is just as puzzling.) These names seem to point to some kind of Anglian overlordship or sporadic influence in the area at a fairly early date. The evidence is too patchy on the ground to represent anything more than that.

For Sunwick BWK there is no early evidence. It is tempting to relate the name Snuke, about five miles to the south-west on the River Tweed, to Sunwick. Early forms for that name are *Snuke* 1550, *Snwik* 1578 (1582), *Snwke* 1609, *Snuik* 1621, *Sneuck* 1652. However, there is no real evidence that these two names are identical in origin, although the absence of early forms for Sunwick is strange. It very likely derives from OE *swīn-wīc* 'pig farm', although without proper documentation this is difficult to establish, especially as there is no identical equivalent in England, only several other compound names containing OE *swīn*, and as no English name shows the development *swīn- > sun-*, the only similar instance being Somborne HMP < OE *swīnburna*. Sunwick is, however, almost certainly a name in *-wīc*. Its meaning can be paralleled by many English examples of *wīc* combined with the name of a domestic animal, like Bulwick NTP 'bull farm', Chelvey SOM 'calf farm', Cowick DEV, YOW 'cow farm', Gatwick SUR and Gotwick SSX 'goat farm', Shapwick DOR, SOM and Shopwyke SSX 'sheep farm', and others.

Morphologically, all modern Scottish names in OE *wīc* end in *-(w)ick* and not in the palatalised form − *(w)ich* which is so common in the Midlands and in the south of England (Greenwich, Swanage, West Bromwich, etc.). This is in keeping with the observation that in England, too, palatalisation has not been carried through to the same extent in the north, although it is sometimes recorded. It is unlikely that Anglo-Norman eleventh and twelfth-century forms like *Berwich* 1136, etc., *Beruvich* 1162-5, *Berewich* 1167 for Berwick, *Bordewich* 1165-9 for Borthwick, and *Hatheruuich* 1094 for Hedderwick mean anything else but *-wik* in pronunciation. *Berwiche* 1128 and *Berewyce* 1120 (=*Berwike*) as well as *Barwykke* 1124-30 for Berwick may be reduced forms of the dative plural *berewīcum* because of the numerous unpalatalised plural names in England. It is therefore possible that many of the Scottish names in *-wīc* (the earlier examples anyhow) may have been originally plural in form, referring to a collection of dwellings. Later sporadic spellings like *Borthwyke* 1391 for Borthwick ROX and *Borthwike* 1362 for Borthwick MLO, are hardly reflexes of the same phenomenon as they only occur once each and alternate with *Borthewyk* and *Borthwik*, respectively, in the same period. Similarly *Fyschewike* 1095 for Fishwick is not conclusive, especially as it appears in a fifteenth-century copy. Generally speaking, the Scottish documentary evidence is too late to allow any definite conclusions as to the grammatical number of the names involved. On the other hand, it in no way contradicts what is known about names in *-wīc* in Northern England.

Only one modern spelling indicates the loss of the *-w-* in pronunciation, Darnick; it is, however, also implied in Hawick, with *haw- < *haga-*. For North Berwick, it is first shown in *North Berrick* (1690); for the Midlothian Borthwick, *Borthik* alternates with *Borthuik* in the last decade of the fourteenth century, and *Borthic* and *Borthuic* in 1473, Fenwick ROX has *Fynnik* in 1547 and Fenwick AYR does not show a -*w*- in spelling till the *Finwick* of 1687, obviously not a pronunciation spelling. Prestwick, although the modern pronunciation is [ˈprestwik] has *Prestik*, *Prestike*, and *Prestick* in the sixteenth and seventeenth centuries. *Fischik* 1548 also shows loss of -*w*- in pronunciation.

As regards the meaning of *wīc* in place-names, only one of the many English possibilities is really relevant in Scotland, 'dependent farm', with the possible exception of Prestwick in which -*wick* may mean 'dwelling' rather than 'farm', and Fishwick which seems to refer to a building for a particular occupation, in a non-farming sense. Berwick 'barley farm or grange', Birswick 'byre farm', Handwick '(?) cock-farm', and Sunwick 'pig-farm' imply certain agricultural activities. Borthwick, if meaning 'home farm', would also belong to this category, or if signifying 'wood dwelling', to the next group which also comprises Darnick 'hidden dwelling', Fenwick 'mud dwelling', Hedderwick 'heather dwelling', and Hawick 'enclosed dwelling' in which reference is made to the geographical surroundings of the places involved. Although the neutral translation 'dwelling' has here been used, these places may be regarded as 'dependent farms' (probably 'dairy-farms') as well, and even Prestwick may belong here. It would, however, be wisest to leave the question of the exact meaning open. Either the specific agricultural purpose of the place or the rather remote situation suggested by qualifying words such as 'hidden', 'mud, marshland', 'heather' and 'wood' point to places that were originally of minor importance, but a distinct upward change in status has occurred for some of these, notably for Berwick-on-Tweed, but North Berwick, Borthwick MLO, Fenwick AYR, Hawick and Prestwick are nowadays also quite important towns or parishes, or both. The modern status is here probably due to the fact that names in *wīc* apply to comparatively early English settlements. The instances from the Border Counties, are all situated on or near large streams and on low-lying ground. Several of them are in the valleys of the Tweed, Teviot and Borthwick Water.

From the map (Map 3) it is clear that, with the exception of the Ayrshire and Angus examples, names in -*wīc* occur well within the area outlined by the geographical distribution of other early English elements. Many of these names are therefore undoubtedly early and belong to the first few centuries of Anglian settlement in Scotland. However, some of them, as in England, where such names clearly continued to be coined after *wīc*-names had reached Scotland, may be post-Conquest. Handwick and Hedderwick ANG may be classed as such, but both Prestwick and Fenwick AYR, particularly the former, are possibly earlier. On the whole, these names have all the hallmarks of a fairly settled population engaged in profitable agriculture, especially cattle-grazing and dairying, and they are therefore not likely to have been coined before the eighth century, i.e. at least two or three gener-ations after the siege of Edinburgh in 638. It may be possible to refine their chronological status by examining their geographical relationship to names in OE -*hām*, for instance, or to names in -*ing(a)hām* and -*ingtūn*. The last word on place-names in -*wīc* as evidence for Anglian

4   Anglian-type Crosses (650 - 850)

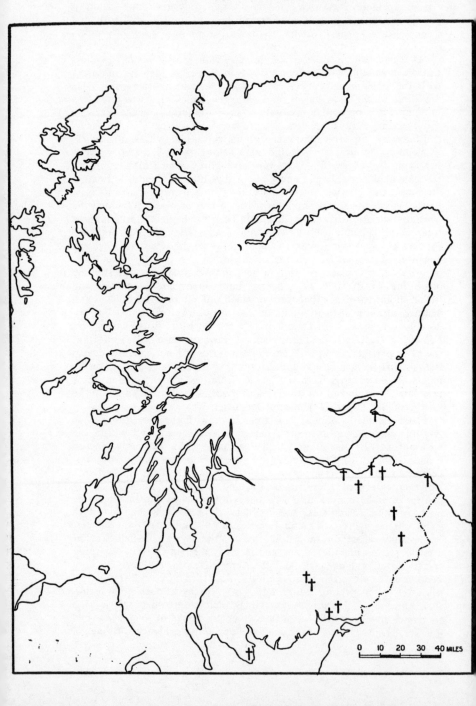

settlement in Scotland has therefore hardly been spoken, especially in view of the fact that there may be other Scottish names ending in -*wick*, mainly because in some cases it is doubtful whether the name in question belongs to this category. The Kirkcudbrightshire parish name Southwick, for instance, does not show a medial -*w*- until the sixteenth century (*Southuic* 1507), whereas earlier spellings, like *Sutheyk, Sutheyc, Suthayc, Suthayk, Suthaik, Suthayck, Sothehack, Sotheayk* show no hint of it. A similar name is recorded for Cunningham in Ayrshire (*Southhuik* 1576, *Southweik* 1596, *Southuik* 1614; *Southheuk* 1661, *Southheuck* 1685), which at least in its earlier forms seems to indicate that the second element might be -*wīc*.

While it is, of course, not to be expected that the early English place-nomenclature of Scotland will mirror the personal and dynastic details of the historical events briefly surveyed on p. 68, and while the linking of place-name evidence with historical events in the process of the Anglian occupation of the Border Counties and the Lothians is difficult and of a comparatively vague nature, certain connections can be made with the findings of archaeology. In view of the observation that the principal archaeological check on the expansion of Northumbrian power is provided by the fine Anglian sculptured crosses of Ruthwell, Hoddom, Closeburn, Aberlady, Abercorn, Morham and so on, which are generally assigned to the 200 years between *c.* AD 650 and *c.* 850, it is informative that a map showing their Scottish distribution (Map 4) coincides remarkably well with this distribution of the Early English place-name elements. Maybe it does not have the amazing congruency which emerges for the settlement area of the historical Picts when names beginning with *Pit*- and the location of symbol stones are plotted side by side (see p. 154 below); but when comparing evidence provided by two completely different lines of investigation continuously hampered by chance survival and late records, one cannot ask for too much delicacy. Nevertheless, on the whole there is no doubt that the archaeological and place-name evidence tally in a most satisfactory manner and certainly do not contradict each other.

This then, in brief, is the story place-names have to tell with regard to the Anglian advance in the Scottish border counties and beyond: Not to be dated before the official acceptance of Christianity in 627, then settlements near the coast and in the valleys of the important rivers evidenced by -*ingahām*, -*ingtūn* and -*hām*, this picture consolidated by the analysis of other early place-name elements like *worð*, *bōðl*, and *wīc*, with some settlements higher up the river-valleys, obviously as part of a secondary occupation, but still in the fertile valleys and not in the hills. East Lothian and Berwickshire, i.e. the whole coast line from near Edinburgh to the present Scottish-English border, combining with Roxburghshire in forming the main early settlement area of the Angles, and this again to be seen as the northern part of the whole of the kingdom of Northumbria, or at least Bernicia, with the Tweed not a divide but a central life line. As always, the toponymic evidence does not provide a consecutive narrative but affords glimpses only, but even through these glimpses a better view of Anglian Scotland in the seventh, eighth, and perhaps ninth, centuries may be obtained.

6
Scandinavian Names

Although English names in many parts of Scotland follow upon Gaelic names — oust them, translate them, adapt them — other languages like Norse and Cumbric also precede English in different areas of the country. This presents a methodological dilemma which cannot be totally resolved in a crabwise move through Scottish toponymic history, but commonsense suggests that one particular group of languages be thoroughly examined before another is investigated. Sticklers for methodological neatness may have their well-founded and convincingly-argued reasons against such a procedure, but what can be done if the place-names created by a certain language form an adstratum to English names in one place, a superstratum in another, and a substratum in most places, sometimes without any contact with English because of an intervening language? Linguistic stratification is never neat and tidy, even if a particular presentational arrangement gives the appearance of a natural order. It is consequently not surprising that those place-names on the Scottish map, which can be traced to Scandinavian-speaking settlers, do not form a homogeneous group, either in their chronological arrival or in their geographical distribution, or, put somewhat differently, that the Scandinavian place-names of Scotland arrived in different places at different times and must be ascribed to several settlement movements rather than to one continuum. It is therefore quite misleading to accommodate a representation of all names of Scandinavian origin on one map, as has sometimes been attempted, since such a map, unless very carefully executed in its temporal and spatial complexity, will have little to convey beyond the general notion of where at one time or another place-names were created by people speaking a Scandinavian language. This book therefore tries to elucidate the toponymic evidence for Scandinavian settlement in Scotland through a series of cartographic representations, some showing only a part of the country. There is not a single corner of Scotland in which English place-names are not to be found, but this cannot be said of any other linguistic contribution including the Scandinavian one.

Just as the study of the evolution of the Scandinavian place-nomenclature has to be pursued with caution, so the terminology employed in describing the linguistic people who coined this nomenclature has to be chosen carefully. It has become customary to refer to them all as Norsemen, and to their language as Norse, apart from Norn, the later derivative dialect spoken in the Northern Isles until at least the eighteenth century. Sometimes the same people are called Vikings with special emphasis on their non-linguistic qualities, or are, in a mixture of both appellations, termed Norse Vikings. It is perfectly permissible to assume that the Vikings spoke Norse, i.e. a western Scandinavian language which may be called the ancestor of both Norwegian and Icelandic; (Old) Norse may also be legitimately used in designating the language spoken by the Scandinavian settlers of the Northern and Western Isles and of some of the adjacent parts of the Scottish mainland. It is not appropriate, however, to use it with the same degree of confidence of the originators of Scandinavian place-names in the Scottish south-west or of the Scandinavian contribution to the toponymy of south-eastern Scotland, since one group of settlers may have close links with Ireland and the Isle of Man, and the other must be regarded as connected with the Scandinavian, and partly anglicised, stratum in the population of the North of England where East Scandinavian, especially Danish, influence is at least possible and cannot be disregarded. In order to keep an open mind and allow for all possibilities, *Scandinavian* is the most appropriate epithet to serve as the umbrella term describing all place-names coined or shaped by one or other of the Scandinavian languages, while a more limited terminology may be employed whenever geographically or historically relevant.

Any investigation of the Scandinavian contribution to the Scottish place-nomenclature has to be concerned with three major areas of influence: the Northern and Western Isles, the Scottish south-west, and the Scottish south-east. Of these three, the first, i.e. Orkney, Shetland, and the Hebrides, has the strongest historical documentation with regard to Scandinavian overlordship and settlement.

The principle of using toponymic material for the investigation of settlement sequence in the northernmost part of Scotland, both in historic and in prehistoric times, is of course not new; one partial, but in its geographical restriction excellent, treatment is the chapter 'Farm-name Chronology' of the late Hugh Marwick's *Orkney Farm-names*. In fact it is this very study which suggested the plan to extend Marwick's approach to Shetland and other areas in which Norsemen are known to have settled, and three of the four elements finally chosen for this more comprehensive survey are amongst those examined by Marwick, whose principal interest was in such words as *kví, setr, land, garðr, bólstaðr, staðir, skáli, bú,* and *býr*. A summary of his findings appears on pp. 248-9 of his book, but his conclusions have been even more concisely summarised by the late F.T. Wainwright:

> ... the *quoy*-names are comparatively late, and few of them are likely to have arisen before 900; the *setr*-names as a group are much earlier, some arose before 900 and some arose after that date; earlier still as groups are the *land*-names, the *garðr*-names and the *bólstaðr*-names, and these with few exceptions arose well before the end of

the ninth century; and earliest of all are the *býr*-names which
represent the original settlements of the Scandinavian *landnámsmenn*.
Individual examples of *land, garðr* and *bólstaðr* may also go back to
the original settlements, and so too may other names, especially old
seaboard names like Elsness, Westness and Sandwick which, having a
geographical significance, do not lend themselves to classification
under elements.

In accepting the broad outlines of the chronological sequence offered
by Marwick, Wainwright adds that it is a sequence of place-name
formations extending from the beginning of the ninth century to the
end of the Middle Ages and he has — partly because of historical and
archaeological evidence — no hesitation in putting the beginning of
Norse settlement in the Northern Isles about AD 800. This appears to
be the most acceptable date, even if it is not wholly undisputed, since
others have considered the possibility of attempts at Norse colonisation
of the Scottish islands as early as the seventh century. Certainly there
is nothing whatsoever in our place-name material which would contradict
acceptance of Wainwright's dating.

As it would be difficult to examine in turn each of Marwick's nine
elements in the wider context of Norse settlement in Scotland, a choice
has to be made. This choice should be mainly influenced by two
factors: first, only elements which also occur in significant numbers
outside Orkney are eligible; second, such elements must be unambiguous
pointers to speakers of a Scandinavian language. As far as the first
criterion is concerned, *land* and *bú* turn out to be unsuitable. From the
point of view of ambiguity, *garðr* has to be eliminated because it, or a
closely related cognate, frequently occurs as a loan-word in Gaelic
place-names in the Hebrides, as well as in bilingual Norse-Gaelic names.
Of the other six elements, *býr* and *skáli* had to be reluctantly discarded
after close scrutiny — *býr* because its sporadic occurrence in southern
Scotland and the dense cluster of names containing this element in
Eastern Dumfriesshire do not easily admit of a reliable interpretation of
the Scottish evidence as a whole. Whereas Marwick always finds it in
conjunction with an 'original' settlement and classes it as his earliest
element, it survives into the post-Norman period in the south
(Lockerbie DMF) where it seems to be altogether unconnected with
the spread of Scandinavian settlement from the north. Such uncertainty
makes the few Hebridean examples not very reliable evidence for what
we are trying to establish. Since *skáli* functioned essentially in minor
names, or as a common noun applied to certain buildings and having
at first no more than local currency, while remaining alive and productive long after the ninth century had ended, it is not the best of
generics on which to base a conclusive argument. This leaves *kví, setr,
bolstaðr,* and *staðir,* but because of the essential interest in settlement
history, only words primarily referring to permanent human settlement
should be examined; as *kví* originally meant a 'cattle fold', it seems to
be less appropriate than the other three. Its obvious lateness also speaks
against it, although its distribution and use in place-names would be well

worth studying in some detail.

In order to gain some kind of perspective, at least one of the most common elements occurring in Norse names referring primarily to natural, rather than man-made, features should be examined and plotted alongside *setr, bolstaðr,* and *staðir, dalr* 'valley' appears to be the most suitable and most easily recognisable word for this purpose. Apart from certain local conditions in Orkney there is no linguistic reason why names containing *staðir* should not have been coinable from the very beginning of Scandinavian settlement in Scotland. There are at least 2500 *staðir*-names in Norway, and Iceland is supposed to have 1165, but it is difficult to believe that these most common names exclusively had their origins in the division of parent farms, as would be undoubtedly true of certain parts of Norway where they would be in this sense 'secondary', although Gubrandsdalen, for example, also possesses plenty of independent *staðir*-farms, and so do several other old Norwegian districts, above all those of South-Eastern Norway and Trøndelagen. For Norway it has therefore been concluded that the *staðir*-names are somewhat older than the Viking age, having apparently flourished as early as the ninth century. For linguistic reasons they are, however, not likely to be older than about AD 650-700. Even when taken at its most conservative, this state of affairs allows the assumption that *staðir* was a well-established and somewhat fashionable place-name element when the Scandinavian settlers first reached the Northern Isles, irrespective of its ultimate roots and usage, and this is of course all that really matters. Indeed, it may well be said that as in the case of *setr*, both *staðir* and *bolstaðr*, which in Norway are perhaps secondary generics, are, in Shetland and Orkney anyhow, primary elements. *Staðir* is also, in the absence of suitable criteria for *bú* and *býr*, the earliest element for which a distributional pattern of any significance emerges which is of more than just local value (Map 5).

Staðir 'dwelling-place, farm' is the nominative plural of Norse *staðr*. That it is the plural rather than the singular which is used in the place-names in question is proved not only by the Norwegian evidence but also by the Gaelic pronunciation of Hebridean names of this provenance, as well as by the fact that practically all the modern Orkney examples in this group end in *-ston*, a development (possibly by analogy with English *-ton* < *tūn*) indicative of an older dative plural *stoðum*, used in a locative sense. Earlier spellings often have *-stath* or *-staith*. In the majority of cases the first element is a personal name, pointing to individual ownership of the settlements referred to and making re-naming possible whenever the proprietor changed (as long as the name had not yet altogether lost its qualities as a descriptive, meaningful label). According to the best authorities, there are 37 examples in Shetland, 25 in Orkney, and 25 in the Hebrides. If the total number of dots on our Map 5 is smaller than the sum of these three figures (87), this is due to the fact that not all of these names appear on the Ordnance Survey one-inch map from which scale our basic material has been compiled. Any names not shown, however, do not alter the overall picture which emerges. Shetland provides such names as Gunnista,

5 Scandinavian names in *-staðir*

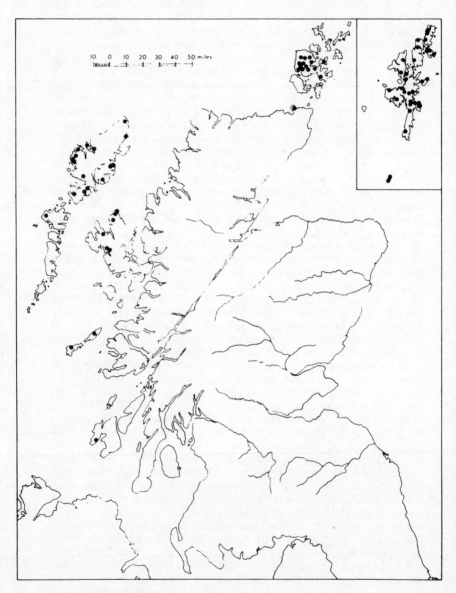

• **Name containing** *stathr*

6   Scandinavian names in *-setr/-sætr*

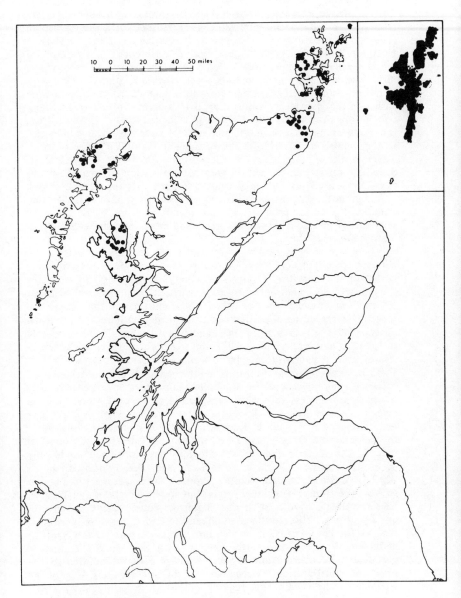

 Name containing *setr*

▮ Shetland, with 124 *setr* names

Wethersta, Colsta, Ugasta, Sotersta, Grista, and Hunsta. In Orkney there are Grimeston, Hourston, Berston, Herston, and Tormiston, as well as Costa, Gangsta, and Yinstay. In the Hebrides we find Skegirsta, Tolsta, Mangersta, and Mealista (Lewis), Scarasta, Bearasta, Unasta (Harris), Connista, Lusta, Shulista (Skye), Hosta (North Uist), Olistadh (Islay). The distribution is such that only Shetland, Orkney, Lewis, and Northern Skye really participate, and if differences in geographical scatter really may mean distinction in time as well — and this whole discussion is based on that premise — then what is comparatively early in Orkney (and Shetland) seems from its coastal distribution to be even earlier in the Hebridean context; or, if it is permissible to transfer any conclusions drawn from the Hebridean evidence to the Northern Isles, *staðir* appears as a place-name element which might have been productive in the naming of farms from the very beginning of Viking settlement. There is little doubt that the *staðir*-map represents the extent of Scandinavian settlement within the first generation or two of settlers from Norway. Thus 850 might not be a bad date for what it shows, although not every name shown must necessarily have existed then. Whether the term 'primary' applies or not, it is an 'early' phase of settlement and one from which further and more extensive colonisation is still to develop.

There are cogent reasons why the *setr*-map must find its place between those of *staðir* and *bólstaðr*. The most persuasive of these is that of the map itself (Map 6). Anybody approaching and analysing the *staðir*, *setr*, and *bólstaðr* maps without prejudice and without information drawn from any other source must see in them a gradual progressive spreading of settlement in this order. Otherwise the virtual absence of *setr*-names from an island like Islay would be extremely difficult, if not impossible to explain, even when geographical, socio-logical, and dialectal factors have been taken into account. The fact that there are seemingly no *setr*-names in the Faroes and in Iceland is of little help here, because the argument, sometimes advanced, that the Scottish *setr*-names are simply a reflection of a later emigration from certain parts of Norway, like Møre and Trøndelag, when two or three generations of Norsemen had consolidated their position as inhabitants of Shetland and Orkney, must be called inadequate from the point of view of the Scottish end-product. Obviously the word *setr* could only be brought to these shores by people who were already using it and for whom it was part of their naming tradition. In that respect it is bound to bear the stamp of regional origin; but in the Northern and Western Isles the distribution is such that it mirrors consolidation and greater density of population in the areas already settled in the *staðir*-period, as well as further expansion in the northernmost part of the Scottish mainland, especially the eastern half of Caithness. In this county in particular, the distribution of *setr*-names is a useful pointer to the period of confrontation between Norse and Gaelic speakers. West of the *setr*-area is the Gaelic *baile*-region, and there is hardly any overlap (compare Map 14). *Setr*-names apparently remained productive longer than *staðir*-names, although many of them may have been coined at the same time as these. If, however, the absence of *setr* from the place-nomenclature of Iceland means anything, then most of the Scottish *setr*-names are older than the colonisation of Iceland. This in turn would place the arrival of this toponymic element in Scotland before the last three decades of the ninth century. Its creative usage must have continued well into those decades, however, and the map distribution may perhaps reflect the position of Norse settlement as it was in the period 880-900, probably nearer the earlier rather than the later date. Many of the names are probably older, some are likely to be younger.

In this respect the map, although overcrowded in those areas in which *setr*-names occur most densely, is again based only on what can be culled from the one-inch map. It has been claimed that there are 170 examples in Shetland, 34 in Orkney, at least 56 in Caithness, and 60 in the Outer and Inner Hebrides, but the last two figures seem rather large in the light of the material available in the Scottish Place-name Survey. If they are correct, however, they are presumably an indication only of even greater density rather than of wider distribution. Another point must be borne in mind: as far as our modern anglicised place-name spellings and pronunciations are concerned, it is impossible to distinguish between old Norse *setr* and *sœtr*. These two words are cognate and both originally referred to pastoral (by all accounts temporary) dwellings and herding activities; *setr* developed the meaning 'dwelling' in general, whereas a *sœtr* is 'a shieling'. Apart from some subtle aspects of Lewis Gaelic pronunciation, there is no way of distinguishing between these two by purely phonological means. Two other factors can, however, be usefully exploited when a distinction is to be made: (*a*) the meaning of the first element in compound names containing *setr* or *sœtr* as the second part, and (*b*) the geographical position and present status of the name in question. If the first element is the name of an animal like cow, sheep, or horse, and if the name applies to a site (or settlement) far from the beaten track, the word it contains is likely to be *sœtr*. If, on the other hand, there is no reference to any domestic animal and if the name is that of a prosperous farm or village on alluvial land in a favourable situation, then *setr* is almost certainly the word involved. The scatter shown on Map 6 and this discussion make no distinction between these two generics, as both of them must be seen in a primarily pastural context and as both of them most likely arrived in Scotland together (if, in fact, any distinction was made in the language of the Norse colonists).

The modern reflex of *setr* or *sœtr* is usually *setter* or *-ster* in Shetland and Orkney. Representative of the many Shetland examples are: Setter, Voxter, Swinister, Dalsetter, Ellister, Vatsetter, Freester, Huxter, Houstter, Gunnister, Collaster, Kettlester, Stanesetter, etc. In Orkney we find, amongst others, Setter, Mossetter, Inkster, Seatter, Melsetter and Snelsetter. Caithness supplies Seater, Tister, Reaster, Syster, Wester, Thurster, and Thuster, for example; and Hebridean reflexes of *setr/sœtr* are Shader, Grimshader, Earshader, Geshader, Linshader (Lewis), Drineshader, Loch Uiseader (Harris), Uigshader, Gerashader, Sheader (Skye), Loch Eashader (North Uist) and Ellister (Islay). *Shader,* in all these cases, is evidence that the names in question have passed through Gaelic before passing into the mouths of English speakers. Another group of names which has apparently undergone the same process, only with different results, is that of the Sutherland names ending in *-side*, Gaelic *-said*, like Linside (Gaelic *Lionasaid*), Loch Coulside (Gaelic *Culasaid*), Fallside (Gaelic *Fealasaid*), Sandside, and Gaelic *Horasaid* and *Bracsaid*. If these names really belong here, the *s*-forms (rather than *sh-*) seem to favour a nonpalatal vowel following in the original because in Gaelic *s* is palatalised into *sh* by a following palatal vowel like *e* and *i*; but non-palatal vowels like *a, o, u* do not change it. Is this, in fact, *sætr* rather than *setr*? But why only here in Sutherland? Until these names have been convincingly analysed, no final verdict can be given, and they are therefore absent from our maps. However, attention must be drawn to their existence: they are all situated in parts of the country in which Norse influence is also otherwise apparent.

Orkney farm-names containing Old Norse *bólstaðr* occupy relatively central positions in their various parishes; they are situated on good old fertile ground, and the large size of so many of them shows them to have been relatively early settlements. Everything points to them being earlier than the tenth century, at least in Orkney, and some *bólstaðr*-names may be as old as the Norse settlements themselves, although it would naturally be difficult to isolate such individual names. What is much more important from our point of view is the fact that *bólstaðr* seems to have remained a creative name-forming element for a considerable time and was used wherever permanent settlements were formed by the Norsemen. As the map shows (Map 7), it has a much wider distribution than either *staðir* or *setr*. Indeed, it can be stated with confidence that a distribution map of names containing *bólstaðr* – like the one presented here – is the map of Norse settlement in the Northern and Western Isles and on the adjacent mainland, when such settlement was at its most extensive and Norse power at its height. All other place-names elements considered fall within the *bólstaðr*-area. Some of these became productive later, others ceased to be used earlier, but none add anything to what the *bólstaðr*-names teach us – a Scandinavian settlement area from the northernmost point of Shetland to the southernmost tip of Islay, with large parts of the coastal areas of Sutherland and of the eastern half of Caithness added.

In Shetland *bólstaðr*-farms are said to have an average size of half the *staðir* ones, and they have therefore been called 'peasant settlements par excellence'. It would however be wrong to pay too much attention to the historical fact that in Norway the split-up farm consisted of several *ból*, or lots, and to think too much in terms of size and division of older, bigger units. In the new Norwegian settlements of the Viking times too, *bólstaðr* probably functioned as an ordinary word designating 'farm', as is borne out by the fact that during the eighth century along the whole of the west coast of Norway *bolstaðr* was *the* farm. What was true of Norway itself must also be envisaged for the area of Scandinavian colonisation in Scotland, and Scottish *bólstaðr* names

7   Scandinavian names in *-bolstaðr*

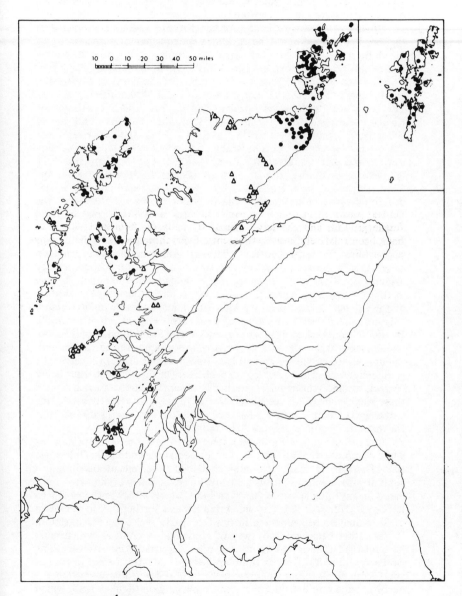

Name containing *bólstathr*

● in form *bister, bster, bost, bus*
△ in form *boll, pol etc.*

may be regarded as independent creations without linguistic or economic links with other farm-names. Where such connections do exist, they are not likely to alter the conclusions.

Perhaps the most difficult problem for the historian interested in this problem would be the detection of *bólstaðr*-names, for they appear on modern maps and in local usage in a number of disguises. The most common form in the Northern Isles is *-bister,* as in Kirkabister, Norbister, Isbister, Symbister, Hoglibister, and Lumbister (Shetland), and Mirbister, Sandbister, Ellibister, Kirbister, Swanbister and Tuskerbister (Orkney). The form *-bist* is, however, also not infrequent in Orkney (Eastabist, Kirbist, Grimbist, Geldibist, Wasbist), and *-bust* (Grobust) and *-buster* (Wasbuster) occur there too. In Caithness, *-bster* and *-pster* represent the original *bólstaðr* (Lybster, Brubster, Scrabster; Strompster, Achilipster, Achkeepster) and sometimes all that is left of the element *ból* is a bilabial nasal before the final *-ster* (Camster, Stemster, Rumster, Thrumster), making the distinction between *staðir* and *bólstaðr* names difficult for the uninitiated. In the Hebrides, Lewis and Skye share the modern *-bost* form which is not unlike some of the forms found in Orkney (Habost, Shawbost, Leurbost in Lewis; Carbost, Culbost, Breabost in Skye). Further south, Islay has developed the form *-bus* (Coullabus, Cornabus, Kinnabus, Risabus) which is, however, comparatively recent because even in the seventeenth-century documentary evidence spellings in *-bolls, -bols, -bollis,* and the like abound. The loss of the *-l-* in the Islay names is compensated for by the complete absence of the *-st-* in other areas (Unapool, Eriboll, and Learable in Sutherland, Ullapool and Arboll in Wester and Easter Ross respectively, Crossapoll, Heylipoll, and Kirkapoll in Tiree), and in the Sutherland names Embo, Skelbo, and Skibo the *-l-* and the *-st-* have disappeared in the modern spelling although the *-l-* can still be traced in the modern local Gaelic pronunciation and in documentary evidence. On the whole it is probably correct to state that the *-er* ending is absent in those areas in which there was Gaelic influence on the Norse language, apparently producing a stronger stress on the first syllable of *bólstaðr*. This would also account for the *bolls > boll, poll, pool > bo* reduction.

Very little linguistic comment is necessary for our next map (Map 8) which presents the distribution of place-names ending in Old Norse *dalr*. There is no reason to think that it has ever meant anything but what it still means in Norwegian today, i.e. 'a valley'. The map is not based on anything anybody has ever done before, either in the Northern Isles or in Norway; it is also not intended as a further link in our chain of Scandinavian settlement history in the parts of Scotland in question. It has rather been added by way of contrast — a contrast which must be explained if it is not to be taken as a contradiction of everything we have said so far, for, as the map clearly indicates, names in *-dalr* — apart from being found wherever *staðir, setr* and *bólstaðr* are at home — occur in large numbers in other areas, especially on the mainland, which according to what we have seen so far cannot be said to be part of the Norse settlement area proper. In this respect it must be remembered that *dalr* primarily refers to natural features, although the name of a

8   Scandinavian names in *-dalr*

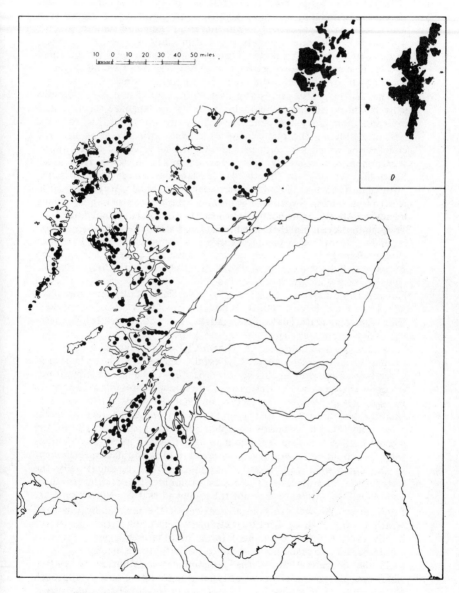

 Name containing *dalr*

Area of frequent occurrence

valley was quite often, at a later date, transferred to a settlement situated in it. A distribution map of *dalr*-names is therefore not a map of permanent Norse settlement but rather of the sphere of Norse influence. It includes those areas adjacent to permanent settlements in which seasonal exploits such as hunting and fishing and summer grazing were carried out, and probably the odd military raid or friendly visit. In most of those undertakings Norsemen must have been accompanied by Gaelic-speakers as otherwise the names concerned would not have come down to us because of a break in communication.

The *dalr*-map also serves as a useful reminder that it is not permissible to throw all names belonging to the same language together and interpret them along the same lines. Anybody who does this, runs the risk of distorting the picture and of reading into any given material conclusions which it cannot provide. Of the hundreds of names represented here we can only give a few examples: Arisdale, Hevdadale, Southdale, Wormadale (Shetland), Muslandale, Knugdale, Durrisdale, Stoursdale (Orkney), Tresdale, Berriedale, Lambsdale, Weydale (Caithness), Helmsdale, Swordale, Ospisdale, Mudale (Sutherland), Udale, Ulladale, Attadale (Mainland Ross-shire), Borrodale, Scamadale, Udal (Mainland Inverness-shire), Glen Scaddle, Easkadale, Carradale (Mainland Argyllshire), Dibadale, Breinadale, Grundale (Lewis), Laxadale, Rodel, Rainigadale (Harris), Udal, Gramsdale (North Uist), Loch Borosdale (Benbecula), Lochboisdale, Hellisdale (South Uist), Allasdale (Barra), Skipisdale (Mingulay), Bracadale, Bernisdale, Keistle (Skye), Papadil, Dibidil (Rum), Cleadale (Eigg), Sorisdale (Coll), An Coireadail, Scallastle, Glen Libidil (Mull), Liundale, Brosdale (Jura), Tormisdale, Glenastle, Margadale (Islay), Etterickdale, Ardroscadale (Bute), Glenashdale, Glen Ormidale (Arran).

Names in -dale south of the Forth-Clyde line have been treated as ending in the English cognate (Clydesdale, Dryfesdale, Liddesdale) and/or as being irrelevant in this context. *Staðir, setr,* and *bólstaðr* do not occur in that region. On the basis of the evidence presented, the names in *staðir* (Map 5) provide a picture of what the Norse settlement area was like before and up to the middle of the ninth century, whereas *setr*-names (Map 6) speak of consolidation and expansion well into the second half of that century. The map of *bólstaðr* in its various disguises (Map 7) supplies an overall visual impression of Scandinavian *settlement* in the north and west when at its most extensive; and finally the distribution of *dalr* (Map 8) serves as a reminder that 'settlement area' and 'sphere of influence' are not the same and that the Norsemen must have known the western coastal districts of the mainland from Cape Wrath to the Mull of Kintyre extremely well even if they never (or hardly ever) had any permanent farms or other settlements there. It would be risky to read any more out of, or into, these maps.

If the consideration of the geographical distribution of certain significant place-name elements or types seems a rather austere approach to the study of Scandinavian place-names in the Northern and Western Isles, and to the study of any kind of place-name anywhere in Scotland, for that matter, then a brief parenthetic excursion is perhaps in order which reminds us that there are, of course, other ways of looking at the same evidence. One of these would be to examine with special care and interest, the semantic burden of *whole* names, with an eye on what these might tell about the quality of the general life of Norse-speaking people in the areas just delineated. In such an examination, the value of the non-generic half of compound names, as historical and socio-logical raw material would become immediately apparent. One might, for instance, take the numerous Scandinavian village names of Lewis and ask oneself what one might discover, by patient detective work, about life in Lewis, and by analogy also about life in other Hebridean islands, from, let us say,·the ninth to the thirteenth centuries, even in the potential total absence of written records or archaeological remains. Even without pursuing such a venture to its full extent, one would arrive at the following basic and skeletal conclusions.

First of all, there is evidence of permanent settlement in names like Bosta 'farm' and Habost 'high farm'. Such farms seem to have been owned privately and individually, as the many names with personal names as their first elements testify, like Swanibost 'Sveini's farm', Tolsta 'Tholf's farm', Grimshader 'Grim's farm', and others. Female ownership is not excluded, if the explanation of Eoropie as 'Jorunn's farm' is correct. The use of enclosed pastures or fields is indicated by names like Garrabost 'enclosed farm' and Croigary 'pasture of the cattle-fold', the latter pointing to the keeping and breeding of cattle. The same Norse word *kví* 'cattle-fold' appears in Quier 'folds' and out-side Lewis in Quinish (Mull, Harris) and Quishader 'headland, and farm, of the cattle-fold', respectively. Reference to the crops grown is made at least in Lionel 'flax-field' and Linshader 'flax-farm' on the one hand, and in Cornabus 'corn-farm' on the other; only it is not immediately clear from the place-name evidence alone what crop the word corn actually referred to at that time.

Horses too, as well as cattle, were kept, as names like Rossal 'horse-field', Hestaval 'horse-hill', Hestam 'horse-islet', and Roisnish 'horse-headland' tell us. Some of these horses seem to have been kept on islands for grazing for at least part of the year. This is indicated by Hestam. The same is true of other farm animals. The many islands called Soay must have received their names from the fact that sheep were grazed on them, and Lampay and Lamalum, both 'lamb-island', Haversay 'he-goat-island', and some of the Calvas 'calf-island' may speak of a similar practice for lambs, goats and calves, although in some instances at least Calva seems to mean a small island off a larger one. Geshader 'goat-farm' may be an indication that some farms were particularly interested in the breeding of goats, and in names like Galson and Griosamul the keeping of pigs is recorded. For summer pasture animals were, of course, not only ferried to islands, but also taken to shielings on higher and less-accessible ground. This practice is apparently implied by names like Soval 'sheep-hill', Hestaval 'horse-hill', Neidalt 'rough hill ground for cattle', and others. The Lewis name Shader and the many names ending in *-ary* or *-airidh* directly tell us of the existence of such shielings.

Apart from such reconstructed farm-life, there are references to fortifications in Borve 'fort' and Boreray 'fort-isle', for instance, and the famous Kisimul, off Castlebay, in Barra, also seems to mean something like 'castle-isle'. Brue, in Lewis, tells of an old bridge, and Kirkebost, Kirkipol and the like, of the presence of the church. The importance of fishing in both river and sea is reflected in such names as Laxay 'salmon river' and Shiltenish 'herring promontory'. This is not a bad little picture, considering the rawness and paucity of the evidence.

One other point is perhaps worth making with regard to the close parallels in naming between a home country, in this case Norway, and a colonial region, let us say Shetland. In my view, it can be demonstrated quite clearly that when the Norsemen arrived in Shetland almost 1200 years ago they not only carried with them in the vocabulary of their language a large number of words suitable for the naming of geographical features of all kinds, whether natural or man-made, but also a stock of actual names which could be drawn upon whenever applicable. The giving of Norse names to places in Shetland – and this statement has, of course, more general implications and could be said to be true of all areas into which speakers of a new language move in large numbers – was therefore not entirely a process of creating appropriate distinguishing labels from suitable lexical items. Although this spontaneous creation did, naturally, take place, there must have been also many occasions when a ready-made name from the homeland was pulled out of the onomastic bag, simply because such and such a feature always had such and such a name at home. In some cases, there may have been an element of nostalgia involved as well but, on the whole, the use of this kind of commemorative naming is usually overstressed by scholars describing early naming processes, perhaps because of the important part it has played in the naming of settlements in the New World across the Atlantic, in more recent times. Naturally, it is not always easy to decide which aspect of the act of naming is involved, but in cases like Lerwick, Dale, Tingwall, Linga, Breiwick, Twatt, Voe, Melby, Houlland, all of which have not only close but identical parallels in Norway, and sometimes several of these, it would be prudent to consider the possibility of onomastic rather than linguistic naming, i.e. that a ready-made name was re-applied rather than freshly created, or, putting it more abstractly, that there are connotative names as well as denotative ones, a fact which rather blurs the distinction usually made between word and name, on the basis of that distinction.

As in the review of the Northern and Western Isles, a scrutiny of the Scandinavian place-names of south-west Scotland will have to be restricted to a few selected generics. In view of the fact that quite a number of name categories, apart from individual names of Scandinavian origin, offer themselves for investigation, it is important to choose the most suitable and numerically most prolific in order to have a fairly dense network of names and to avoid drawing conclusions from insufficient evidence. This does not mean that certain peculiar or isolated or important individual names might not be excellent onomastic pointers, perhaps simply because of their individuality, but they cannot have the same force for a historically oriented inquiry as groups or types of names which occur more frequently in a given area. Guided by this principle of selection, it is appropriate to look at names in *-by*, representing names of human settlements, names in *-fell*, as examples of mountain-names, and names in *-thwaite*, showing the impact of human activities on the region, while at the same time supplying one of the so-called west Scandinavian 'test-words', like *beck* < *bekkr*, which as the fourth generic under review provides the hydronymic ingredient. Finally, one group of what has come to be known as 'inversion compounds', i.e. Germanic compound names showing Celtic word order with the generic preceding the specific, has to be discussed: names beginning with *Kirk-*. Unfortunately, therefore, names containing elements like *-holm* (ON *holmr*), *-garth* (ON *garðr*), *-gill* (ON *gil*), *-grain* (ON *grein*), or *-dale* (ON *dalr*) cannot be examined in the same detail although there are many examples of most of them, especially of the *holm-* and *gill*-names, in the Scottish south-west.

For this examination, there is no need for maps covering the whole of Scotland, since the distribution of these name types outside the south-west is negligible or irrelevant or both, and can therefore be ignored. It is, on the other hand, of the utmost importance to show at least the northernmost parts of England on these maps because the use of the present Scottish-English border as a line of demarcation in connection with toponymic evidence about a thousand years old is both restrictive and misleading, having hampered the proper investigation of material such as the names reviewed in this section for far too long. Such anachronistic boundaries have no place in this kind of study, apart from their convenience as cartographic markers for modern readers.

Names in *-beck* (ON *bekkr* 'a stream'), although they are found in four counties — Dumfriesshire, Roxburghshire, Lanarkshire, and Kirkcudbrightshire — form geographically a much closer cluster than such an enumeration indicates, with Dumfriesshire forming the centre and the examples from the other counties situated just across the Dumfriesshire-border. In most cases, the names still apply to watercourses, in others they now serve as names of human settlements on the banks of these streams as well, or as those alone. In others again they have become part of the name of another geographical feature, like *Elbeckhill* in the parish of Wamphray DMF. The defining elements in these names are usually of non-Scandinavian origin, mostly Anglo-Saxon but also Norman, as in *Butcherbeck Burn* (*Bochardbech ante-*1329), and Gaelic, as in *Gillemartinebech* of 1194-1214, now 'lost', or *Craigbeck*. Some Scandinavian elements occur, as for instance in *Allerbeck* whose earlier form *Elrebec* (*c.* 1218) points to an original ON *elri bekkr*, or possibly in *Fishbeck* and *Greenbeck* where *Fish-* and *Green-* might represent the Scandinavian cognate rather than the Anglo-Saxon word. Despite their paucity, it is significant that genuinely Scandinavian compound names in *-beck*, i.e. compounds in which the specific element is also Norse, do occur in our region, pointing to settlements by speakers of a Scandinavian language or languages.

The majority of names, i.e. those with specific elements other than Norse, is more difficult to assess. The question is whether they indicate that a Norse language was still spoken up to and after the Norman invasion or whether the word *beck* passed into the local Lowland Scots dialect and remained productive in this way. There are probably examples illustrative of both sides of this question: *Beck*-names containing Anglo-Saxon or Gaelic personal names, like *Archerbeck* and the 'lost' *Gillemartinebech*, may have been coined by Norsemen living in the neighbourhood of these streams, and even *Bochardbech* may belong here. On the other hand, names like *Mere Beck, Kings Beck, Muckle Hind Becks, Muirbeck,* and such as *Beckfoot, Beckhall, Beckton,* and *Beck Burn,* with tautological addition of Scots *burn,* are indicative of the second alternative and must have been created by English rather than Scandinavian speakers. Even *Craigbeck* may contain the Scots loan-word *craig* rather than its Gaelic original, and in *Allerbeck* the Anglo-Saxon term replaced the Norse one. Neither the *Dictionary of the Older Scottish Tongue* nor the *Scottish National Dictionary,* however, mentions a word *beck* in the meaning of 'stream, water-course', and it may well be that this word was never really established in local dialect usage, something which cannot be said of the north of England where, in some districts, *beck* has replaced earlier *burn* in toponymical and appellative usage. Alternatively, *beck* may have been obsolete in the local Dumfriesshire dialect by the time the, rather scanty, early literary sources begin.

On the English side, *bekkr* is extensively used throughout the so-called Danelaw and in the north, except for Northumberland, replacing Old English *brōc* and *burna.* In this respect, *Linburn Beck* DRH contrasts significantly with pleonastic usage of *beck,* with *Beck Burn* KCB. There are at least 67 instances of *beck*-names in the neighbouring Cumberland where it is said to be the most common stream-name element among names which have survived, and 80 in Westmorland. The North Riding of Yorkshire shows 39, and Lancashire has at least 7. There is also one in Derbyshire, just across the Yorkshire border. It has, on the other hand, not been noted in early names in Northumberland and Durham. Interesting modern reflexes are *Claveg* and *Strenebeck* in the Isle of Man.

It is obvious that the Scottish *beck*-names in and near Dumfriesshire are part and parcel of the Northern English group of names containing the same element; they form the most northerly section of the more general *beck*-area. Further proof of this is to be found in the fact that there are identical equivalents on both sides of the border: The Scottish *Merebeck* has at least 3 equivalents in Cumberland and one in the North Riding of Yorkshire; apart from the *Troutbeck* in Dumfriesshire there are 4 in Cumberland and one in Westmorland; *Ellerbecks* occur in Cumberland (4), Lancashire and the North Riding of Yorkshire, as well as in Dumfriesshire, represented by the *Allerbeck* mentioned above, and by Elbeckhill whose first part is *Elrebec* in 1194; and

Butcherbeck (*Bochardbech ante*-1329) links up with *Butcherby* in Cumberland.

In addition, the English examples show exactly the same kinds of compound as our Scottish instances: (1) Genuine Scandinavian names, (2) names in which the first part of the compound is of Germanic but not of Norse origin, and (3) names compounded with Norman-English elements. There seems, however, to be a much higher percentage of names belonging to the first category, i.e. genuine Scandinavian names on the English side of the border, and the Scottish names look as if they are, on the whole, a little later than their English counterparts. Only names in which the defining element is without doubt of Norse origin as well, can, of course, be taken as proof of Scandinavian settlement.

The danger of looking narrowly at both the Scottish or the English material in isolation is also obvious in the case of names in *-bie, -by* (ON *býr* 'a farmstead, a village'), names which denote primarily human settlements, and not water-courses. *Býr* is an element whose ultimate etymology and original meaning have been widely discussed but do not concern us here; in the Scottish south-west it is always connected with permanent buildings and could either be translated as 'farm' or as 'hamlet' or 'village', according to the size of the settlement.

As was the case with *beck*-names, the Scottish stronghold of names in *-bie, -by* is Dumfriesshire (Map 9). There are, however, a few scattered outliers in other parts, as the distribution map indicates, and there is a pronounced little cluster in Ayrshire, in the Ardrossan area. *Býr* also occurs in a few individual examples from Argyllshire and the Hebrides, as well as in Caithness, but as it has never been an important ingredient of the Norse contribution to the place-names of the Western Isles and the adjoining mainland, the names in question are apparently unconnected. MacBain lists most of them in his paper on 'The Norse Element in the Topography of the Highlands and Islands'.

Apart from an almost identical geographical distribution of their main group, the Scottish *by*-names resemble *beck*-names with regard to the linguistic origin and semantic categories of their specific elements. Again, fully Scandinavian names stand side by side with names containing Anglo-Saxon, Norman and Gaelic elements, in particular personal names. Their English counterparts are numerous, and although more widespread than names containing *beck,* conform on the whole to the pattern outlined for those. The same English counties which are noticeable centres of *beck*-names, are also full of names containing *by*. The North Riding of Yorkshire has 150 of them, Cumberland over 70; there are at least 15 in Westmorland, and Lancashire produces three more than this number; Derbyshire has a minimum of 10 *by*-names. Scottish-English identical equivalents are numerous, the most remarkable example being *Sowerby* which is on record in all the English counties mentioned, except Westmorland and Derbyshire, and appears twice in south-west Scotland as *Sorbie* – one in Dumfriesshire and one in Wigtownshire – and, in addition to two further instances from Ayrshire and Fife (!), also occurs four times in Argyllshire, including one example each from

9 Scandinavian names in *byr* and *fell* in Southern Scotland

● Name containing *byr*
o Name containing *fell*

the islands of Mull and Tiree; *Surby* (Isle of Man) also belongs here. Perhaps the frequency of this particular name whose original form must have been an ON *saur-byr* 'mud village' or 'swamp village', provides an insight into the type of colonisation undertaken by the Scandinavian settlers responsible for all these names, for the above interpretation, if correct, speaks of hard-working newcomers trying to make a living out of poor soil, under adverse conditions (Or could *saurr* sometimes refer to the mud flats covered by water at high tide and dry at low tide?) One other explanation must, however, be borne in mind, i.e. one which has been put forward for the Icelandic counterparts of Scottish and English *Sowerbys*. Partially based on the significant distribution of the Icelandic examples, and on their association with the goddess Freyja, it interprets them as centres of a fertility cult. If this interpretation can be confirmed, the significance of this group of names in the study of pagan religious practices amongst the Scandinavian settlers in this country could be considerable, but caution is obviously called for.

Another common name is *Crosby* 'cross-farm', attested for all four English counties under consideration, for the Isle of Man, and appearing on the Scottish map as *Corsby* – with metathesis – in Wigtownshire, Ayrshire, and Berwickshire. The *Newbys* and *Al(d)-bys* are common to both the Scottish south and the English north, and the Dumfriesshire *Mumbie* (*Monieby* 1552), has its English counterpart in the Yorkshire *Monkby*, whereas the Wigtownshire Applebie is paralleled by places of the same name in Westmorland and Derbyshire. There are several identical parallels of this kind (cf. *Bombie, Canonbie, Denbie, Ėsbie*, etc.) which do not require discussion in this context. A notable absentee from the Scottish contingent is *Kirkby*.

The overall picture, however, is the same as that established above for names in *beck*. Again the Scottish group of names forms the northernmost part of a much wider scatter south of the border and cannot be ascribed to the same stratum of settlers that created the few *by*-names in the Inner Hebrides and in Argyllshire. In the very south of Scotland and particularly in Dumfriesshire, it seems more than likely that the burn flowing past a *by*-place will be a *beck*, especially when the settlement name was given by Norwegians; but Danish settlers also used this word while it also continued in living use as a place-name element after the Norman conquest.

Whereas *thwaite* is the form in which ON *þveit* 'a clearing, a meadow, a paddock' normally appears on English maps, this is rare in Scotland although *Thorniethwaite, Murraythwaite,* and *Crawthwaite* are relevant examples. The usual modern Scottish spelling is *-that* as in *Cowthat, Howthat, Lairthat, Murthat, Slethat* and *Twathats* (plural), or *-what(e)* as in *Butterwhat, Harperwhat, Robiewhat, Thorniewhats, Raggiewhate,* and possibly *Dalwhat* although it is by no means certain that the second element in this name is in fact *þveit.* Modern *Branteth* is *Brandthwaite* in 1516-7, and other earlier written forms are *-thet, -thweyt* (and *-thweytes), -twayt, -pheit, -weit* and *-wat.* This variety indicates that the history of the written forms of the Scottish names has not been as stereotyped as the main two modern alternatives *-that* and *-what* might lead one to believe, and the difference between Scotland and England in this respect is also not as great as the fairly consistent Modern English *-thwaite* might suggest, for both earlier spellings and modern pronunciation link the English with the Scottish evidence, where a spelling convention apparently divides it: A name like *Great Crosthwaite* in Cumberland, for instance, shows practically the whole range of the above spellings in its earlier forms recorded between 1150 and 1750, and the modern pronunciation [krosθat] refers it straight away to the Scottish *-that* group of names. Similarly, *Curthwaite* in the same county is [karθat], and *Branthwaite* is pronounced [branθat].

The linguistic unity of the Scottish and English evidence becomes even more obvious on the lexical level. The majority of the specifics which feature as first elements in the Scottish compound names containing *þveit,* appears in the same combinations in England, i.e. many of the Scottish *þveit*-names have identical equivalents south of the present border. This applies to names like *Murthat* and *Murraythwaite* in Dumfriesshire and *Moorfoot (Morthwait, -thwayt -thuweit* 1142) in Midlothian, for there are two *Moorthwaites* and two *Murthwaites* in Cumberland and an additional *Murthwaite* in Westmorland, all of which derive from ON *mór* or OE *mōr* 'moor'. *Slethat (Slachquhat* 1459-60, *Slaithwait* 1516-17) is identical with *Slaithwaite* [slauwit] in the West Riding of Yorkshire; these two names have as their first element ON *slag* 'blow', with the whole compound meaning something like 'clearing where timber was felled'. *Butterwhat* is also paralleled by the West Riding name *Butterthwaite* which is explained as 'clearing with rich pasture', from OE *butere* 'butter'. *Thorniethwaite* 'thorn clearing' repeats the Cumberland and West Riding *Thornthwaites* all of which might well contain ON *þorn* 'thorn-tree' rather than its Old English equivalent, as the Old Danish name *Thornthwed* shows. Even the plural *Thorniewhats (Thornythaite* in 1583, however!) occurs in England as *Thornythwaites* in the West Riding of Yorkshire similarly recorded in the sixteenth century as *Thornethwayte.* For˙ the two *Howthats (Holthuayt c.* 1218) there is the parallel *Hoathwaite (Holtwayt* 1272-80) in Lancashire, both from ON *holr* (or OE *hol*), meaning 'clearing lying in a hollow'; and it is just possible that *Heithat* is identical with *Haithwaite* in Cumberland and *Haythwaite* in the North Riding. In those the first element could be either OE *heg* or ON *hφy, hey 'hay'* which would give them a meaning like 'clearing where hay is cut'.

Three 'lost' names, too, have identical equivalents in England: (1) *Appiltretwayt* of 1317 which is compounded with ME *appel-tre* 'apple-tree' also occurs in early Lancashire documents as *Apiltretuait* and *Appeltrethwayt;* here the English word may have replaced an earlier ON *apaldr* of the same meaning. (2) *Brakanepheit* (1194-1214), also *Brakansweit (post* 1275) is the same as several *Brackenthwáite* in Cumberland and one in the West Riding, as well as *Brackenfield (Brakenthwait,* etc. in 1269) in Derbyshire, 'bracken clearing'. (3) *Langesweit (post* 1295) is the 'long clearing', like *Langthwaite* in the North Riding and Cumberland, and *Lanthwaite (Green),* also in the latter county.

In other instances, for which there is no identical equivalent for the whole name in England, the first part of the compound occurs in conjunction with other generic terms of Norse origin in English place-nomenclature. *Carthat,* for example, which apparently contains ON *kjarr* 'brushwood, marsh', can be compared with Kirkgate *(Kergate* 1275), a street-name in Wakefield, containing *kjarr* and ON *gata* 'road, street'. *Lairthat,* a compound of ON *leirr* 'clay' and *pveit,* has the same first element as *Lear Ings (Leyrynge* 1439) in the West Riding. Similarly, both the Scottish *Raggiewhate (Ragaquhat c.* 1544) and the Yorkshire *Ray Gill* contain OE *ragu* 'moss, lichen'; *Cowthat* and *Cow Gate,* again in Yorkshire, share the Old English word *cū* 'cow' as a first element; and the 'lost' *Blindethuayt* of *c.* 1218 has a parellel in the Lancashire *Blind Beck.* In these last two names the first part could be either ON *blindr* or ME *blind* 'blind, hidden'. Another thirteenth-century 'lost' name, *Litelsweit,* shows the same hybrid formation as the Yorkshire *Littlethorpe* and˙possibly the Cumberland *Little Dale.*

This leaves a handful of names like: *Branteth (Brandthwaite* 1516-17), possibly containing ME *brant* 'steep', or OE *brand* 'place cleared by burning', or even ME *brame* 'bramble' which has been postulated for the two Cumberland *Branthwaites,* pronounced [branθat] ; then *Twathats (Thwathweytes* 1304), apparently Middle Scots *twa thwaytes* 'two clearings'; *Harperwhat* 'Harper's clearing', *Robiewhat (Roberquhat* 1542) the first element of which may have developed from a Norse personal name like *Hroðbiartr* or *Hróðbiorg*; also *Crawthat,* from (?) OE *crawe* 'crow', and the strange, now 'lost', *Panthawat* (1516). In these instances the first element is either difficult or obscure. or it is a personal name or significant word which is apparently not on record in conjunction with any Scandinavian generic term in English place-nomenclature. These exceptions by no means spoil the picture; their small number rather emphasises the strong link between the Scottish and English *þveit*-names which can be postulated on lexical and morphological, as well as phonological grounds.

As is the case with *by* and *beck*, *thwaite* must have remained productive as a place-name generic for many a century and can probably tell very little about the immediate and direct linguistic impact of the first Scandinavian settlers on the areas in which it occurs. This is especially true of the English north where it is still alive in the regional dialects in the meaning of 'a forest clearing', although the south of Scotland does not seem to share this dialect usage. As the examples have demonstrated, *thwaite*, like *beck* and *by*, enters into many a hybrid compound which might have been formed at any time after the anglicisation of the Scandinavian settlement area, presupposing some period of bilingual co-existence. Its very limited geographical distribution is, however, linguistically of considerable significance, even if only by indicating the borders of the area where, for a time, it penetrated into the active local dialect vocabulary. A less likely, but possible, alternative explanation would be that its existence was restricted to place-names in this part without any reflection in local appellative usage at any time.

From a distributional point of view (Map 10), place-names containing *þveit* are strongly associated with those in *bekkr* and *býr* although their scatter is not identical with that of either of the two.

In England it occurs most frequently in the usual four counties, the respective figures being about 80 for Cumberland, 60 for Westmorland, 40 for Lancashire, and 30 for the North Riding of Yorkshire; it is also common in the western parts of the West Riding but is rare in the remaining Danelaw counties (4 in the East Riding, 7 each in Nottinghamshire and Derbyshire, including 3 field-names in the latter). It is doubtful whether their particular geographical distribution is only due to the abundance of forest and waste-land in the north-west of England, as has been maintained. Undoubtedly the location of *thwaite*-names is connected with such topographical conditions but, in addition, the particular type of settler, i.e. his way of conquering unprofitable land and of increasing his area of land under cultivation, must be taken into account too. This would be the response to the natural habitat of the same settler who, as far as can be established, built most of the *bys* in this area and called the streams near them *becks*.

In Scotland, the county of Dumfries is the obvious centre and even here the distribution is limited to the so-called 'Norse parishes', as *þveit*-names occur almost exclusively in its eastern half. It is doubtful whether the most north-westerly example shown on the map, *Dalwhat* (*Dalquhot* 1511), does in fact belong here, although some think that it stands for ON *dal-þveit* 'thwaite in the valley' but others explain it as Gaelic *dail chat* 'field of wild cats'. An interesting outlier is *Moorfoot* in Temple parish in the county of Midlothian, better known probably in conjunction with the Moorfoot Hills. From its early forms it becomes clear that the substitution of *-foot* for *-thwaite*, or the like, is not older

10   Scandinavian names containing *þveit* and *Kirk-* in Southern Scotland

•   Name containing *thveit*
●   Name containing *kirk*

than the seventeenth century, with a form *Morfat* of 1559-60 paving the way. Not shown on the map are the two or three examples from the Northern Isles. In Orkney there are two farms called *Twatt,* one in Stenness and one in Birsay, and there is also a township named *Twatt* in Sandsting, Shetland. The word apparently does not survive in the place-names of the Hebrides or of other parts of the Scottish mainland where Scandinavians are known to have settled.

If the map were extended to the southern parts of Lancashire and of the three Ridings of Yorkshire, as well as into Nottinghamshire and Derbyshire, a complete picture of the English evidence would emerge. As it is, even if these more southerly English *þveit*-names were added, these names would in no way invalidate the contention that the southern Scottish names ·do not form a separate entity but must be seen and studied together with the English material. What is really significant is that Northumberland and Durham are completely empty of names in *þveit*, as far as the evidence at present available goes. One wonders, however, whether a detailed examination of the· place-names of these two counties along the lines of the English Place-name Survey might not produce some minor name or field-name just north of the Tees, containing this element; but even if such names are found, the borders of the *þveit*-country, as it emerges from the map, will not be substantially altered.

If the distribution of *þveit* and *býr* in those counties in which both·of them are found is compared, it becomes apparent that the two distribution patterns are by no means congruent. Whereas there are instances of names in *-thwaite* and *-by* occurring closely together, *þveit*-names on the whole cover areas in which *býr*-names are not particularly common, and *vice versa*. In general, *býr*-names, especially when traceable directly to Scandinavian speakers, must be the primary settlements whereas *þveit*-names are associated with the secondary development of less promising ground, usually on a higher level. This is perhaps not quite so obvious, at least not on a map of this scale, in Dumfriesshire as in some of the English counties, especially in Cumberland and Westmorland but also in the North Riding of Yorkshire.

As a term particularly applied to hills, ON *fell*, or *fjall*, appears frequently in south and south-west Scotland as *fell*. Map 9 shows that *fells* are much more widely distributed over this part of Scotland than the three categories discussed so far. The different emphasis, however, is worth noting. Particularly striking is the large number of instances in Wigtownshire, as well as the frequent occurrence of this element in Kirkcudbrightshire. There are no *becks* and no *þveits* in these two counties, and a mere three *bys* in coastal districts meagrely represent an element so common in other areas once occupied by Scandinavians.

Not unexpectedly, Westmorland furnishes the highest number of *fell*-names in England; the relevant English Place-name Society volume lists 32 of them, whereas Lancashire has 7, the North Riding of Yorkshire 2, and Cumberland has at least 21; there are 9 in Northumberland and 2 in Durham, In the Isle of Man there are *Snaefell, Stockfield* and *Masool*. Significantly, the two names in the North Riding are both located in the most westerly corner, close to the Westmorland and West Riding borders. Similarly, the West Riding examples are all in its western half.

It looks as if only very few of the names containing this element can be said to go back to the Scandinavian settlers themselves. Very often the first element is the name of another geographical feature in the vicinity, in many cases of English or Gaelic origin, which gave its name to the *fell*, amongst them *Balmurrie Fell* and *Glenkitten Fell* WIG and *Ewenshope Fell* DMF. Even *Borgue Fell* WIG probably belongs to this late category, although *Borgue* is, of course, purely Scandinavian itself, going back to an original ON *borg* 'a fort, a stronghold, a fortified hill, a fort-shaped hill'. However, *Borgue Fell* is not an original compound dating from the time of early Scandinavian settlers; rather *Borgue* had already been in use as a well-established place-name before the hill was called after it. It is quite possible that this *fell* was the original *borg*, the 'fortified or fort-shaped hill', that gave its name to the human settlement nearby. An exact parallel is the place-name *Burrow* < *Borg* in the Isle of Man.

The English examples show similar signs of lateness, although Gaelic elements are completely lacking, of course, and it seems that − as was to a lesser extent true of *beck* − this is a toponymical element whose ultimate Scandinavian origin cannot be doubted but which passed into the local dialect as a loan-word before becoming one of the distinctive features of the place-nomenclature of south and south-west Scotland, as well as of north-west England. Only when Lowland Scots began to supersede Gaelic in the south-west, did this element enter Wigtownshire toponymy and did it reach the North Channel in a westward movement. Nevertheless, its seedbed must again have been the area straddling the

Solway Firth, i.e. the Scottish county of Dumfries and the English
county of Cumberland. The earliest example on record, mentioned by
the *Dictionary of the Older Scottish Tongue,* stems from 1448, and the
Scottish National Dictionary quotes literary examples from the beginning
of this century.

The *fell*-country, then, appears to be the most north-westerly of all
the distribution patterns mapped, taking in the whole of Galloway and
Carrick which names in *þveit* and *bekkr* do not enter and where there
are only one or two *býr*-names near the shores of the Solway Firth. It is
not really part of the Danelaw, partly for linguistic reasons, one
presumes, and partly because a word like *fell* is bound to occur in hilly
country only. The great majority of this group of names cannot be
called Scandinavian as they have obviously been coined by English
speakers, mainly using other geographical names as first elements
although not exclusively so. *Fell*-names are very much a secondary
toponymic stratum and, as the primary names employed in creating
them are of a variety of linguistic origins and more or less accidentally
compounded with *fell*, it would be useless to look for identical pairs
south of the border. Quite clearly only very few of them can have been
given by settlers speaking a Scandinavian language, and *fell* has to be
regarded as an English dialect word borrowed from Scandinavian, rather
than as a Norse element.

ON *fell, fjall* is, of course, a well-known feature of the hill nomenclature of the Hebrides where it normally appears as *-val*, but also as *-al*
usually after *s(h)*. Examples would be *Liaval* (Lewis), *Bleaval* (Harris),
Eaval (North Uist), *Stulaval* (South Uist), *Hartaval* (Barra), *Heishival*
(Vatersay), *Roineval* (Skye), *Orval* (Rum), *Oiseval* (St Kilda), and on
the other hand *Roishal, Uishal* (Lewis), *Haarsal* (South Uist), *Preshal*
(Skye), and *Minishal* (Rum). It also occurs in the Northern Isles where
its reflexes are often *Field* in Shetland (cf. *Fugla Field, Hamara Field,
Mid Field, Tonga Field, Valla Field*) and *Fiold* in Orkney (cf. *Fibla
Fiold, Low Fiold, Sand Fiold, Vestra Fiold*), but these are examples of
primary Scandinavian names, unconnected with *fell* as found in south
and south-west Scotland (apart from the ultimate etymological identity
of the generic, of course).

The group of names containing Norse *kirkja* 'a church', illustrates a
phenomenon which has come to be known as an 'inversion compound',
in this instance a Germanic compound name showing Celtic word-order.
Apart from having produced the current Scots equivalent of English
church, kirkja does, of course, feature in Scottish place-names in the
'normal' (not inverted) way in cases like *Whitekirk* ELO, *Muirkirk* AYR,
Mearnskirk RNF, *Falkirk* STL, *Brydekirk* DMF, *Ashkirk* SLK, and
Selkirk itself, where it is preceded by the specific element. It is also
itself extremely common as a specific and is then followed by the
generic term, as in *Kirk Burn* LAN, *Kirkcleuch* DMF, *Kirkhill* ABD,
and many others, but these are genuine Germanic compounds which do
not fall into the category under discussion. Not in this category either
are names of the type *Kirkliston* WLO, *Kirknewton* MLO, *Kirk Yetholm*
ROX, etc., which is paralleled by names like *Kirk Deighton, Kirk*

Hammerton and *Kirk Leavington* in Yorkshire; these are, in a way, shortened versions of the more elaborate **Kirktown of Liston, *Kirktown of Newton*, etc., or of some such fuller name, although they may be structurally allied to the 'inverted' names.

True 'inversion' is shown by such names as *Kirkbride* WIG and KCB, when contrasted with *Brydekirk* DMF, or *Kirkoswald* AYR, in contrast to *Oswaldkirk* YON. Both these names also have exact parallels in Cumberland. But even if they cannot be contrasted with actual examples of 'normal' Germanic word-order, names compounded of other saints' names and *kirk* nevertheless qualify for this category, and instances like *Kirkchrist, Kirkcolm, Kirkcowan* in Wigtownshire, and *Kirkanders, Kirkcormack* and *Kirkcudbright* in Kirkcudbrightshire belong here. With regard to them, it has been possible to plot all the Scottish and English examples on one map, (Map 10). It is absolutely clear from this distribution that these names are limited to the south-west of Scotland and to the very north-west of England, but that their scatter significantly differs from that of names in *beck, by, pveit,* and *fell*. Whereas these latter name-groups form rather extreme and small appendices to the large bulk of English names containing the same elements, 'inversion compounds' with *Kirk-* show exactly the opposite distribution of weight. They are essentially a south-west Scottish feature, with a few scattered additional instances from the English county immediately adjacent to that part of Scotland. The emphasis lies no longer on Dumfriesshire but on Wigtownshire and Kirkcudbrightshire, and practically all the names are to be found in coastal districts or in easily accessible river-valleys. As recent research has made abundantly clear, the linguistic background of the Galloway names in *Kirk-* is predominantly Gaelic which must have been established in Galloway between the sixth and ninth centuries, before the Norse settlement began. There is, however, also the possibility of the simultaneous arrival (from Ireland?) of Norse and Gaelic speakers in Galloway, and it looks as if, to a certain extent, these may have been responsible for the creation of the first of these 'inversion compounds' in *Kirk-*. It seems to be equally obvious, on the other hand, that not every *Kirk*-name of this type goes back to these early times, say the early tenth century. Names like *Kirkmaiden, Kirkmadrine* and *Kirkmabreck*, which contain Gaelic *mo* 'my', may well be part translations of an earlier **Kilmaiden, *Kilmadrine, *Kilmabreck*, made, at an early date, by Scandinavians who, because of their acquaintance with Irish, understood the function of *mo*. However, since one of the *Kirkbrides* in the Rinns of Galloway is still locally known as *Kilbride*, and since *Kirkcormack* KCB is sometimes *Kilcormack* in records and *Kirkpatrick (-Fleming)* appears as both *Kirkepatric* in 1189 and *Kilpatrick* in 1296, it is difficult to imagine that all *Kirk*-names go back to the earliest period of Scandinavian, or rather Norse-Irish, settlement from Ireland. A similar case is *Kirkdominie* AYR, which is still on record as *Kildomine* in 1404 in a manuscript charter. In 1541 the Register of the Great Seal refers to a *Kilquhonell* in Carrick, the modern *Kilwhannel*, which takes its place beside the *Kirkeonnels* of Dumfriesshire and Kirkcudbrightshire.

Examples from other parts of Scotland support this consideration, although purely documentary evidence is not always conclusive; *Kirk-michael* R O S. was known in Gaelic as *Cill Mhicheil,* and the old name of the parish of Strath in Skye is said to have been *Kilchrist* or *Christiskirk* in 1505, but *Kirkchrist* in 1574. *Kilmorie* in the island of Arran, is *Kilmory* in 1483 but *Kyrkmorich* in 1595, and the Manx Gaelic version of *Kirk Bride* in the Isle of Man is Killey Bridey; similar Manx versions seem to have prevailed for all the *Kirk*-names in the Isle of Man while Manx was still extensively spoken in the island.

It appears to be self-evident from all this that there is bound to be amongst the *Kirk*-names a number of late part-translations in which *Kirk-* replaced *Kil-*. Other *Kirk*-names may have been formed at a later date following an established pattern. Some may be much later than the time during which a Scandinavian language was still current in the area. Sometimes the second element may provide some clue as to the originators of a certain Kirk-name. The information it supplies may not always be of a linguistic nature, and that seems to be why linguists have, until recently, paid so little attention to the hagiological implications of the saints' names that form the second parts of these compounds, apart from their linguistic analysis.

Names like *Kirkbride, Kirkcolm, Kirkconnel, Kirkcormack, Kirk-mirran, Kirkpatrick,* etc. obviously point towards the Irish church, and *Kirkmabreck, Kirkmadrine,* and *Kirkmaiden* are just as clearly basically Gaelic in thought and construction. Even if such a form has not actually come down to us on record, it can be more or less assumed that the original first element in these names was *Kil-,* rather than *Kïrk-*. These are essentially Gaelic names, with a Gaelic religious background, and there does not seem to be any reason why they should be attributed to Scandinavians, unless as part-translations adopted by Norse incomers when they reached this Gaelic-speaking area. In some cases, however, it seems to be more plausible to assume that *Kirk-* supplanted *Kil-* not in Scandinavian, but in Anglian mouths. In this respect, names like *Kirkoswald* and *Kirkcudbright* may be keys to a solution of this problem. Both, St Oswald, the Northumbrian king and saint who was slain in 642, and St Cuthbert, the influential seventh-century missionary and Bishop of Lindisfarne who belonged to the Lothians or the Scottish Borders, are great figures of the church in the English north-east, and although their cults very probably reached south-west Scotland before the arrival of the Scandinavians, one would hesitate to attribute the linguistic origin of these commemorations to the Norse newcomers.

This does not mean that all *Kirk*-names of this kind are completely un-Scandinavian; the implication is rather that a number of them may be post-Norse in their present form. They and other 'inversion compounds' undeniably speak of linguistic contact between Scandinavian and Gaelic speaking people in our area, but do not necessarily prove that the Norse raiders and settlers imported this type of name from the Viking colonies in Ireland, the Isle of Man and the Hebrides from where they are supposed to have reached the shores of north-west

England and south-west Scotland. There is, of course, the evidence of 'inversion compounds' containing first elements other than *Kirk-*. Several of these are to be found in the part of Scotland under discussion. *Crossraguel* AYR, for instance, again points to a religious context (apart from its vicinity to *Kirkoswald*), and *Torthorwald* DMF, containing Gaelic *torr* 'a hill' and the ON personal name *þorvaldr*, must have been coined by Gaelic-speakers describing the property of a Scandinavian neighbour; this again stresses the fact that the inhabitants of this area at this time must have been predominantly Gaelic. A possible example of complete adaptation of the Gaelic principle of word-order is *Westerkirk* DMF, which is on record as *Wathstirkir* in 1305; it is probably to be derived from ON *vað* 'a ford' and the personal name *Styrkárr*. There are a few others, but on the whole the Norse 'inversion compound', which shows total adoption of the Gaelic principles of formation, is the rare exception rather than the rule.

In general, the Scandinavian impact on the place-nomenclature of the Scottish south-west is much purer and shows no signs of the strong influence of Goidelic speech on the language of the Norse immigrants which it has been claimed to possess. Purely Norse names which show no trace of Irish influence whatever are, for example, *Borgue* KCB (*Borg* 1469) < ON *borg* ' a stronghold'; *Stoneykirk* WIG (*Stennaker* 1534) < ON *steina aker* 'field of stones'; *Applegarth* DMF (*Apilgirth 1275*) < ON *apaldr(s) garðr* 'apple-orchard', which has two identical parallels in Yorkshire (in all cases OE *æppel* 'apple' has probably later replaced ON *apaldr* 'apple tree'); *Float* WIG (*Flot* 1540) < ON *flot* 'a piece of flat ground'; *River Fleet* KCB < ON *fljót* 'a river' (but possibly OE *flēot* 'an estuary'); *The Wig* WIG < ON *vík* 'a bay'. In addition there are the four elements discussed above, as well as numerous other names containing either one or two Scandinavian words. The distribution and the importance of these elements may vary, but their ultimate connection with Scandinavian-speaking immigrants cannot be denied, although it may be well to remember that many individual place-names may not have been introduced by the people from whose language they are derived.

In summing up these preliminary but substantiated findings, it should be stressed again that the distribution of the elements *bekkr*, *býr*, and *þveit* suggests close connection with a larger area south of the English border, particularly Cumberland, Westmorland, Lancashire, and the North Riding of Yorkshire. A substantial proportion of the names containing these elements may go back to the original Scandinavian immigrants, others must definitely be ascribed to later periods; some of them are post-Norman. The case of *fell* is slightly different in so far as this element does not seem to have entered the toponymy of the Solway region during the early period of Scandinavian settlement, but rather as a local dialect word borrowed from Norse, peculiar to north-west England and south-west Scotland. In the latter area, it forms a later stratum in place-nomenclature, occurring in comparatively young formations and overlaying older Gaelic, Scandinavian and Anglian strata.

The names containing these elements are not due to Irish-Norse settlers from Ireland, but to a different stratum of Scandinavian settlement. It is difficult to believe that Dumfriesshire should have been settled direct from Ireland or the Hebrides. It rather looks as if it was settled by Scandinavians a little later than the larger region in Northern England, when the Norse sphere of influence expanded. There is a certain West Scandinavian flavour about these names — if 'test-words' mean anything — but there is also *Denby* DMF, which in 1304 is recorded as Daneby; this is paralleled by four *Danbys* in the North Riding of Yorkshire, and it looks as if the presence of a sporadic East Scandinavian (Danish) element has to be taken into account in the Norse population of these parts of the British Isles. The movement of this Norse settlement must have come from south and south-east of the Solway and from across the English border, rather than direct from across the Irish Sea. That, at least, seems to be the verdict of the place-names evidence in this area, as derived from the distribution patterns.

The 'inversion compounds' in *Kirk*- have to be interpreted differently. They cannot be separated from an essentially Gaelic background. Some of them may be attributable to Norsemen from Viking colonies in Ireland and in the Isle of Man, who reached Galloway and parts of Carrick from the early tenth century onwards and, seemingly, also settled in the extreme English north-west. One would like to exclude the Hebrides from the possible places of origin of these Scandinavian settlers, as, apart from one example in the Isle of Skye, there does not seem to be the slightest indication of a development of a similar type of compound name. It is very likely that Gaelic speakers from Ireland arrived simultaneously with the Norse immigrants and reinforced the Irish-Gaelic element in the nomenclature under review; such an explanation would also satisfactorily account for certain names of Irish-Gaelic origin in the north-west of England. The first *Kirk*-names, depicting commemorations of Irish saints, and the wide-spread juxtaposition of *Kil*- and *Kirk*-names in the Scottish south-west, may be due to close linguistic contact between these two groups of settlers, as well as with the already existing Gaelic-speaking inhabitants of the district. The first cases of substitution of *Kirk*- for *Kil*- (and *vice versa*?) may also be ascribed to this early period, but once the pattern had been established and once kirk had gained sufficient currency in the Anglian dialect of the district, the precise linguistic background of *Kirk*-names becomes obscure, and they must be taken to have been created, re-created and translated for a number of centuries, owing to this threefold linguistic contact Gaelic-Norse, Gaelic-English, rather than to genuine bilingualism.

It would be of considerable interest to see what a closer analysis of all types of 'inversion compounds' in the place-nomenclature of this area may have to say on the movements of people and their languages into this part of Scotland, and particularly on the immigration of Scandinavians which is practically unrecorded. It would also be desirable to establish a more factual knowledge as to the geographical origin of these Scandinavians, beyond the rather vague speculations on which one has to rely at present. The more one studies such toponymic elements as *bekkr, býr, þveit,* and *fjall,* as well as the more complex 'inversion compounds' in *Kirk-,* the more one becomes aware of the lack of, and consequently the need for, a comprehensive survey of Scandinavian place-names in these islands. This would lend a new dimension to the study of Scandinavian settlement and influence not only in Scotland but in the whole of Britain and Ireland. Such a project would demand co-operation amongst the place-name scholars of the British Isles and would also require extensive consultation with Scandinavian toponymic experts: it should not be beyond realisation of international and interdisciplinary scholarship.

Outside Orkney, Shetland, and the Hebrides, on the one hand, and the Scottish south-west (mainly Dumfriesshire and Galloway) on the other, toponymic evidence for Scandinavian settlement in Scotland becomes exceedingly scarce. There are certainly no other parts of the country which can compare with the areas already surveyed, concerning the density of name material, echoing in its turn extensive settlement, at one time or another, by people speaking a Scandinavian language. Repeated claims have nevertheless been made for the presence of Scandinavians elsewhere in Scotland, on the basis of surviving place-names, and although these frequently derive from the confusion of OE *wīc* 'dependent farm' with ON *vik* 'bay', ME *firth* 'estuary' with ON *fjörðr* (its Norse 'ancestor'), or OE *næss, ness* 'promontory, headland' with the cognate ON *nes,* they cannot be completely ignored, especially in view of the fact that more scattered and less direct evidence does exist for Scandinavian influence outside the two main, and most obvious, areas. This is particularly true of the Scottish south-east where there are some names in *-bie,* and several place-names in which a Scandinavian personal name combines with an English generic, two name categories which may well throw some light on the otherwise poorly-recorded Scandinavian ingredient of settlement history in south-east Scotland, mostly in the Border Counties and the Lothians.

Though small in number, place-names containing ON *býr* as a generic are obviously of special significance, since it is unlikely that this element was ever used by English-speakers in the creation of new names. Begbie ELO (*Bagby* 1458), probably identical with Bagby YON (*Bagebi* 1086), is 'Baggi's farm'; *Baggi* is found as a personal name in Old Norse, Old Danish and Old Swedish. While Blegbie ELO (*Blackbie, Blaikbie* 1659) may contain OE *blæc* 'black' or *blāc* 'pale, bleak', its specific element is more likely to be the Old Norse cognate of the latter, *bleikr* 'pale, livid' or the personal name *Bleici* which derives from this adjective. Corsbie BWK (*Crossebie* 1309) is identical with several English places named Crosby in Cumberland, Westmorland, and Lancashire, all reflexes of an Old Scandinavian *Krossa-býr* 'farm with crosses', ON *kross* itself being a loan from Irish. The most prolific personal name associated with a place-name in *-bie/-by* is *Hundi,* as in Humbie ELO (*Hundeby c.* 1250), MLO (*Humby* 1546), WLO (*Hundeby* 1290), and FIF (not recorded before the sixteenth century). There is also a Humbie in the Renfrewshire parish of Mearns but no details are known to the author. In England, the name occurs in Lincolnshire as Hanby (*Hundebi, Hunbia, Humbi* 1086) and Humby (*Humbi* 1086). In all likelihood it means 'Hundi's farm', from Old Scandinavian *Hunda-bȳr*. With Pogbie ELO (*Pokby* 1238-70) may be compared Pockley YON (*Pochelac* 1086) and Pockthorpe YOE (*Pochetorp* 1086), which seem to be Poca's (Pohha's)*lēah* (forest, glade) and *thorp* (farm), respectively. In Schatteby BWK (so in 1300, now 'lost') the first element may be an Old Norse personal name *Skati* or the noun *skata* 'skate'. An interesting hybrid is Smeaton MLO (*Smithetun* 1124-53, *Smithebi* 1153-65, *Smetheby* 1232, *Smithetune* 1234), since the substitution of *-by* for *-tūn* is unique in this area. It is a good indicator for the presence of a Scandinavian language as a temporary adstratum or superstratum.

In the cases of Begbie, Corsbie, the four Humbies, and Schatteby — and there is no reason why the not so well-documented Pogbie should not also be included in this list — the first elements, whether personal name or appellative, are undoubtedly also of Scandinavian derivation and therefore point to Scandinavian origin for the whole name. Consequently, they are evidence of small pockets of Scandinavian settlers in the areas concerned, and presumably a Scandinavian, rather than an English, dialect must have been spoken there for a while. There is, however, no evidence that these small groups of people were, as has sometimes been asserted, of Danish, or Eastern Scandinavian, extraction. The elements involved are either neutral in that respect or indicate Norse rather than Danish influence.

The only other Scandinavian word directly involved in the formation of place-names in this region is the isolated example of *þveit* 'a clearing, a meadow, a paddock' in the name of the Moorfoot Hills (*Morthwait, -thwayt, -thuweit* 1142) in which the first part could be either ON *mår* or OE *mōr* 'moor'. As in the case of *bȳr*, the main *þveit*-area of Scotland is otherwise Dumfriesshire, and one might perhaps look for linguistic and ethnic affinities in that county and the Solway Firth region.

This total of nine, or maybe ten, names in which both elements are, or could be, of Scandinavian origin, consists of names occurring either singly or in small clusters. Of the latter, the Humbie group (Humbie, Blegbie, Pogbie) would be a good example. The main impact of the Norse language on the place-nomenclature of south-east Scotland is, however, to be found in a different type of name formation, i.e. in names which cannot be ascribed to Scandinavian-speakers but contain Scandinavian personal names as their defining elements. A fairly common name in this category is Bonnington MLO (Ratho parish: *Bondingtona c.* 1315), MLO (City parishes: *Bonyngtown* 1465), ELO (*Bondingtoun(e)* 1329-71), LAN (*Bondingtoun* 1329-71), and PEB (*Bonnestoun c.* 1380, *Bondingtoun* 1329-71); it also appears as Bonnytoun WLO (*Bondington* 1315).

There are additional Bonningtons in Fife and Perthshire, and there is recorded evidence for places of this name in Angus, Ayrshire, Berwickshire and Renfrewshire. Most of the names in question are probably derived from the Scandinavian personal name *Bóndi*, as in Bonby LIN (*Bundebi* 1086, *Bondebi* c. 1115) and Bombie DMF (*Bundeby* 1296, *Bomby* 1329-71). This is a common name although it was known in Norway rather as a by-name than as a Christian name. There is, however, also the appellative noun *bond* 'a peasant or serf; a bondman' which goes back to ME *bond, bonde, bounde*, OE *bonda*, ON *bonde* 'householder, etc.'. In most cases .it is impossible to say whether a personal name or an appellative applies. If the former is preferable, the meaning is 'farm of Bondi, or of Bondi's people; if the latter, a hybrid compound noun, meaning 'peasant farm' or the like, might be considered as the lexical base.

It is difficult to say whether Brotherstone ·MLO (*Brothirstanys* 1153-65) belongs to the category under discussion. It could simply be 'twin stones', from OE *brōðor*, or it might contain an Old Norse personal name *Bró'ðir*, as in Brothertoft LIN, Brotherton SFK (*Brodertuna* 1086), Brotherton YOW (*Broðertun* c. 1030), or Brotherwick NTB (*Brotherwyc* 1242). The generic element is, of course, OE *stān* 'stone'. The personal name ON *Kolbrandr*, Old Swedish *Kolbrand* of Cockburnspath BWK (*Colbrandespade* c. 1130) is also contained in the Swedish village-name Kolbrandstorp. Colinton MLO (*Colbanestoun* 1319), Covington LAN (*Uilla Colbani* 1189-96, *Colbaynistun* 1212), and Cobbinshaw MLO (*Colbinshaw* 1512) have as their first elements the ON personal name *Kolbeinn*, an adaptation of the Irish name *Columbán*. The generic in Cobbinshaw is OE *sceaga* 'wood'. Corstorphine MLO (*Crostorfin* c. 1128) has to be seen as an 'inversion compound' of Gaelic *crois* 'cross' and a personal name which is ultimately ON *þorfinnr*; a meaning 'Torfinn's crossing' would be appropriate. Four place-names formed with the Old Norse personal name *Dólgfinnr* are Dolphington WLO (*Dolfingtoun* 1490-91), Dolphinston ROX (*Dolfinestone* 1296), Dolphinton LAN (*Dolfinston* 1253), and Dolphingston ELO (*Dolphinstoune* 1680). The same personal name occurs in such English names as Dolphenby CMB (*Dolphinerby* 1283) and Dolphinholme LNC (*Dolphineholme* 1591). A Middle English derivative of ON *Ísleifr* is the first part of Elliston ROX (*Iliuestun* 1214-49), for in 1220 *Johannes filius Yliff de Ylistoun* grants land to Dryburgh; this information places the creation of the place-name approximately at the end of the twelfth or the beginning of the thirteenth century. Illieston WLO (*Ileustune* c. 1200) has the same etymology, as does the *Domesday Book* entry *Isleuestuna* for Suffolk.

For the East Lothian name Gamelshiel (*Gamelshields* 1505) and its first element, the Old Norse personal name *Gamall* (Old Danish, Old Swedish *Gamal*), a helpful chronological reference is provided by the Cumberland name Gamblesby (near Melmerby; *Gamelesbi* 1177) which in its earliest record is described as *terram que fuit Gamel filii Bern*. *Gamall* is also the specific element in another Cumberland Gamblesby (*Gamelesby by Ayketon* 1305) and in the two Nottinghamshire Gamstons (both *Gamelestune* in 1086). In the 'lost' Midlothian name Auchtiegamel (thus 1773) the personal name is combined with the Gaelic land-measurement *ochtamh* 'an eighth part' In Gilston MLO

(*Gillystoun* 1288), 'Gille's farm', the personal name in question is probably the same as in Gilby LIN (*Gillebi* 1139) and Gilsland CMB (*Gilleslandia c.* 1185), i.e., *Gille* < ON Gilli < Old Irish *gilla* 'servant'. As the earlier spellings show, modern Graham is a re-interpretation of ON *Grimr* in Graham's Law ROX (*Grymeslawe* 1296). In England, this name is found frequently in records of the tenth century and also occurs often in place-names such as Grimesthorpe YOW, Grimsargh LNC, Grimsbury OXF, Grimsby LIN, and Grimscote NTP, Grimston, which is quite common, has in England become the prototype for names of English settlements taken over by Scandinavians. *Grimr* is also well known in the place-names of the Northern and Western Isles of Scotland. The second element in Graham's Law derives from OE *hlāw* 'a rounded hill'.

For Gunsgreen BWK (*Gownisgrein* 1580) 'Gunni's green', England offers such parallels as Gunby St Nicholas and Gunby St Peter LIN, Gunness LIN, Gunthorpe LIN, NFK, RUT, and Gunton NFK, SFK, *Gunni* is described as a Danish tenant in *Domesday Book*. Hailisepeth BWK, in Lauder (thus *c.* 1222, *Ailinispeth c.* 1230), is now 'lost'. If *Ailin-* stands for *Ailiu-*, the personal name contained in this compound may well be ON *Eilifr*, as in Allithwaite LNC (*Hailiuethait c.* 1170); if *Ailinespeth* is genuine, the Lancashire name Elliscales (*Aylinescal c.* 1230) might be compared. On the basis of its early spellings, it has been convincingly suggested that Ingliston MLO (*Ingalstoun* 1406) is 'Ingialdr's farm'. The personal name in question is also seen in Ingoldisthorpe NFK, Ingoldmells LIN, Ingoldsby LIN, and possibly in Ingleston DRH (*Ingeltun c.* 1050) and Ingleton YOW (*Inglestune 1086*). Similar in composition to Corstophine and Auchtiegamel is Kirkettle MLO (*Karynketil* 1317, *Karketile* 1474) 'Ketill's cairn', a compound of Gaelic *carn* 'cairn' and a personal name *Ketill* which not only occurs in Kettlestoun WLO (*Ketlistoun* 1147-53) and Kettleshiel BWK (*Ketelschel c.* 1269) but also in a great number of English place-names, such as Kettleby LEI, LIN, Kettleburgh SFK, Kettleshulme CHE, Kettlesing YOW, Kettlestone NFK, Kettlethorpe LIN, YOE, and Kedleston DRB.

The earliest recorded form of Lyleston BWK (*Liolfstoun c.* 1222, *Lyalstoun c.* 1230) points to a personal name *Li(g)ulf* as a first element but although adjudged a Scandinavian name probably of Old Norse provenance, the exact etymology of this name is still doubtful. Recorded evidence for Milsington ROX (*Milsintoun* 1654) is too scanty and late to permit a definitive analysis of its first element which may be an Old Norse personal name *Mylsan*, possibly a shortened adaptation of Old Irish *Maelsuithan*; this name probably appears in Melsonby YON (*Malsenebi* 1086). The Old Norse name *Ormr* is the specific in several place-names, including two Ormistons in Roxburghshire (*Hormiston* [p] 1214-49, *Ormistoun* 1452), Ormiston MLO (*Ormystoun* 1211-26), Ormiston ELO (*Ormeston* 1628), Ormistoun PEB (*Ormstoun* 1603), and the unrecorded *Ormscleugh Syke* MLO. Since it is a very common personal name in medieval England, it also occurs in many English place-names, like Ormsby NFK, YON, North and South Ormsby LIN,

Ormside WML, Ormskirk LNC, and Urmston LNC (*Urmeston* 1212, *Ormeston* 1284). Oxton BWK (*Ullfkelistoun, Hulfkeliston* 1206 [*c.* 1320], *Ulkilstoun c.* 1220 [16th], *Ulkestoun* 1273, *Ugistoun* 1463-64, *Uxtoun* 1654) is a good example of a name which has become unrecognisable within four centuries. Modern *Ox-* and the seventeenth-century *Ux-* are reductions of the Old Norse personal name *Ulfkell,* itself a slightly shortened form of *Ulfketill* which is well recorded but perhaps not native in Old Norse.

In contrast to Oxton, the later spellings of Ravelston MLO (*Railstoun* 1363, *Raylistona* 1364, *Ravilstoune* 1494) seem to be closer to the original first element than the earlier ones. *Ravil-* and *Ravel-* are likely to go back to an earlier *Hrafnkell,* or possibly *Hrafnulfr,* both frequently found in *Domesday Book. Hrafnkell* would be a reduction of *Hrafnketill.* Because of the lateness of the recorded evidence, both Rousland WLO (*Rusland* 1540-41, *Rousland* 1582) and Snaberlee Rig ROX (*Snebirly* 1654) are uncertain candidates for the name category under discussion. If the development of the former is the same as that of Rusland LNC (*Rulesland* 1336), it is possible that the first element is the Old Norse personal name *Hrolfr,* or perhaps *Hroaldr.* The latter may possibly contain an Old Norse personal name *Snæbiorn,* but since Domesday Book mentions this only for Yorkshire, this can be no more than a conjecture. Swanston MLO (*Swaynstoun* 1214-40), on the other hand, is clearly 'Sveinn's farm', although in the seventeenth century it was re-interpreted as *Cygnea domus vulgo Swanston,* i.e. as 'farm where swans are'. An identical name is *Swainston* IOW (*Sweyneston* 1255), and other English names containing the same personal name are Swainsthorpe NFK, Swainswick SOM, and the two Swainbys in the North Riding of Yorkshire. The development *Swain-Swan-* is shown by Swanland YOE (*Suenelund* 1189) and Swannington LEI, NFK. ON *Sveinn,* Old Danish and Old Swedish *Sven,* is common in both Scandinavia and Britain.

It is just possible that the first element of Thorlieshope (Tower) ROX (*Thorlishoip, Thirlishoip* 1569) may be a Middle English form *Thorli* of the Old Norse personal name *poraldr,* although the late spellings are not reliable. *poraldr* occurs in the English place-names Thoralby YON (*Turoldesbi, Toruldesbi* 1086) and Thorlby YOW (*Torederebi, Toreilderebi* 1086); it also appears four times in *Domesday Book.* Thurston ELO (*Thureston* 1292) is identical with Thurston SFK (*Thurstuna, Torstuna* 1086); they both mean '*pori's* or *puri's* farm. The personal name in question, which would be *porir* in Old Norse and is an old and extremely frequent name well documented in *Domesday Book,* also occurs in such English place-names as Thoresby LIN, NTT, YON, Thoresthorpe, Thoresway (both LIN), etc. The personal name involved in Toxside MLO (*Thocchesheved* 1142) may be either OE *Tocca* or ON *Toki* as in Tockholes LNC and Toxteth LNC; the second element is clearly a misunderstood OE *hēafod* 'height'. Ugston ELO (*Ugston* 1478) possibly contains the same first element as Ugthorpe YON, either *Ugga* or *Uggi.* The latter is a known Old Norse personal name but is not with certainty evidenced in

Domesday Book. The first element of Ulston ʀ o x (*Ulvestoun* 1147-52) is the very common personal name, ON *Ulfr*, which occurs in many English place-names, such as Ulceby (two in Lincolnshire), Ulleskelf ʏ o w, Ullesthorpe ʟ ᴇ ɪ, Ullswater ᴄ ᴍ ʙ, ᴡ ᴍ ʟ, and Ulverscroft ʟ ᴇ ɪ. There are many instances of this personal name in *Domesday Book.* For Yorkston ᴍ ʟ o (*Yorkistoun* 1354) a personal name *Jorek* from ON *Jorekr* has been suggested as the first element; although this name is not evidenced in *Domesday Book*, it apparently occurs in Yorfalls ʏ o ɴ (*Yorcfal* 1335).

The evidence just paraded, incomplete and patchy of necessity, is sufficient to answer a number of questions. First of all, it is quite obvious that none of the names in this category were given by Scandinavians. Generics like OE *-tūn, -stān, -paeð, -hlāw, -sceaga, -grēne, -land, -lēah,* and *-hēafod* point to speakers of English as originators of the names in question, whereas Corstorphine, Auchtiegamel, and Kirkettle clearly show Gaelic influence both in word-formation and derivation. Considering these names as total formations there can, therefore, be only one verdict: they are non-Scandinavian in origin. However, the whole group is of course characterised by the fact that the specific element in each name is, or at least may be, a Scandinavian personal name, implying the possibility of a sizeable influx of Scandinavians into south-east Scotland.

What is the nature of the personal names involved? In order to determine whether they are basically Danish or Norse, some information about the dialectal provenance and local distribution of Scandinavian names in England may prove useful. Of the names in question, *Bóndi, Tóki,* and *þór-* are of West Scandinavian origin because of their phonetic shape; in addition, *þórfinnr* is only found in West Scandinavian sources. The only name for which East Scandinavian origin might be claimed, *Ulfkell,* belongs to those that are found all over England, like *Grímr, Ketill, Sveinn, Tóki,* and *Ulfr,* and can therefore be said to have lost its peculiar Eastern qualities. Names like *Dólgfinnr, Hrafnkell, Kolbeinn* and *Ligulf* only occur in north-west England and are consequently more likely to be of western than eastern Scandinavian provenance. *Kolbeinn,* like *Mylsan* and *Gilli,* has strong Irish connections, probably reaching England with Norsemen from Ireland. *Sveinn, Gamall* and *þórfinnr* are also found in Ireland. On the negative side, none of the names only found in (*a*) Lincolnshire, (*b*) Lincolnshire and Yorkshire, (*c*) East Anglia, are amongst the names under scrutiny. Admittedly, *Gunni* is expressly called a Danish tenant in *Domesday Book,* and the first part of Thurston may be Old Danish *þurir* rather than ON *þórir,* but the bulk of the evidence points to names which are either of west Scandinavian origin or are neutral as far as their dialectal provenance is concerned. It would therefore be totally incorrect to speak of a Danish linguistic element in the place-names of the Scottish south-east.

Nevertheless, whatever their ultimate origin may be, it is more than likely that most of the personal names listed had, by the time they reached Scotland, become so anglicised that it is questionable whether the people bearing these names were in fact Scandinavians. *Dólgfinnr*, for instance, is in all respects a West Scandinavian name but it is recorded fact that its English derivative *Dolfin* was the name of at least two members of the Northumbrian family of Dundas in the thirteenth century. *Johannes filius Yliff de Yliston* was mentioned under Elliston as being recorded for 1220. *Ligulf* witnessed a Durham charter about 1100, *Lyulf* was the son of Uhctred (1119-24), and in 1174 we have *Liulfo filio Macus.* In 1147-50, Crailing in Roxburghshire is called *villa Orme,* and a little earlier (1127) there is record of *Orm presbitero de Edenham. Gille, *Thorli, Ulf,* and a number of others are probably to be looked upon as Middle English rather than Old Norse names by the time they appear as elements in Scottish place-nomenclature.

The conclusion would therefore have to be that the group of names just discussed is in a completely different category from the *by*-names mentioned earlier on. In the majority of cases these were, in spite of the ultimate Scandinavian origin of the personal names involved, simply English place-names coined by English speakers using what were at that time English elements. In those instances, in which the bearer of the name may still have been a person of Scandinavian descent, speaking a Scandinavian language, he is likely to have been of Norse rather than Danish extraction.

In more general terms, the complexity of the Scandinavian contribution to the Scottish place-nomenclature has become quite apparent. Not only are there three major geographic areas providing quite distinctive regional nomenclatures, but within each area subtle, but important, distinctions exist among a variety of name-types, pointing to a considerable chronological range, on the one hand, and to a variety of linguistic relationships, on the other, ranging from the *staðir*-names of the Northern and Western Isles to the 'inversion compounds' of the south-west and the anglicised Scandinavian personal names in the place-names of the south-east. Any emphasis placed on the heterogeneity of these names is, however, in no way a crude denial of ultimate links which exist behind this variety and which allow the use of the umbrella term 'Scandinavian' for all the ingredients. Certain *býr*-names, like *Sowerby,* for example, have a much wider scatter than could normally be expected from Scandinavian names of regional dominance in the south-west. Similarly, the final etymological identity of the element *fell* with the *-vals* and *-als* of the Hebrides, the *fields* of Shetland, and the *fiolds* of Orkney is a non-regional feature. To this might be added the identity of *Tinwald* DMF, *Dingwall* ROS, and *Tingwall* ORK, SHE, ON *þing-vollr* 'assize-field, or parliament-site', a name which declares that the legal organisation of the Scandinavian settlers in Scotland and elsewhere must have been much more homogeneous than their naming processes and social relations with others; a name which also proclaims them to be part and parcel of such Scandinavian colonial settlement wherever it occurred, whether it be documented by the place-name Tynwald in the Isle of Man or by the

Icelandic *þingvellir,* quite apart from identical equivalents in the Norwegian homeland. Here is unity underlying heterogeneity. In this connection, it is worth remembering that these Scandinavians were people who were in need of land and who were ready to settle down and lead their lives in a society governed by law, whenever they had the opportunity to do so. The Scandinavian place-names of Scotland certainly are proof of that attitude.

7
Gaelic Names

After the disintegration of Roman power in Britain, the comparative powerlessness and petty factionalism of the native princelets even in the larger kingdoms created a political situation which of necessity attracted power- and land-hungry foreigners to the shores of the British mainland. Whereas 450 (or some year during the preceding decade) is usually given as the date of the first large-scale Saxon invasion of southern England, the third quarter of the same century is regarded as the time when Gaelic-speaking Scots from Ireland first established a dynasty in Dal Riada, comprising much of present-day Argyll. Initially, contact with the homeland, especially Ulster, remained close and continuing but after a few generations the Scots of 'Scotland' gained more and more independence, their warriors and settlers spread, by the middle of the ninth century their ruler had become King of the Picts, and two hundred years later Gaelic was spoken throughout Scotland, with the exception of the extreme geographical north dominated by Scandinavians, and the south-eastern-most territories of the Angles bordering on English Northumberland. After this period of most extensive Gaelic-speaking settlement and power in Scotland, the arrival of a Norman dynasty and administration signals the beginning of the decline of Gaelic linguistic domination, a decline whose sad and regrettable, but unmistakable, final stages we witness in our own life-times, it seems.

Throughout this rise and fall of Scottish Gaeldom, summarised rather simplistically in the preceding paragraph, Gaelic place-names were created by Gaelic-speakers, and are, albeit to a very limited quantitative and geographical extent, still being created in the 1970s. They form the stratum which directly underlies English place-nomenclature in most parts of Scotland, and their creation over a period of over 1400 years, together with their anglicisation during about half that time, has provided Scottish toponymy with much of its distinctive 'Scottishness', perhaps best expressed by such names as *Auchenshuggle* (Glasgow), *Auchtermuchty* FIF, and *Maggieknockater* BNF, names which simply do not occur in other parts of the British mainland but provide a historical and linguistic link with Ireland. Both Irish and Scottish Gaelic, as well as the almost extinct Gaelic of the Isle of Man, derive from Goidelic, a branch of Insular Celtic, although the stage of the language preceding the divergence into Irish and Scottish Gaelic is best called 'Common Gaelic'. Common Gaelic, then was the language spoken by the Scots newcomers from Ireland and therefore also the linguistic backcloth to the earliest Gaelic contribution to the Scottish nomenclature. Scottish Gaelic has, of course, continued to develop phonologically, morphologically, lexically, and syntactically since those beginnings and even during the seven hundred years in which its dominance has declined.

At first sight, the Gaelic stratum in the Scottish place-nomenclature, a layer 1400 years 'deep' in places, appears to be almost impenetrable with regard to the further isolation of strata within the stratum, since most lexical items used toponymically seem to have been employed ever since the first Gaelic place-name was coined in Scotland, while still being productive now, both in Scotland and in Ireland. The difficulty in pin-pointing elements to which more limited chronological usage may be attributed is especially frustrating in the search for criteria which might be helpful in recognising pre-Norse Gaelic place-names in those parts of Scotland — mainly the Hebrides and the adjacent mainland — in which Norse became a linguistic adstratum and subsequent superstratum, practically blanketing the earlier Gaelic place-nomenclature where the distribution of Norse place-names, particularly settlement-names, is at its densest, as for instance in the island of Lewis. The isolation of Gaelic *sliabh* 'a mountain' as an early element (see pp. 39-46), mainly on the basis of its geographical distribution in relation to historical information provided by documentary evidence, constituted a breakthrough in this respect, leading not only to a visual impression of the extent of early Gaelic-speaking Scotland but also to the discovery of a second primary settlement area, besides Dalriadic Argyll, of Gaelic Scots from Ireland, in areas of Galloway facing the Ulster coast, a discovery later confirmed by archaeological finds. The role which the study of place-names played in that connection, by giving a lead to other disciplines, cannot be over-emphasised in an academic climate, which tends to ascribe to toponymic evidence a supportive rather than a pioneering role. The materials offered in this and the last two chapters, their analysis and the arguments resulting from that analysis should for ever dispel the doubts apparent in that attitude, regarding the reliability of independent onomastic evidence and the insights it furnishes.

The distribution of *sliabh* in Scottish place-names, mostly hill-names but secondarily also settlement-names, reflects the geographical extent to which Gaelic was spoken in Scotland a few centuries after the Dalriadic settlement, mainly in Galloway, Argyll (with special emphasis on Islay and Jura) and in the upper reaches of Tay and Spey. The exact point in time at which *sliabh* ceased to be productive toponymically is, of course, impossible to determine but it should be put well before the ninth century when Gael and Norsemen confronted each other in the Hebrides and Caithness, and when Gaelic had already begun to infiltrate Pictland. *Sliabh* is conspicuously absent from all these areas, and the seventh century might well be considered as the end of the use of this element in place-names, at least in the northern areas of its geographical scatter. Because of the detailed coverage of *sliabh* in Chapter III, it is not necessary to repeat the discussion of this generic, and reference should be made to Map 1 for the cartographic representation of the names in question.

Before an examination of Gaelic place-names, from the point of view of Scotland as a whole, it is necessary and salutary to focus on the evidence place-names can provide for the history and geographical distribution in southern Scotland, i.e. south of the Forth and Clyde, because of the extreme dearth of other linguistic source material. In fact, we know next to nothing about the phonology, morphology, syntax, and vocabulary of Gaelic in southern Scotland from any kind of text or other documentary evidence. In particular the spoken language has eluded us altogether since it was extinct by the end, or perhaps even by the middle, of the seventeenth century even in the remotest parts of Carrick where it seems to have lingered longest. Whereas it has been possible to record the Gaelic forms and contemporary pronunciation of some Ayrshire place-names from native speakers of Gaelic in the island of Arran, these recordings can obviously only faintly mirror the actual Ayrshire Gaelic pronunciation of these names and, although extremely valuable in themselves, are no substitute for any information at first hand.

In order to avoid the use of uneven criteria, the discussion will focus on two groups of place-names (those containing Gaelic *baile* and *achadh*) which have a direct connection with a settled population, and on a short analysis of another category (that beginning with *Kil-* < *Cill-*) which might possibly supply both a glimpse of the cultural background and an opportunity for dating some of the earlier settlements. The selection of the Forth-Clyde line as the northern boundary of 'Southern Scotland' of necessity results in a certain amount of artificial distortion, in so far as what is not unreasonable in the east leads to the not entirely justifiable inclusion of parts of Stirlingshire and Dunbartonshire in the centre and west which otherwise might well have been thought not to belong here. However, the relative artificiality of the line chosen is not considered to be a factor which will distort the relevant part of the evidence. Only the distribution of names to the east of the Firth of Clyde will be shown in detail on the maps, whereas the hatching covering the adjacent parts of the counties of Bute and Argyll merely indicates the presence of our names in these areas without showing their exact position or density.

(*a*) *The distribution of Gaelic* baile. *Baile* is not only the most frequent but also the most instructive of Gaelic settlement terms, for whether it is translated as 'village', 'hamlet', 'town', 'home', or 'farm', it always refers to a permanent type of human settlement, the inference being that, wherever it occurs, it is indicative of a well-settled Gaelic-speaking population, as it takes quite a number of people speaking a certain language to create, use, and sustain place-names in that language. Examples of *baile*-names found in the region under discussion are:

Ayrshire: Balbeg, Balgray, Balkenna, Ballantrae
Wigtownshire: Baldoon, Balgown, Balminnoch, Balwherrie

Kirkcudbrightshire: Balcary, Balmaclellan, Balmingan
Dumfriesshire: Ballaggan, Baltersan
Lanarkshire: Balbackie, Balwaistie
Selkirkshire: Balnakiel
Peeblesshire: Bellaman (with Ballaman Hill)
East Lothian: Balgone, Ballencrieff
Midlothian: Balerno, Balleny
West Lothian: Balbardie, Balgreen, Balmuir
Renfrewshire: Balgreen, Ballageich (Hill)

For those familiar with the geography of the southern Scottish counties, even the numerical evidence behind this list makes impressive reading, for a total of at least 74 names in Ayrshire and Galloway (Ayrshire 39 or 40, Wigtownshire 25, Kirkcudbrightshire 11) set against 25 names from the remaining counties, half of which figure is supplied by Renfrewshire (6) and West Lothian (6), make the enormous difference in density immediately apparent. Even this count is not exhaustive, however, since other secondary sources add to the Ordnance Survey evidence at least another 12 names for Wigtownshire, seven for Kirkcudbrightshire, and another five for Dumfriesshire. For the visual presentation (see Map 11) other known evidence, purely historical, has been included (although 'lost' names like *Balnebucht* twelfth century, *Balbaghloch* 1331, *Ballentrodoch* 1237, *Balgrwmy* 1593 in Midlothian, and *Balgrenagh* and *Balnegrog*, both 1336 and in East Lothian, could not be plotted accurately), even at the risk of unevenness. An analysis of this map shows quite clearly that this type of name is densest on the ground in western Galloway (= Wigtownshire) and the southern parts of Ayrshire, mainly Carrick but also Kyle. Kirkcudbrightshire and the parts of Dumfriesshire west of the Nith also still display a fair density as does to a certain extent Renfrewshire. While the northern regions of our map, from Dunbartonshire through Stirlingshire into West Lothian obviously belong to, and link up with, the more northerly regions not shown on this map, the rest of the Scottish south is very sparsely represented. Lanarkshire has at least some examples in the upper reaches of the Clyde and its tributaries, and there are some outliers in eastern Dumfriesshire, but in the Lothians from Edinburgh eastwards and in the Border Counties proper, *Bal*-names are extremely scarce, to the complete exclusion of Berwickshire. This evidence leads one to distinguish roughly four zones: (I) Galloway, including the southern parts of Ayrshire and the parts of Dumfriesshire west of the Nith; (II) Northern Ayrshire, Renfrewshire, the Clyde valley, and Dumfriesshire east of the Nith and west of the Esk; (III) Dunbartonshire, Stirlingshire, West Lothian, perhaps the western half of Midlothian; (IV) the Border Counties (Peeblesshire, Selkirkshire, Roxburghshire, Berwickshire) and East Lothian with the eastern half of Midlothian. Zones I and III obviously presuppose full-scale settlement of Gaelic speakers for a long period, Zone II would indicate a shorter and less dense settlement, and Zone IV a mere sprinkling of Gaelic-speaking settlers for a very short time.

(b) *The distribution of Gaelic* achadh. Gaelic settlement-names beginning with *baile* are only rivalled in number by those beginning with *achadh*, but it must be remembered that although most of these are now names of towns, hamlets, farms, etc., they must have started out originally as field-names. They are therefore not always direct evidence for settlement, but rather point to ancillary agricultural activities of the settlers. This is an important distinction which must not be obscured by the present status of such names. In the Scottish south, as in other parts of Scotland, the anglicised form is usually *Auchen-* or *Auchin-*, i.e. it includes the Gaelic definite article preceding the second element in a stereotyped form which no longer allows one to say whether it represents the feminine genitive singular or the genitive plural. In fact, the simplification seems to have gone even further, because *Auchen-* appears before personal names in the genitive (Auchenfedrick DMF: [*Auchinfathrik* 1505] = *Achadh Phadruig* 'Patrick's Field') and even before adjectives (Auchenroy AYR: Gaelic *ruadh* 'red'; Auchenbegg LAN: Gaelic *beag* 'small'; Auchenreoch KCB: Gaelic *riabhach* 'brindled'; Auchenbrack DMF: Gaelic *breac* 'speckled'; etc.). Whether this development took place during the end-phase of Gaelic in these parts, when inflexional features were breaking down, or whether it should be ascribed to the process of anglicisation is difficult to· say, but the most plausible general explanation would be that a bilingual situation was responsible for such changes. It certainly looks as if the anglicised form *Auchen-* was regarded by non-Gaelic speakers as a fixed element, having become an indivisible morphological unit which had swallowed up the former definite article altogether.

Auchenfedrick DMF has, of course, been explained as *Achaidhean Phadruig* 'Patrick's field', and a diminutive *achadhan* has been invoked for Auchenreoch KCB. It would, however, be strange if in practically every case in which an adjective forms the second element, either the plural or the diminutive were to have been used instead of the normal singular. In all the 'one-inch' material from Dumfriesshire, for instance, there is not a single example in which the anglicised form of the name does not begin with *Auchen-*. It would therefore be preferable to ascribe this phenomenon to a levelling process in a bilingual or even post-bilingual situation, rather than to a phonologically correct reflex of the original monoglot Gaelic form.

The Ordnance Survey one-inch maps supply, amongst others, the following names:

Ayrshire: Auchairn, Auchenbrain, Auchengarth, Auchinleck, Auch-millan

Wigtownshire: Auchabrick, Auchenree, Auchleach, Auchnotteroch

Kirkcudbrightshire: Auchencairn, Auchenfad, Auchenreoch, Auch-nabony

Dumfriesshire: Auchencairn, Auchengyle, Auchenlone, Auchentaggart

Lanarkshire: Affleck, Auchenglen, Auchingray, Auchrobert

Midlothian: Auchendinny, Auchindoon

West Lothian: Auchinhard

11   Names in *Bal-* in Southern Scotland

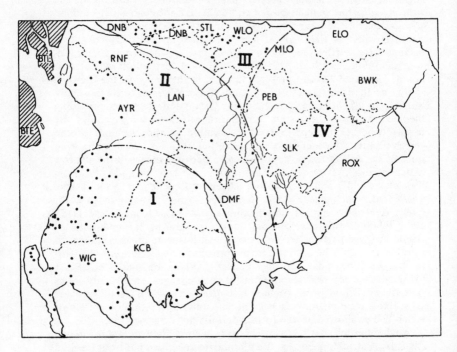

Renfrewshire: Auchans, Auchencloich, Auchentiber, Auchmead

From a purely numerical point of view, names beginning with *Auchen-*, etc., by far outnumber those beginning with *Bal-*, i.e. on the one-inch Ordnance Survey sheets for southern Scotland there are only 113 *baile*-names, but 165 in which *achadh* is the first element. Again it is worth remembering that these are the minimum figures and that in Galloway alone there are at least another 12 names in Wigtownshire and two in the Stewartry, according to other sources, while there may be as many as 36 additions for Dumfriesshire.

Important in this context is the observation that the larger number of names is confined to a smaller area (Map 12), leaving bare completely the eastern half, namely the Border Counties east of Dumfriesshire and, apart from one example in West Lothian and two in Midlothian, also the Lothians (Auchencraw in Berwickshire is *Aldenecraw* in 1333; this still makes it a potential Gaelic name, but one containing a different generic). In addition, the proportions within the area covered differ considerably. Ayrshire is still at the top of the list, but has proportionately a smaller number of names. Within this county, *achadh*-names are found in parts from which *baile*-names are noticeably absent, particularly in Cunningham. Wigtownshire shows a proportionate and absolute decrease, compared with Map 11 but in the other four

12   Names in *Auch-* in Southern Scotland

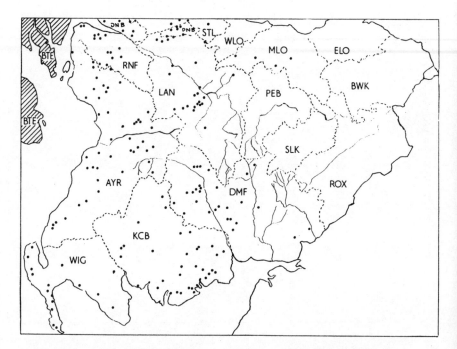

counties the distribution is very much denser, with the increases being
especially marked in Kirkcudbrightshire (34 against 11), Dumfriesshire
(28 against 5), and Lanarkshire (23 against 5). Within the region of
the six western counties, therefore, there is a remarkable shift of
emphasis towards the east, and whereas the counties strongest in
baile-names (Ayrshire and Wigtownshire) are not neglected, the other
four are definitely *achadh* rather than *baile* counties.

Bearing in mind the semantic differences between *baile* and *achadh* –
the former always implying permanent settlement, the latter originally
agricultural activities ancillary to such settlement – the case may be
argued for a distinction between primary (*baile*) and secondary (*achadh*)
settlement names. The question whether this may also be interpreted as
a chronological sequence of 'earlier' and 'later' cannot be answered
from the distributional evidence alone, but there is nothing in this
distribution which would contradict such an assumption. Taken
together, on the other hand, the presence of *baile-* and *achadh*-names
in the six western counties is an indication that here, at one time or
another, people whose language was Gaelic both lived in permanent,
non-seasonal dwellings *and* tilled the soil, brought in the harvest,
milled the corn, grazed the cattle, etc. In contrast, the limited presence
of one group of names (*baile*) and the absence of the other (*achadh*)

13   Names in *Kil-* and *Kirk-* in Southern Scotland

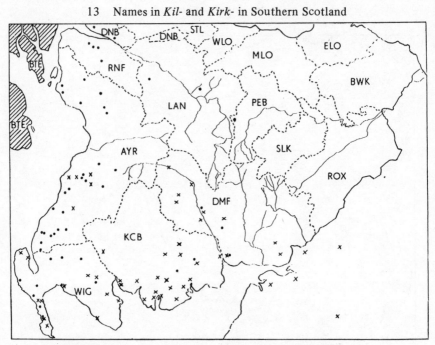

• Names in *Kil-*   × Names in *Kirk-*, with historical *Kil-* forms
× Names in *Kirk-*

in the other six or seven counties is surely a reflection not only of
the smaller numbers of Gaelic speakers in the east but also of a
difference in status of these speakers, who are also non-seasonal
settlers as in the west but apparently lack any direct connection with
agricultural and pastoral activities, having presumably been landowners
rather than tillers of the soil.

In terms of the four 'zones' established for the distribution of
baile-names, this would mean that, whereas there is very little difference
in Zones I and III, from the point of view of the occurrence of
achadh, major changes are to be found in Zones II and IV, in the
former a sizeable increase in number and density, in the latter complete
absence. In Zone II however, the increase is much more marked west
of the Clyde than to the east of it.

(*c*) *The distribution of Gaelic* cill. If *baile*-names imply non-seasonal
settlement and *achadh*-names reflect primarily agricultural activities,
names beginning with *Kil-* (< Gaelic *cill*) point to a background of
Christian religion, or more tangibly to the presence of churches and
churchyards, or at least hermits' cells. The fact that they are Gaelic
names must mean that, even if some of them might be considered to be
part-translations or adaptations of earlier British names, they are the
linguistic expression of more than mere proselytising activities of

individual Gaelic missionaries either in isolation or in small groups, amongst a Cumbric-speaking population. *Kil*-names must have been given by sizable Gaelic-speaking Christian communities, mostly in commemoration of a particular saint or of a missionary who was a follower of, or had taken the name of, such a saint.

The main difficulty in establishing a reliable distribution map of names in this category (Map 13) lies in the fact that it is not always easy to sift the *cill*-names proper from those which in their anglicized form look identical but, when properly examined, are found to contain such elements as *coille* 'wood', *cuil* 'nook', or the like. *Cinn* 'at the end' has also in one or two instances become *Kil*-, and sometimes *cill* is the original generic in names now beginning with *Kirk*-. In addition, there are such names as Kilbank, Kilburn, Kill Brae, etc., for which early documentation is lacking but which are to all intents and purposes English names of natural features containing an unidentifiable first element. Are they to be regarded as part-translations, as has sometimes been done, so that such names as Kell Burn and Kill Burn are considered products of an earlier *Allt na Cille*? As such an assumption can hardly ever be proved, these doubtful names have been omitted from our compilations, and the list which follows only contains names of which it can be said with reasonable certainty that they incorporate Gaelic *cill.* One of the main criteria in this respect has, of course, been the presence of a saint's name as the second element, another the present status and significance of a name.

Examples in this category are:

Ayrshire: Kilantringan, Kilbride, Kilmarnock, Kilpatrick, Kilwhannel

Wigtownshire: Kildonan, Kilfillan, Killumpha, Kilquhockadale

Kirkcudbrightshire: Killymingan, Kilmichael

Dumfriesshire: Closeburn (*Kylosbern* 1200), Kilblane

Lanarkshire: (East) Kilbride, Kilcadzow

Peeblesshire: Kilbucho

Renfrewshire: Kilbarchan, Kilellan, Kilmacolm

That the distribution of *Kil*-names is more restricted than that of both the *Bal*- and the *Auchen*-names is at once apparent, since the list contains few or no entries for the counties not bordering on either the Firth of Clyde or the Solway Firth. Indeed, only Ayrshire and Wigtownshire and, for its size, Renfrewshire show a reasonable representation. The map immediately confirms this impression (Map 13), and reveals not only the Peeblesshire name Kilbucho but also the Lanarkshire Kilcadzow on the east bank of the Clyde as outliers with very little connection with the rest of the group. Even East Kilbride is made to look less out of place only by the fact that the two names just mentioned are so much further east.

On a purely distributional basis, the scatter of *Kil*-names may be regarded as either an early or a late feature of the spread of Gaelic in this area, but as there is no compelling reason why it should be the latter, and as all other evidence points in the direction of the former, the conclusion must be that the distribution of this type of name reveals an earlier state of affairs than that of either of the other two elements. Examination of the northern counterparts of this name-type provides a clear indication that these are not likely to be younger than the year 800 (see p.144) and the question arises whether *Kil*-names must be earlier than 800 in the south as well. On the whole, their virtual restriction to 'Zone I', coupled with the location of *Kil*-names in Scotland as a whole, is an indication that the distributional picture of Map 13 represents the spread of Irish ecclesiastical influence within a Gaelic-speaking context not later than the last few decades of the 8th century, perhaps earlier, but undoubtedly in pre-Norse times.

For how long has this influence lasted or, in onomastic terms, when was it first possible for *Kil*-names to have been created? Apart from some evidence not contained in the names themselves, there is a certain amount of guidance in the second elements of these names — the saints' names involved. Obviously no name of this kind can be earlier than the lifetime of the saint commemorated, and as most of the identifiable saints (Brendan, Brigid, Ciaran, Ciannech, Faolan, Findbarr, etc.) died in the sixth century and others (Mo-Ernoc, Donnan, Mochutu) in the seventh, the creation of the majority of these place-names should not be put much before the second half of the seventh century. This would allow for up to 200 years for these names to have arisen, a comparatively short time which perhaps accounts for the instability of many of them under late Norse influence when, in many cases, *Kil-* was translated or replaced by *Kirk-*. The original number of *Kil*-names must therefore have been much greater, and, in order to indicate the geographical relationship between *Kil-* and *Kirk-*, names of the Kirkcowan type have therefore been incorporated in Map 13. This would give Kirkcudbrightshire and Dumfriesshire (west of the Nith) a much more realistic representation as Norse influence was quite clearly strongest there. In general, the scatter of the so-called 'inversion compounds' in *Kirk-* simply represents a section of the map depicting *Kil*-names.

A comparison of the three distributional pictures suggests that *Cill*-names represent a comparatively early phase of Gaelic settlement, not earlier than the seventh, but also not later than the middle of the ninth century. *Baile*-names may have arisen during this early period, but they continued to be coined much longer and, in one way or another, found their way into almost the whole of southern Scotland. *Achadh*-names would follow in the wake of *Baile*-names, but only in those areas where Gaelic-speakers were working the soil. They would normally require a denser Gaelic-speaking population, and in Zone II in particular are probably later than *Baile*-names. In tabular form the position would look something like this:

Table II

Name Type	Zone I	Zone II	Zone III	Zone IV
Cill	X	(X)[1]		
Baile	X	X	X	X
Achadh	X	X	X	

How does this rather abstract picture, only indicating relative sequences, fit into what is known of the actual historical framework of the times? The spread of Gaelic in southern Scotland is, of course, intimately linked with the fate of the other linguistic groups in the same region, chiefly the Cumbrians and the Angles, but also the Norsemen. It is, therefore, possible that the areas of density here called 'Zones' (p.124) are perhaps reflections of differing relationships with such groups. As far as the Cumbrians are concerned, a good summary of the extent of their political unit, Strathclyde, is contained in Jackson's statement that it 'was essentially the basin of the Clyde; its capital was on the hill of Dumbarton Rock, and its ecclesiastical centre was Kentigern's foundation at Glasgow . . . at the minimum it must have consisted of Lanarkshire, Renfrewshire, Dumbartonshire, and parts of Stirlingshire and Ayrshire'. After reoccupying Dumfriesshire, which had been taken from them by the Angles in the seventh century, at the beginning of the tenth century and holding it for about a century, the Cumbrians finally ceased to exist as a separate nation early in the eleventh century when they became part of a larger Scotland. Their language may have lingered on for another hundred years or so.

The military and political events affecting the fortunes of the Scottish south appear to leave little room for any major Gaelic influence until this complete breakdown of the kingdom of Strathclyde, or at least until the middle of the tenth century. The only two important events recognised by most historians as being linked with the Gaelic language are the activities of the Irish Church in Northumbria, especially in Galloway and Dumfries, in the seventh century, and the arrival of the so-called *Gall-Ghoidhil*, people of mixed Norse and Gaelic stock, first towards the end of the ninth century from Argyll and Bute, and later from Ireland. Otherwise, in the absence of any really tangible evidence, the expansion of Gaelic into Cumbria and the Lothians is usually ascribed to an aristocratic superstratum, at least initially, and it is also generally recognised that there was no sudden displacement of the English-speaking population in the Lothians. Explanations given are, however, not very specific in their accounting for the presence of place-names of Gaelic origin in the various regions of the south. The main problem appears to be that a fairly large number of Gaelic place-names seems to have arisen in a comparatively short time, particularly in Strathclyde where, as elsewhere in southern Scotland, we must reckon with considerable Anglo-Norman and presumably also English influence from the twelfth century onwards. Certainly one century would not be enough to account for the considerable number of *Auchen*-names, and even if Gaelic is assumed to have continued as the daily means of communication of the majority of people for another century or two, before it declined rapidly under the strong pressure of English, this would hardly have permitted the creation of so many Gaelic names. Scholars trying to interpret this situation are in a similar dilemma elsewhere.

It is therefore necessary to ask whether political boundaries are by definition linguistic boundaries and whether the rise and fall of languages are, in the Dark Ages, of necessity linked with the rise and fall of kingdoms. Is it realistic to wait for 1018, i.e. Duncan's accession, before a major influx of Gaelic-speakers into the still existing kingdom of Strathclyde becomes possible? If it is true that, whereas the decline of political strength may frequently be accompanied by the deterioration of the language connected with this power, the rise of a language can happen long before there is any manifestation of political superiority, it is more than likely that there was Gaelic linguistic influence in Strathclyde even before the eleventh century. Furthermore, not all linguistic developments are immediately discernible in political terms, although commonsense guesses might be made to interpret a situation in such terms. A migration from Dal Riata to Galloway in the middle of the eighth century is, for instance, inferred by some from the Pictish oppression of Dal Riata on the one hand and the 'open and masterless' position of Galloway on the other; others find it difficult to believe such a suggestion because they see no reason why the English should not have been strong enough to repel any such movement at that time, whether from Ireland or from Argyll. The former view appears to be preferable, because English power was probably not very strong in these areas at the best of times and certainly not in a time of near anarchy in Northumbria (see p.159 below).

In a further move amongst the politically uncharted, disagreement has to be voiced with the idea that Gaelic must have been established in Galloway before the Cumbric period, but the presence of hill-names containing the Gaelic word *sliabh*, anglicised *Slew-*, is evidence of an early settlement of Gaelic-speakers mainly in the Rinns of Galloway (see pp.39-46 and 122), which may well have been the beginning of the existence of Gaelic in southern Scotland, placing the settlers at roughly the same time as the Dalriadic settlement of Argyll, with the same kind of close connections with Ireland which this 'colony' had until the middle of the seventh century. The work of Irish missionaries in Galloway and Carrick and the coastal regions along the Solway Firth and the Firth of Clyde would create a new phase. Although largely working amongst Cumbric speakers initially (*Kirkgunzeon, Kilwinning*), they would not have come exclusively to an area in which at that period the language was Cumbric, but would soon have had the advantage of being backed by speakers of their own language who would gradually spread from their first restricted settlement area to the north and west along the coast, with perhaps further Gaelic speakers coming in from Arran, Bute, and Kintyre. *Kil*-names are not dedications by missionaries speaking a foreign language but commemorations by people to whom *cill* was the natural word for a church-like structure. In all probability, these *Kil*-names existed when the *Gall Ghoidhil* arrived in large numbers, reinforcing Gaelic to a certain extent and also introducing Norse linguistic features. The part-translation of many of the *Kil*-names into *Kirk*-names must partially belong to this period, and also the creation of a number of new *Kirk*-names according to the old pattern (see also p.109 above). It is interesting in this respect that these *Kirk*-names, as far as Scotland is concerned, only occur within a slightly extended *Kil*-area. Since about half the *Kirk*-names are attached to parishes, whereas *Kil*-names neither are nor ever have been parish-names, both name-types serve as toponymic pointers to the status of Norse- and Gaelic-speakers in that region, for elsewhere *Kil*-names are frequently used to denote parishes such as Kilbirnie, West Kilbride, Kilmarnock, Kilmaurs, and Kilwinning in northern Ayrshire, East Kilbride in Lanark- shire, Kilbarchan and Kilmacolm in Renfrewshire, Kilbucho in Peebles- shire, Closeburn in Dumfriesshire, and several other names in such counties as Argyll, Bute, Dunbarton, Inverness, Ross, etc. The southern Ayrshire names Kirkmichael and Kirkoswald, as well as Kirkconnel, Kirkmahoe, Kirkmichael, and the two Kirkpatricks in Dumfriesshire, would bear out this observation. *Kil*- does not to any extent penetrate into Strathclyde and Lothian (Kilcadzow, Kilbucho, and perhaps East Kilbride are notable exceptions), an indication that Gaelic had not made any inroads into Cumbric-speaking Strathclyde territory by the ninth century. In other terms, it was still confined to Zone I, plus the western parts of Zone II.

The next phase in the spreading of Gaelic could be generally identi- fied with the distribution of *Bal*-names, although it is evident that this is a very composite picture. Names containing *baile* may, by and large, be said to confirm the presence of Gaelic speakers in the *Kil*-areas, to be indicative of a process of consolidation in these parts, and to speak of further expansion from the ninth century onwards. They must have been given at different times, under differing conditions, and must have come from various areas of origin. On the whole, they are quite clearly not as late as their Irish counterparts would imply, for it has been shown that in Ireland there is no evidence of its use as an element in the formation of place-names before the middle of the twelfth century, and that many *baile*-names are fourteenth-century translations of English names in *-tun*. That they undoubtedly form a superstratum to earlier English names in the Solway Firth area and in Carrick is illustrated by such a name as Dalswinton DMF which in 1295 has a side-form *Baleswyntoun*. Both *Dal*- and *Bale*- are obviously later addi- tions to an English name in *-tun*. The Ayrshire name Dalmellington may have to be interpreted similarly, and such an explanation would not be surprising in view of the fact that Maybole (*Maybothel* 1189- 1250, *Maibothel* 1204-30), consisting of Old English *mæge* 'kinswoman, maiden' and *botl* 'dwelling', is not far away, an early English name which appears as *Meibothelbeg* and *Meibothelmor* in 1185-96, i.e. with the later Gaelic additions of *beag* 'small' and *mór* 'large'. There are, of course, other early English pre-Gaelic names in the Solway Firth area, but they are not very thick on the ground and do not give the impression of a region densely settled by speakers of English at that stage.

If the suggested explanation of Balnab near Whithorn as *Baile an Aba* 'the abbot's land or house' is correct, this name may be of considerable antiquity because Whithorn ceased to be an abbacy about AD 800. After the restoration in the twelfth century it became a priory. Balnab, therefore, may well be one of the earliest *baile*-names in the south of Scotland, dating back to the eighth century. There is

another Balnab near Glenluce Abbey, but this cannot be older than
the twelfth century as Glenluce was founded by the Cistercians in the
last decade of that century. In general, however, *baile*-names are as
difficult to date as English *tūn*-names, apart from their first recorded
form and the potential datability of some of the second elements. In
Strathclyde they are not numerous enough to be indicative of a period
of dense Gaelic-speaking settlement, and although some may, of course,
belong to the post-1018 period, others may well have reached the
Clyde valley with earlier infiltrators from the west (and north), perhaps
at the same time as the isolated *Kil*-names, or a little later. The fairly
impressive number of names north of the Clyde from Dumbarton to
Edinburgh must be linked with an influx of Gaelic speakers from the
Scoto-Pictish kingdom further north. They may have been created any
time between the ninth and twelfth centuries. The two names in the
northernmost corner of East Lothian, on the other hand (Balgone and
Ballencreiff), are likely to be the result of intimate contact with the
other side of the Firth of Forth, particularly in view of the fact that
the twelfth-century earls of Fife possessed land in East Lothian, as well
as the 'earl's ferry' which formed a direct link between Elie and North
Berwick; the nearby place-name Earlsferry is still a reminder. These
two names may therefore be regarded as being of twelfth-century
origin. Balnakiel in Selkirkshire is a puzzle. There seems to be no early
record of it, and its modern form, with its formal preservation of the
genitive of the definite article, is difficult to reconcile with the evidence
presented by other anglicisations. If it is genuine, however, it must
belong to the period of temporary Gaelic overlordship over 'Lothian'
from the second half of the tenth to the beginning of the twelfth
century, when a Gaelic-speaking aristocracy must have formed a good
proportion of the landowning classes, whereas the population in general
remained English-speaking. It is in this context, too, that such names as
Gilmerton, Congalton, Gilchriston, Malcolmstone, Makerstoun, etc.,
have to be placed, i.e. names given by English-speakers to villages or
estates owned by 'Scots'.

By and large, the Clyde-Nith line (or rather the watersheds to the
east of these two rivers) may be said to have formed an important
barrier in the eastward movement of Gaelic speakers. To the north
this movement was halted by the Angles, to the south by the Norse
whose presence in Dumfriesshire east of the Nith as the northernmost
'outpost' of the Scandinavian settlement area of northern England is
evidenced by names in *-by* and *-thwaite* (see pp. 101-107 above). Even
when purged of all names of doubtful authenticity, the not inconsiderable number of Gaelic names of natural features in the Border Counties
and the Lothians is, in view of the scarcity of *Bal*-names and the absence
of *Auchen*-names in these areas, also to be ascribed to the temporary
Gaelic overlordship already mentioned, and although such names
indicate that Gaelic must have been to a certain degree current in
Lothian, the place-name evidence does not allow any notion of general
currency, or consequently, of extensive settlements of Gaelic-speaking
people, especially since in the counties of Roxburgh and Selkirk,

and in parts of Berwickshire, Gaelic may have disappeared in the twelfth century.

The rather long survival of Gaelic in Peebles seems to have been just as much caused by an influx of Gaelic-speakers from the north through West Lothian and Midlothian as across the watershed from the Clyde valley. It is in this respect that names beginning with *Auchen*- are so instructive because they are completely absent from all those counties for which temporary overlordship of the Scots over the English may be postulated. This must be partly due to the fact that *Auchen*- names are on the whole later than *Bal*-names, or perhaps one should say that they became fashionable later, at a time when any Gaelic influence there had been over these English-speaking areas was in decline, whereas Gaelic was in the ascendancy in Strathclyde; for doubtless most of the *Auchen*-names were introduced into the former Cumbric-speaking kingdom after it had lost its political identity at the beginning of the eleventh century. The picture in Dumfriesshire (28 *Auchen*-names against 5 beginning with *Bal*-, or a total of 64 against 10) is also most easily explained in this way, and *Auchen*-names are likely to have been created as long as Gaelic remained the everyday language of the majority of the population in the area west of Clyde and Nith, and to the north of the Clyde. The end of this phase is difficult to ascertain as not enough information is as yet available, but a thorough scrutiny of the phonology of anglicised place-name forms and an examination of the medieval personal names, especially the first appearance of English names in these parts, should allow the establishment of some kind of chronological framework. Until this work has been done, however, it can only be surmised that the decline of Gaelic in Strathclyde must have begun in the fourteenth century at the latest, and that Gaelic is unlikely to have been spoken there after the sixteenth, or even the fifteenth, century. The position in Galloway and Carrick has already been outlined (p. 123).

Summing up the situation in the Scottish south, it must again be stressed that in the period under discussion the borders of political units are not necessarily also the borders of linguistic people, although frequently the two coincide. On the basis of names beginning with *Slew*- (*sliabh*), *Kil*- (*cill*), *Bal*- (*baile*), and *Auch*- (*achadh*), it can further be argued that the distribution of these elements represents phases of the spreading of Gaelic in southern Scotland, only seldom charted or hinted at in conventional historical documentation. The distribution maps give a visible account of the rise of Gaelic in the Scottish south: from small beginnings in the sixth century in the Rinns of Galloway (*sliabh*), via ecclesiastical activities in the coastal areas of Solway and Clyde from the seventh to the ninth centuries (*cill*); backed by increasing Gaelic-speaking settlement, perhaps supported by new incomers from Bute and Kintyre and also Ireland, and making small-scale inroads into Strathclyde from the west and the Lothians from the north and north-west from the tenth to the beginning of the twelfth centuries (*baile*); to more intensive settlement of Strathclyde and Dumfriesshire after 1018 (*achadh*). They also point quite clearly to the

fact that Gaelic was never at any time the language of everybody south
of the Forth-Clyde line, and that as far as 'Lothian' is concerned, there
is at most evidence of a temporary occupation and of the presence of a
landowning Gaelic-speaking aristocracy and their followers for something
like 150-200 years.

The non-toponymic evidence, both linguistic and extra-linguistic,
for the history and nature of Gaelic-speaking settlement north of Forth
and Clyde is, of course, so much better than in the south, but naturally
both the amount and the quality of the available information vary
from area to area. Near the east coast, for instance, in counties like
Aberdeen, Kincardine, Angus, Kinross, Clackmannan, and Fife the
situation is not unlike southern Scotland, whereas the Hebrides and
parts of the adjacent mainland still offer limited but adequate opportunity for field-work amongst live speakers of local Gaelic. In central
Scotland the situation differs from place to place but diligent search has
produced good Gaelic-speaking informants in many localities, ranging
from individuals to sizable communities. This is true, for example,
of areas like upper Banffshire, Badenoch, Glen Urquhart, Strathtay,
Atholl, and the Trossachs, as well as of many localities in Ross-shire
and Sutherland. In the island of Arran everyone of the small surviving
group of Gaelic-speakers has been recorded, and similar work is being
done in nearby Kintyre. Direct contact with the living language provides
welcome opportunities for the observation of name behaviour, while
also removing doubts and false etymologies caused by ambiguous
anglicisations of Gaelic names. Although there is always the risk of
anachronistic falsification in the projection of present circumstances
into the past, twentieth-century place-name evidence, especially the
modern Gaelic pronunciation of names, frequently backed by written
documentary sources, nevertheless throws much light on the meaning
and development of our Gaelic place-nomenclature. It also provides an
opportunity for the study of the Gaelic treatment of non-Gaelic names,
both past and present, even in areas, like the Borders, in which Gaelic
was never spoken to any large extent, and the existence of parallel
Gaelic names is revealed, like *Cill Chuimein* for Fort Augustus INV,
Bun Ilidh for Helmsdale SUT, or *Baile Bhoid* for Rothesay BTE.
Since such a large proportion of our Scottish toponymy is Gaelic
in origin or shows Gaelic influence, it is reassuring to know that the
systematic study of that toponymy began and is carried out while so
much Gaelic evidence is still rescuable.

In view of this rather happy situation, it is not necessary to treat
the relevant place-names north of the Forth-Clyde line with the same
painstaking detail as their southern counterparts, although some com-
mentary is required in conjunction with maps 14-16. The first of these,
Map 14, quite clearly supports the contention that *baile*-names occur
wherever Gaelic has been, or still is, spoken in Scotland. In fact, there
is no other Gaelic place-name element which might serve to the same
extent and with similar accuracy as a toponymic marker for the area
of permanent settlement of Gaelic speakers in this country. A map
depicting the geographical distribution of *baile* is a map of Gaelic-

14   Gaelic names containing *baile*

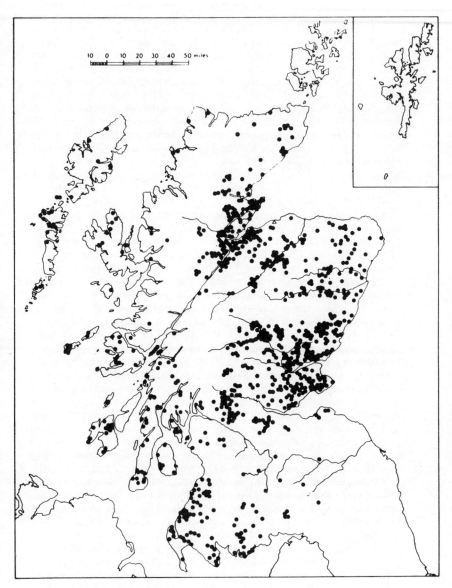

• Name containing *baile*

speaking settlement. Quite rightly, therefore, the only parts, in addition
to the Borders, in which it is not found are Orkney and Shetland and,
on the mainland, the eastern half of Caithness — areas which used to be
thoroughly Scandinavian, as a comparison with the maps showing the
distribution of Norse *setr/sætr* and *bolstaðr* demonstrates (Maps 6 and
7; see also p. 90). Especially in Caithness the contrast between the
distribution of *baile* and *achadh*, on the one hand, and of *setr/sætr*
and *bolstaðr*, on the other, indicates a line of demarcation, if not
confrontation, between Gaelic-speaking and Norse-speaking, between
Celtic and Scandinavian settlers. If this historical line of demarcation
has any chronological significance, it must be evidence for ascribing
the earliest Gaelic settlement in this northernmost part of Scotland
and neighbouring areas to the ninth century, even if not all the *baile*-
names, or any of them, were created at this early date. This would
allow about four centuries for the expansion of Gaelic from the small
beginnings in Dalriadic Argyll to almost total coverage of the Scottish
north, and would find support in the military, political, and dynastic
history of the time, since Kenneth MacAlpin defeated the last king
of the Picts in 840, a victory which also accounts for the presence of
Gaelic place-names in the Scottish north-east, i.e. in former Pictish
territory, from the ninth century onwards.

That the density of *baile*-names is not the same everywhere north
of the Forth and Clyde is due to the nature of the terrain which in
some areas would not permit the kind of permanent settlement to
which Gaels would give names beginning with *baile*, while in others
attracting settlers to good alluvial land in major river-valleys, or the like.
That this is not the whole story and that *baile*-names, or settlements
bearing such names, were not only created in response to the natural
habitat, is, however, attested by the distribution of *baile* which quite
clearly flourished in a linguistic environment in which Gaelic was
preceded by Pictish and succeeded by Lowland Scots, but led a less
vigorous existence in the Scottish west and north-west, Scottish
colonial territory of the Norsemen. It has been calculated that out of
about 125 names of villages and isolated crofts in the Isle of Lewis, for
instance, 99 are 'decidedly Norse, some few are of doubtful origin,
and the rest are post-Norse', the conclusion being that 'a logical
consequence of this would be to infer that the areas in question were
completely Norse, linguistically speaking, during a considerable period
(probably in the eleventh century), or very nearly so, and that Gaelic
was introduced or reintroduced, afterwards'. What is true of Lewis may
also, to some degree be said of other islands and mainland areas in which
Norsemen settled although the Gaelic dialects of Lewis are claimed to
be 'unique in that they are the result of the adoption of the Gaelic
language by a previously Norse-speaking population'. It is difficult to
imagine any other linguistic reason, apart from Scandinavian influence,
for the comparative dearth of *baile*-names in areas which were for
several centuries under Norse domination. The post-Norse nature of
some *Bal*-names is also proved by the incorporation of Norse elements
as specifics after the Gaelic generic, as in *Baile an Lōin* (several) ROS

'settlement of the damp meadow' (*lōn* is a Gaelic borrowing from
Norse *lōn* 'quiet water'), Balmainish (Skye) 'Magnus' settlement', or
Ballantrushal, Gaelic *Baile an Truiseil* (Lewis) 'settlement of the
Trusel(-stone), possibly from Old Norse *þurs* 'goblin, ogre'. In most
instances, however, the whole name is thoroughly Gaelic, and there is
no way of knowing in what chronological relationship to the Norse
period these names would stand.

In terms of 'zones', Zone I in the Scottish south-west is matched by
a similar extensive zone in the north-east, stretching from Fife to
Easter Ross and reaching into central Scotland along all the important
waterways. In this context, the southern Zone III is now clearly seen
as the southern-most appendix of this dense north-eastern distribution,
proclaiming the Forth, but not the Clyde, to be less of a dividing line
than might have been expected. Zone II, comprising all areas in which
baile-names do occur but not at all densely, extends strictly to the west
of Zone I right to the western seaboard and the Hebrides, whereas
Zone III (paralleling the southern Zone IV) includes those areas in which
no names beginning with *baile* are to be found, i.e. the Northern Isles
and neighbouring Caithness. Although no conclusion with regard to
absolute dating can be reached, in many parts of Zone II less density
may also imply a chronologically later stratum, but such an implication
would be difficult to support in areas like, let us say, Kintyre or
eastern Sutherland and western Caithness. On the whole, the greater
density of names in Zone I probably means consolidation of permanent
settlement over a longer and sustained period of time, and probably
also the building of permanent homesteads and farms on less productive
soil. This period, during which *baile*-names were created, must have
included a protracted span of bilingualism, as the time in which Gaelic
was the only language in the counties between the Firth of Forth and
the Moray Firth was comparatively short, perhaps from the tenth to
the twelfth century. It is difficult to conceive of the several hundred
baile-names as having been coined during this monoglot period. Minor
names excepted, even 700 or 800 years of English have not produced
many more equivalent names.

As it might be of special interest to know something about the
semantic structure of place-names in an area in which three languages
followed each other in fairly rapid sequence (Pictish-Gaelic-English),
here are some *baile*-names from the Dundee region, roughly the
drainage basins of the Tay, the Esk rivers, and Bervie Water: Balchalum
PER is 'Calum's stead', Baldinnie FIF is the 'stead near the height'
(Old Irish *dind*), Baldornoch PER is 'pebbly stead' (Gaelic *dornach*),
Baldragon ANG is probably 'the dragon's stead' (Gaelic *dreagan*),
'dragon' being a complimentary word for a 'hero'. Balfour ANG contains
the same element Gaelic *pór* 'pasture' (Welsh *pawr*) as Pitfour below;
Balgay PER is Gaelic *Baile (na) Gaoithe* 'stead of the marsh' (or wind?),
Balgonie PER is perhaps 'dogs' stead' (from Gaelic *con*), Balgour PER.
'goats' stead' (Gaelic *gobhar*), and Balgowan PER 'smith's stead' (Gaelic
gobhainn). The three Balgrays in Perthshire may have had horse-studs
(Gaelic *greagh*), Balhagarty KCD must be the 'priest's stead' (Gaelic

15 Gaelic names containing *achadh*

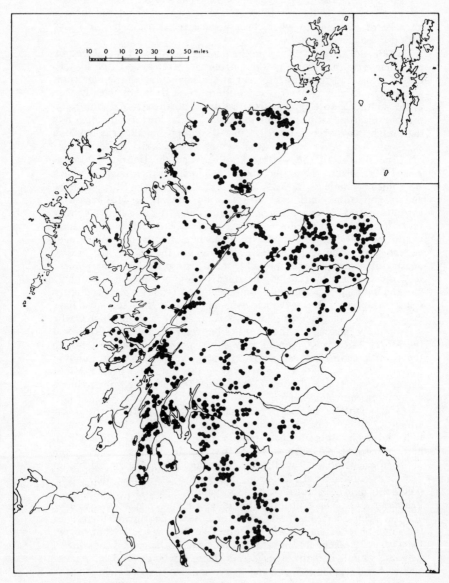

• Name containing *achadh*

sagart), and the personal name *Cathalan* in Balkaithley FIF is also evident in Pitkeathly PER. Ballindean FIF and PER are best interpreted as *Balie an Deadhain* 'the dean's stead', Ballintuim PER is *Baile an Tuim* 'stead of the knoll', the personal names in Balmakewan KCD and Balmalcolm PER are obvious, and Balmuckety ANG has a second element better known from Auchtermuchty FIF: *muccatu* 'piggishness'; pigs were raised here. Balnabriech ANG is the 'bank-stead' (Gaelic *Baile na Bruaich*), Balnacree PER the *'boundary-stead'* (Gaelic *crioch*), Balnaguard PER the 'craftsmen's stead' (Gaelic *Baile na gCeard*), and Balnamoan PER and Balnamoon ANG contain anglicised forms of the Gaelic word for 'peat' (*moine*). Even from this limited selection a picture of intensive agricultural and pastoral activities emerges, with personal ownership of farms, not at all unlike the impression one gets from the equivalent Pictish evidence. *Baile*-names from other parts of Scotland confirm this picture.

The map devoted to the distribution of place-names containing Gaelic *achadh* 'field' (Map 15) both agrees with and differs from the *baile*-map, in so far as it shows *achadh*-names as occurring in practically all areas in which *baile*-names are found, but also somewhat beyond them. The different emphasis in the distribution pattern is best summarised by saying that Zone II contains many more names beginning with *achadh* than names beginning with *baile*. Undoubtedly, *achadh* with its primary reference to fields rather than buildings did become an element in settlement-names much later than *baile*, originally mainly through the transference of field-names to settlements. As a rule of thumb, it might therefore be claimed that the majority of *achadh*-names is relatively later than the majority of *baile*-names. In fact, one wonders how many *achadh*-names were coined for, or transferred to, settlements before the ninth or tenth centuries; probably very few, in spite of the fact that there are quite a number of them in the area of the original Scottish *Dail Riata*; these could, after all, easily be later. Similarly, the ascription of names containing *achadh* to settlements on less desirable ground is explained in this way. The map has plenty of examples for this phenomonen. In this respect, *achadh*-names in the north parallel those in the south, and again the terms 'primary' and 'secondary' may be usefully employed in describing the distinction between *baile* and *achadh* in terms of settlement-names. It should also be noted that, whereas *baile*-names are thin on the ground in the Outer Hebrides, *achadh*-names, with only one exception, do not occur there at all, having seemingly never replaced the equivalent Norse term which continues to live as Gaelic *gearraidh* in both toponymic and appellative usage. Here the general dictum with regard to Zone II is reversed, not surprisingly perhaps in view of the linguistic situation in Lewis and other Hebridean islands between the ninth and thirteenth centuries, and the nature and relative lateness of settlement-names beginning with *achadh*. The absence of such names makes the Western Isles almost look like the Northern Isles, in terms of intensive Scandinavianisation.

The most common anglicised form of *achadh* is *Auch-*, as is attested

16   Gaelic names containing *cill*

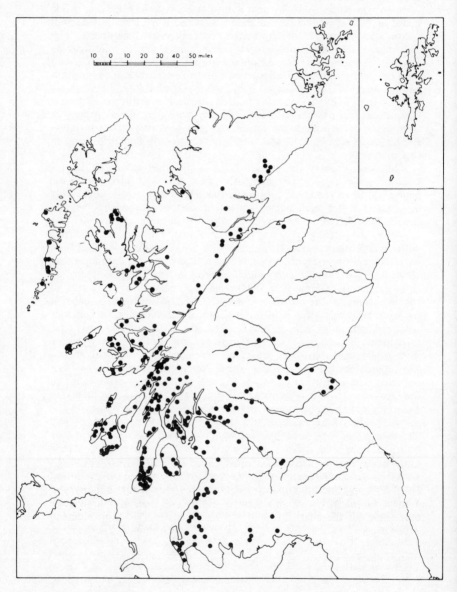

•   Name containing *cill*

by such Aberdeenshire names as Auchlee < Gaelic *Achadh liath* 'grey field', Auchmore < Gaelic *Achadh mór*, 'big field', or Auchnabo from Gaelic *Achadh nam bo* 'field of the cows'. In counties like Ross-shire, closer to live Gaelic, *Ach-* is the more usual anglicised spelling, as in Achmore < Gaelic *Achadh mór* 'big field', Achnahannet < Gaelic *Achadh na h-annait* 'field of the patron saint's church', or Achnegie < Gaelic *Achadh an fhiodhaidh* 'field of the place of wood'. *Auchen-* and *Auchin-* also occur, again mostly in counties like Aberdeenshire, but, in contrast to southern Scotland (see p.125), it appears to represent a genuine combination of *achadh* and some genitival form of the Gaelic definite article and not a morphological element perceived as a simple, single word. Examples would be Auchentend < Gaelic *Achadh an teine* 'field of the fire', Auchinbo < Gaelic *Achadh na bo* 'cow field', or Auchintoul < Gaelic *Achadh an t-sabhail* 'field of the barn' (all in Aberdeenshire). The process of grammatical de-gaelicisation had, it seems, not yet gone as far as in the south, when the nineteenth-century map-makers petrified the name spellings we use today. The only name listed in Alexander's *Place-names of Aberdeenshire*, likely to show some confusion, *Auchendarg*, may well be a diminutive *Achan dearg* 'little red field'.

As in the southern Scottish evidence, the geographical distribution of our third element, *Kil-* < Gaelic *cill* 'church, churchyard' in the north is more restricted than that of the other two generics (see Map 16). *Kil*-names do by no means occur in all areas north of the Forth-Clyde line in which Gaelic still is, or at one time was, spoken. The north-east, from the Tay north-wards and north-westwards to Inverness, is practically as free from these names as the Border Counties and the Lothians, and most parts of Sutherland and Caithness are also empty. In the north and the north-east, therefore, the signs are that, after two or three centuries of linguistic and cultural movement, *Kil*-names had ceased to be created when Gaelic speakers moved into Pictish territory proper (see Map 17 below) on any appreciable scale, and before Gaels and Norsemen stood facing each other in Caithness. Since both these situations came about in the course of the ninth century, *Kil*-names in the northern half of Scotland, like their counterparts in the south, are in general not likely to be much younger than 800. Whether such names stopped being productive for linguistic reasons or because of changes in ecclesiastical policy, organisation or architecture is difficult to establish,, and much detailed research is still needed as to the causes involved. For the time being, one has to be content with the knowledge that any one of these factors, or a combination of more than one, may have been responsible for the death of Gaelic *cill* as a creative place-name element before the end of the first four centuries of Gaelic-speaking settlement in Scotland. After *sliabh* (and *carraig*), *cill* is the second earliest Gaelic place-name generic isolated so far; it is, of course, the old dative-locative of Gaelic *ceall*, from Latin *cella* 'cell, church'.

From a chronological point of view, the saints' names involved as specifics also pass the hagiological acid test, because, as in the south, all identifiable and datable saints, commemorated by *Kil*-names, belong to the sixth, seventh, and eighth century, especially the first two. Adamnan, the ninth abbot of Iona, for example, is known to have died in 704. His name occurs in Killeonan near Campbeltown (but also, for instance, in Rowardennan on Loch Lomond). Angus, the 'saint' of Killanaish in Knapdale, died in 535; Barre of Kilbarr in Barra about 610; Cainnech of Kilchenich in Tiree, and Kilchenzie in Kintyre, Coll and South Uist in 600; Ciaran of Kilchieran in Islay in 549; Mo-Luag of Kilmaluag in Lismore and elsewhere in 592; Kentigerna of Kilchintorn on Loch Duich in 734; Cummein of *Cill Chuimein*, the Gaelic name for Fort Augustus, in 669: St Columba of the numerous *Cill Chaluim Chille* lived from about 521-597, having come to Scotland in 563; Maol Rubha's lifespan is 640-722, and he crossed to Scotland in 671; the most famous Brigid (of Kildare) can be dated about 452-525; etc.

If, as in the case of Kilbrandon (Lorn, Mull and Islay), there are 15 known 'saints' of the name *Brenainn*, or if, in connection with that widespread name Kilbride, one finds 15 female 'saints' called Brigid, or if there are 16 *Faolans* to explain *Cill Fhaolain* (Kilillan in Kintail, Kilellan in Kintyre and in Cowal), 30 *Cronans* to give us a clue to *Cil mo-Chronaig* (Kilmaronag on Loch Etive), and even 218 *Colmans* to choose from to explain Kilchalman in North Uist and Kilmachalmaig in Sutherland and Bute, then it becomes clear that these church names are hardly ever dedications in the modern sense of the word, but rather commemorations of missionaries, abbots and other active churchmen of their time. But even when allowing for later followers bearing the names of saints, there is every indication that dedications to, or rather commemorations of, them were probably made before 800, in conjunction with the element *cill*. There is, of course, no exact way of knowing when names like Kilchrist ARG, Kilmartin ARG and INV, Kilmichael ARG and BTE, Kiltearn ROS, or Kilphedder INV, Kilpheder INV, Kilphedir SUT, commemorating Christ, St Martin of Tours, St Michael, Our Lord, and St Peter, respectively, ceased to be given, but even if such commemorations are technically possible in and after the ninth century, they must be, if linked with Gaelic *cill*, just as restricted as that element. In a situation, in which admittedly no definite proof is possible, *Kil*-names, on the whole, are nevertheless surely the earliest of the three types discussed. It is not unlikely that, whenever they occur in the Hebrides, they may well be exciting fossils from pre-Norse Gaeldom in the Western Isles.

As the Gaelic stratum is quantitatively and with regard to toponymic 'flavour' the most typically Scottish ingredient of our place-nomenclature, or is at least perceived as such, a further excursion into the geographical scatter of other names belonging to this stratum would appear to be in order, particularly since this would also be an excursion away from settlement names. The services rendered by a close examination of the toponymic use of Gaelic *sliabh* in Scotland have been such that it might well be profitable to scrutinise some other generics in Gaelic mountain-names in the same fashion. The number of Gaelic words used as basic elements in hill- and mountain-names is, of course, considerable and a basic list contains generic elements such as *barr, beinn, carn, cioch, cnoc, creag, druim, maol, meall, monadh, ord, sgorr (sgurr), sliabh, stack, stob, stuc, tom, torr*, and *tulach*. Most of the generics, like practically all Gaelic elements, are shown on the modern maps of Scotland in at least two forms, i.e. their original Gaelic spelling and their anglicised form. This gives us pairs such as *barr* and *bar, beinn* and *ben, cnoc* and *knock, druim* and *drum* (or *drim*), *torr* and *tor*, and *tulach* and *tully*. Whatever reasons produced the Gaelic map-spellings on the one hand and the anglicised forms on the other, these were apparently similar for all pairs, and it is therefore sufficient to parade these differences and their reasons for two somewhat divergent examples only, i.e. the elements *cnoc* and *tulach*. Unfortunately it is not possible in this context to explore the distribution of Gaelic hill-names beyond the examination of this particular problem but it is certainly very instructive with regard to the study of strata within a stratum, to which we referred earlier (p. 39).

Gaelic *cnoc* is a geographical term meaning 'hill, knoll, hillock, eminence'. While very prolific in the formation of Scottish hill-names it is an element which is also very common in Ireland. According to the Scottish National Dictionary, the Anglo-Scottish form *knock* (or *nock*) is now obsolete as an appellative except in poetry. A quotation for 1897 reads 'the nearest knock to her place of dwelling'. The distributional patterns for *cnoc* and *knock* (736 and 343 examples, respectively) are in many ways typical of all oppositions involving Gaelic and anglicised forms, although the scarcity of either form in Central Scotland and their relative unproductivity in the Outer Hebrides somewhat distort the picture. What does become obvious however, is the fact that *cnoc* and *knock*, by and large, represent the areas in which Gaelic was still spoken when the Ordnance Surveyors compiled their basic evidence about a hundred years ago, and those in which it had died out. Areas of overlap on the Gaelic-English fringe may be judged to imply the survival of Gaelic in small pockets of individual speakers amongst a majority of English-speakers. Where *knock* occurs in the Highlands and Islands, the use of estate maps and similar cartographic aids by the surveyors may be at least partly responsible for its presence. It must also be remembered that in a number of cases names have been re-gaelicised since the maps were first made, but without constant reference to the first editions or the original name-books it would be difficult to ascertain just how many names have received this treatment. It would be fair to state, however, that subsequent anglicisation has to all intents and purposes never taken place. The two distributions together roughly cover the area in which Scottish Gaelic was spoken when it was the language of most of Scotland, and quite a number of the *knock*-names in the north-east and at least some in the south-west must go back to medieval times, because they must have been coined when Gaelic was either the only or the majority language in these regions. The lack of examples in the upper regions of Strathclyde is noteworthy.

Cnoc/Knock apparently never applied to very high eminences and it would be surprising if any really old names survived. Certainly the semantic picture does not point to any particular antiquity of any of the names. Not only do we find a recent situation with regard to descriptive adjectives, but the frequent naming from features of the surrounding countryside is an even surer sign of relative modernity, resulting in fairly complex grammatical and morphological structures such as *Cnoc a'Choire Bhig*, *Cnoc Allt a'Chait*, *Cnoc Alltan Iain Duinn*, *Cnoc an Tigh Odheir*, *Cnoc na Buaile Salaich*, *Cnoc na Glaic Tarsuinn*, *Cnoc Preas a'Mhadaidh*, *Cnoc Tigh Mhic Fhionnlaidh*, and others. The Mull name *Knockantivore* would also belong here.

Analysing more closely this latter type of anglicised name, it is undoubtedly true that it must ultimately derive from a Gaelic hill-name even if it has only survived as a settlement-name. Only in two cases does it appear possible, however, as far as the one-inch map is concerned, to trace the original name. One instance is the Islay settlement-name *Knockdon* which is situated beside the hill called *Cnoc Donn Mór*, and the other is *Knockdamph* ROS which is quite close to the hill-name *Cnoc Damh*. In the case of *Knockan* (Assynt), a burn called *Allt a'Chnocain* flows past it and gives us an indirect indication of the Gaelic hill-name. Similarly the names *Knock*, *Knock Castle*, and *Knock Bay* in Skye can safely be said to refer to the nearby *Cnoc a'Chaise Mór*. The majority of other instances in which *knock* instead of *cnoc* appears on the maps of present-day Gaelic-speaking areas applies to names of settlements of various sizes like *Knock* (Lewis and Mull), *Knockaird* (Lewis), *Knockanbearach* (Islay), *Knockanrock* (Wester Ross), *Knockantivore* (Mull), *Knockantuim* (North Uist), *Knockhanty* (Kintyre), *Knockintorran* (North Uist), *Knocklearoch* (Islay), *Knockline* (North Uist), *Knocknafenaig* (Mull), *Knocknaha* (Kintyre), *Knockriach* (Kintyre), *Knockrome* (Jura), *Knockroy* (Mull), and *Knockvologan* (Mull). *Knockanteagal* (South Uist) seems to be the only name in this category which has been re-gaelicised recently to *Cnoc an t-seagail*. *Knockangle Point* is a coastal feature of Islay, but wherever the anglicised form appears in a hill-name, the reason is apparently that the second element is of non-Gaelic (Norse) origin as in *Knock Geimisgarave* (Harris), *Knock Gune* (Berneray, Harris), *Knock Mugary* (North Uist), *Knock Noddimull*(Sandray, Barra), *Knock Rolum* (South Uist), and *Knock Smerclett* (North Uist), and *Knock Ullinish* (Skye). A map totally based on local Gaelic oral tradition would obviously look quite different and eliminate practically all these examples.

That *knock* was regarded as at least part of the toponymic terminology of the non-Gaelic Lowlander is shown by such names as *Big Knock* PEB, *East* and *West Knock* ANG, *Easter Knock* ABD, *Low Knock* WIG, *Mill Knock* KCB, as well as the many places called *Knock* or *The Knock*. As some words are peculiarly confined to onomastic usage, these examples do not necessarily imply that *knock* was also used as a general appellative. As a curiosity it might be added that Arran English has produced the noun *cronk* from Gaelic *cnoc*, by adopting both the widespread Gaelic pronunciation of *cn-* as *cr-* and the subsequent strong nasalisation of the vowel.

Scottish Gaelic *tulach* 'hillock, knoll, mount, small green hill, low smooth hill or ridge' is a derivative of Old Irish *tul* 'protuberance, projecting part, swelling' which also has the variant forms *taul*, *tel*, and *til*. Correspondingly, *taulach*, *telach*, *tilach* occur in Old Irish besides *tulach*, but in addition there are the variant forms *talach*, *tailach*, and *tolach*. In fact, the vowel of the first syllable is so unstable that the whole range of Old Irish vocalic monophthongs and two *a*- dipthongs are possible. Whereas Old Irish apparently still reflects an earlier Indo-European situation, later stages of the language adopted a more economical simplification with *tulach* seemingly running out the winner; early forms of the name *Kirkintilloch*, for instance, still show a tremendous variety of vowels in the stressed syllable, as in *Caerpentaloch* tenth century, *Kirkentulach* c. 1200, *Kirkintolauche* 1288, *Kerkintallach* 1306-29, *Kirkintullach* 1399.

At first glance it looks as if the pair *tulach - tilach* sufficiently explains the toponymic usage of our term in Scotland and that the anglicised reflexes *Tully-* and *Tilly-* (with their minor variants) have developed significant geographical distributions from what was once a purely phonological dichotomy. With *i*-spellings forming a very definite distribution area within the distribution of the *u*-spellings; in fact *u*-spellings are rather rare where *i*-spellings are plentiful, as in the region between Dee and Don in Buchan. The distribution of *Tilly-* is quite clearly more much limited than that of *Tully-* and is practically confined to what one might call the Scottish north-east proper, i.e. the area between Tay and Spey. Outliers do occur but only in very small numbers. Historically the situation is a little more complex.

If we look at a number of Aberdeenshire place-names beginning with *Tilly-*, for instance, because these are particularly well documented, we find that the majority of these have earlier *u*-spellings, such as *Twlery* 1544 and *Tullyrie* 1610 for Tillery, *Tulyhafe* 1390 and *Tulyaif* 1511 for Tillieve, *Tulygonyis* 1461 and *Tulygownes* 1505 for Tilligonie, *tuligreg* 1157 and *Tuligirg* 1436 for Tilligreig, *Tulielte* 1234 and *Tulenahilt* 1474 for Tillyhilt, *Tholaukery* c. 1250 and *Tullecherie* 1574 for Tillykerrie, *Tullochourie* 1628 and *Tulliequhorrie* 1638 for Tilly-gourie, and many others. On the other hand, 25 names (including Tilliepestle, Tilligreig, Tillybo, Tillybrex) do not show any *i*-spellings until the last decade of the seventeenth or well into the eighteenth century, the sources being in almost all cases either the Parish Registers or the Poll Book of Aberdeenshire, sources which are presumably close to the local pronunciation. For one name, Tillybirloch, the Poll Book lists both *Tillibrickloch* and *Tullibrockloch* in 1696. That *i*-spellings expressing an *i*-pronunciation (or its allophonic realis-ation) were possible earlier is shown by such forms as *Tillicarne* and *Tillicartin* 1592 for Tillycairn in the Arbroath Liber, *Tillikero* 1597 for Tillykerrie, *Tillioch* 1557 for Tillioch, *Tilliquhroskie* 1597 for Tilly-fruskie, and *Tillentermend* 1534 for Tillytarmont, all in the Register of the Great Seal. The earliest example is *Telanchsyne* 1357 for Tillyching, quoted in the second volume of the *Antiquities of Aberdeen and Banff*. The impression one derives from this documentation is that the *Tilly-*

forms represent a late dialectal change in pronunciation, perhaps to be, dated from the sixteenth century onwards, or a little earlier, but first clearly expressed in the Parish Registers and the Poll Book, compilations less close to, or completely independent of, scribal traditions. This is supported by the fact that only two names of the *Tully*-variety — admittedly much rarer in Aberdeenshire than *Tilly*-names — have isolated *i*-spellings: *Tullynessle* in 1549 (*Tillenessil*) and *Tullikera* in 1455 (*Tillykerak*). *Tulloch*-names which mainly occur in the west of the county never show any *i*-forms. It is therefore clear that, at least as far as Aberdeenshire is concerned the *Tully*–*Tilly* opposition is not based on a Gaelic *tulach-tilach* dichotomy but on a phonological phenomenon within the post-Gaelic dialect of the region. The resulting distribution patterns may therefore be treated as the visual representation of this dialectal development. In their total distribution in Scotland *tulach*-names are confined to central and north-east Scotland, with a few, outliers in Argyll and a lonely Tulloch Hill in Ayrshire. Did *tulach* flourish particularly well on Pictish soil?

With regard to both *cnoc* and *tulach* the following observations apply: In those cases in which Gaelic and anglicised forms exist, these are largely complementary in a geographical sense and presumably reflect fairly accurately the position of Gaelic when the maps were made. If anglicised forms occur in present-day Gaelic-speaking areas, they usually apply to settlement-names derived from the names of nearby hills. In some instances the Gaelic hill-name and the anglicised settlement-name exist side by side on the map; in Gaelic oral tradition this situation is, of course, quite different and this contrast does not exist. In most cases the hill-name does not seem to have survived. Whenever the anglicised form occurs in a hill-name in a Gaelic-speaking region, the specific element of the name is normally of non-Gaelic origin.

A wealth of evidence establishes a Gaelic toponymic stratum in Scotland as having existed from the fifth century to the present day. This stratum is anything but homogeneous, in whatever way one looks at it. The names which are comprised within this layer differ in geographical distribution, historical depth, as well as in the length and time of their productivity. Even the most widespread of them contradict the common assertion that there once was a time when Gaelic was spoken throughout Scotland. In their relationship to other languages, Gaelic place-names were coined before, during, and after the period of Scandinavian domination in certain parts of the country, succeeded or ousted Pictish names in others, and have been progressively giving way to English names ever since the eleventh or twelfth centuries. When Gaelic names first began to be coined in Scotland in the fifth century, other Celtic names already existed in this country, some of them Pictish, some of them Cumbric. The next chapter will be concerned with names belonging to these two strata.

8
P-Celtic Names: Pictish
and Cumbric

One of the two major publications dealing, in recent years, with the people we commonly call the Picts, is very appropriately entitled *The Problem of the Picts*, for if there is any linguistic stratum in Scottish history and prehistory with a greater capacity for raising problematic questions and creating controversy, it has still to be found, despite many of the uncertainties and differences of opinion surrounding the 'Old European' nomenclature (see Chapter IX). Obviously, the problematic nature of so many aspects of Pictish life is at least partly due to the Picts' chronological position in the history of Scotland but also to the paucity of records. Nevertheless, we are not without valuable information. If we view them as archaeological people, for instance, their chief monuments, the sculptured stones, provide us with not inconsiderable insight into their symbolism and ornamentation, and certain facets of their way of life; or, as Isabel Henderson has put it, 'the monumental art of the Picts . . . . is, on any terms, of considerable skill and high aesthetic value.' The Pictish symbol stones afford us more than a glimpse of a culture anything but primitive, and what we know of Pictish political affairs and royal succession certainly supports this impression. From the scanty evidence of the, mostly non-native, sources of Pictish history, we can place them roughly between the third and the ninth centuries; a twelfth-century manuscript tract, *de situ Albaniae*, expressly informs us that Pictland, before it was united with the land of the 'Scots', when Kenneth MacAlpin defeated the last king of the Picts in AD 840, comprised seven provinces which are, on the whole, still recognisable today: *Enegus cum Moerne* (Angus with the Mearns), *Adtheodle et Goverin* (Atholl and Gowrie), *Stradeern cum Menetid* (Strathearn with Menteith), *Fif cum Fothreve* (Fife with 'Kinross'), *Marr cum Buchen* (Mar with Buchan), *Muref et Ros* (Moray and Ross), and *Cathanesia* (Caithness). In general, the picture which emerges portrays a highly-developed culture and a well-organised political and dynastic life.

It is when we attempt to analyse the language which sustained such a culture that our troubles really begin, for if our records are patchy for the Picts in other respects, they are decidedly skimpy with regard to linguistic matters. To begin with, not a single sentence written in the

Pictish language survives, and our main sources for that language are inscriptions, personal names, mostly of kings or other leaders, and place-names. As it turns out, the inscriptions, although generally decipherable and transcribable letter by letter, are in many instances unintelligible to us, and speculation and guesses as to their significance have been rampant, alongside more responsible attempts at their interpretation. Both their geographical distribution and their linguistic opacity seem to indicate, in the view of the best scholars of Pictish affairs, like Professor Kenneth Jackson, the existence of two Pictish languages, one Celtic and the other not. At present, it is impossible to say what the second of these two languages, non-Celtic Pictish, was like and what its linguistic affinities were, and there is certainly no place-name evidence which can be isolated as yet, concerning the identification of this kind of 'Pictish'. Indeed, from a toponymic point of view, it is the absence of place-names belonging to the Celtic variety of 'Pictish' from certain areas which must be termed Pictish on non-linguistic grounds. This absence supports the theory of two completely different linguistic Picts. Or to put it somewhat differently: The archaeological evidence − principally the sculptured stones − for the Picts is not totally matched by the toponymic evidence, in so far as the latter occurs in territory more limited than that indicated by the distribution of finds ascribable, and ascribed, to Pictish material culture, and by early writers. Pictland at one time was larger than the area outlined by the scatter of so-called Pictish place-names.

Before a detailed analysis of these place-names, a brief discussion concerning the name *Pict* itself seems to be in order, since it has been subject to just as much controversy. There is, first of all, no direct evidence that the Picts called themselves by that name (just as there is no reason to believe that the Celts ever referred to themselves by that term); secondly, the earliest classical writers, who otherwise tend to have the best and most reliable information about Scotland in Roman times − Tacitus, Ptolemy, and Cassius, for instance − do not use the term *Picti* (in its Latinised form) but prefer the name *Caledonii*; thirdly, the pseudo-learned etymology which derives the name of the Picts from their supposed habit of tattooing or painting themselves is not acceptable from a linguistic point of view. The classical writer Claudian (about AD 370-410) alone attempts an etymological explanation of the word. In referring to the 'well-named Pict' he is clearly associating the name with Latin *pingo*, 'to paint', 'colour', 'inscribe', while also making no real distinction between the Britons and the Picts, in this respect. Whether the Picts did tattoo or paint themselves is another question which has never been answered in a satisfactory manner, but fortunately it does not have to concern us here, since a Roman learned etymology or soldiers' nickname, even if it did exist, is not likely to have given rise to the name for a whole people.

Although we do not know what the Picts called themselves, there is nevertheless every likelihood that the name by which they were known by their neighbours from about the fourth century onwards, first by the Romans, then by the Norsemen and Anglo-Saxons, did originate in some native name which, at least by that time, no longer had any semantic significance. The Roman *Picti* corresponds closely to the Old Norse *Péttar* or *Péttir* (the *Historia Norvegicae* calls them *Peti*) and to the Old English *Pehtas, Pihtas, Pyhtas, Peohtas,* and *Piohtas* of the Anglo-Saxon Chronicle (as well as to the first elements of the personal names *Peohthelm, Peohtred, Peohtweald, Peohtwine, Peohtwulf,* etc.), and there is little doubt that these linguistic variants do not derive from each other but from a common source — probably a native name. The *-tt-* of the Old Norse form *Péttar* or *Péttir,* as well as of the *Péttlandsfjorðr* 'Pentland Firth' of the sagas (Latinised as *Petlandicum mare*), demonstrates very nicely that the Norsemen must have known of the Picts before their first raids on the Northern and Western Isles in the last decade of the eighth century, since *-ht-* developed into *-tt-* around AD 700. As is to be expected, the Anglo-Saxon forms retain, as in native English words, the consonant cluster *-ht-,* because the fricative *-h-* does, in this combination, not disappear until a much later date (in the fourteenth century at the earliest).

The conclusion we must come to is that either *Pict-* had become something like **Piht-* or **Peht-* by the time the Norsemen and Anglo-Saxons learned their name, or that the original Pictish form was replaced in Early English, similar to the rendering of Latin *-ct-* as *-ht-* in words borrowed into English between AD 450 and 650, as in OE *elehtre* 'lupin' (Latin *electrum*), OE *truht* 'trout' (Latin *trūcta*), or OE *traht* 'passage' (Latin *tractus*). In this connection, it is of interest that the first element of the name of *Pecthelm,* Bishop of Whithorn, who died in 735, is recorded as *Pect-, Peht-,* and *Pecht-.* The modern English form is, of course, derived from, or at least influenced by, the Latinised term *Pictus.* As far as the people so designated are concerned, it is prudent to limit the name specifically to the 'historical 'Picts' (about AD 200-800), rather than to apply it generally to all the peoples who lived in northern Scotland at the time. This is accordingly the way in which the name *Pict(s)* and the adjective *Pictish* are used in this book.

The toponymic evidence for these 'historical Picts' depends on a few generics of different quality and impact; amongst these the element which is now the first part of over 300 names beginning with *Pit-* is undoubtedly the most important. It is practically the only place-name element which can be said to be exclusively limited to the Picts, and its distribution does therefore have considerable significance with regard to an attempt at depicting the settlement area of the Pictish people, i.e. of the speakers of Celtic Pictish.

Also it cannot be denied that, over the decades, the discussion of this element has been stormy, to say the least, ranging from the strongly held opinion that it is of Gaelic origin and consequently signifies the presence of Gaelic-speakers in Scotland much earlier than the Dalriadic settlements from Ireland in the fifth and sixth centuries AD, to the equally strongly held view that it is of entirely unknown origin. More dispassionate analysis has, however, led to the conviction, now widely held by Celtic scholars, that the underlying generic is indeed Pictish. It is on record as an appellative in the twelfth-century *Book of Deer* in its accusative singular form *pet* or *pett*, and as the genitive singular *pette*, and in such references as *Pett in Mulenn, Pett Malduib, Pett Mec-Garnait*, and *Pett Mec-Gobroig*. In the earliest recorded forms of practically all *Pit*-names the generic also appears as *Pet-*, as, for example, in Pitbladdo FIF (*Petblatho* 1481), Pitsligo ABD (*Petslegach* 1426), Pittendreich MLO (*Petendreia c.* 1130), Pittenclerock PER (*Pettincleroch* 1489). *Pett* is cognate with Welsh *peth*, Cornish *peth* 'thing', and Breton *pez* 'piece'; its Gaelic equivalent is *cuid* 'portion'. Extremely important in the unravelling of its origins and history is a Low Latin word *petia* 'piece (of land)' which through French *pièce* has given us the Modern English word *piece*. It is now generally assumed that *petia* is a Latinised version of a Gaulish word which, since the Welsh and Cornish cognates do not seem to have served as generics in the creation of place-names, has suggested to a number of scholars close linguistic connections between Pictish and Gaulish, i.e. Continental Celtic. In form, *pett* could, of course, be generally British, which for Scotland would mean 'Cumbric', but the geographical distribution of the names involved, rules this out. The claim of a close link between Pictish and the Continent is bolstered by the fact that· the modern French place-names Poitou and Poitiers derive from recorded oblique cases of the tribal name *Pictavi*, later *Pictones*. While this evidence does not necessarily prove that the historical Picts of Scotland did in some way emigrate from the area of the French *Pictones* or *Pictavi*, the similarity of the tribal names cannot be ignored, especially when seen in conjunction with the ties created by Pictish *pett* and Gaulish **petia*. One of the big problems in this respect is, of course, the lack of any evidence whatsoever as to the route the Picts may have taken from Gaul to the Scottish north-east, and the limited material available as a basis for forging such a link should therefore not be strained beyond the limits of credulity. It is, on the other hand, very suggestive and satisfying to find that Gaulish **petia*, in the Latin phrase *petia terrae* and Pictish *pett* are identical in meaning: 'a piece of land'.

The toponymic material in which *pett* survives, is formed by a group of some 300 names beginning with *Pit-*. Some of the names belonging to this category are: Pitbladdo FIF 'flourshare', Pitcaple ABD 'horse-share', Pitcarmick PER 'Cormac's share', Pitcastle PER 'castle-share', Pitcorthie FIF 'pillar-stone share', Pitcox ELO 'share of the fifth part', Pitfour PER and ABD 'meadow-share', Pitkennedy ANG 'Cenneteigh's share', Pitkerro ANG 'share of the fourth part', Pitliver FIF 'share of the book, i.e., the Bible', Pitlochry PER 'stony share', Pitlour FIF 'leper's share', Pitlurg ABD 'share of the shank (-like strip of land)', Pitmain (Badenoch, INV) and Pitmedden ABD 'middle share', Pitmurchie ABD 'Murchadh's share', Pitmurthly PER 'portion of the big hill', Pitpointie ANG 'bridge-share', Pitsligo ABD 'shelly portion', Pittencrieff FIF 'share of the tree', and Pittenweem FIF 'share of the cave'.

Map 17 shows that *Pit*-names are found from the Firth of Forth northwards, through Fife, Angus, Kincardineshire, Aberdeenshire, the counties along the Moray Firth into Easter Ross and the southern tip of Easter Sutherland. Westwards, they stretch up the fertile river

17 · Pictish names containing *Pit-*

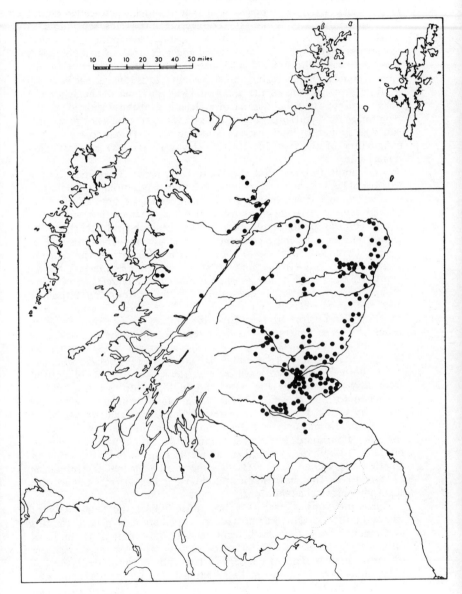

● Name containing *pit*

valleys into Perthshire, and as far as Badenoch. They are crown wit-
nesses for a determination of the area in which the Celtic Pictish-
speaking people lived, and it does not come as a surprise that the area
they cover practically coincides with that in which the so-called Pictish
Class II symbol stones, i.e. symbol-bearing cross-slabs sculptured in
relief, referred to above (p. 150), are found, demanding the logical
conclusion that the people who carved and erected these symbol stones
were the same who created place-names with *Pit-* as a first element.
Such a conclusion is certainly largely acceptable as long as it is based on
separate investigations of the archaeological and linguistic evidence and
does not argue the total identity of archaeological and linguistic people
The images and craftsmanship of the symbol stones does not reveal the
language spoken by their carvers, and *vice versa*. The almost complete
congruency of the two distributions (Maps 17 and 18) is nevertheless
remarkable.

Any simplistic view that the Scottish *Pit*-names were given by the
'historical Picts' is, however, put in question by a potential contradiction
in this evidence. Even from a brief and superficial examination of the
limited sample of names just listed the fact emerges that, while *Pit-*
(from *Pett*) is undoubtedly of *p*-Celtic (i.e. non-Gaelic) origin, the
second elements in these compound names are almost exclusively of
Gaelic derivation, like *capull* 'horse, mare', *caisteal* 'castle', *coirthe*
'pillar, stone', *coig* 'five', *gamhain* 'stirk', *ceathramh* 'quarter', *leabhar*
'book', the personal names *Cormac, Cathalan, Cenneteigh*, and many
others. Of the names quoted, only Pitbladdo, Pitfour and Pitpointie
may contain non-Gaelic Celtic words. Of these three, Pitpointie ANG.
which is *Petponti(n)* in the thirteenth century, is the only name in
which the second element can definitely be said to be of non-Gaelic
Celtic origin, as it has obviously to be compared with Welsh *pont*
'bridge'. In Pitfour PER, recorded as *Petfur* in 1357 and *Pethfoure* in
1358, both Welsh *pawr* 'pasture' and the Gaelic loan-word derived
from it, *pór*, could be the base; and in Pitbladdo FIF the modern
anglicised form is closer to Welsh *blawd* 'flour', whereas the spelling
Petblatho of 1481 indicates a corresponding Gaelic genitive *blatha*. In
both cases the meaning is not in doubt — one means 'pasture share',
the other 'flour share', in themselves interesting agricultural references —
but it is difficult to say whether the whole name is of Pictish origin or
whether the second part is Gaelic. The most plausible interpretation
appears to be that both names passed from Pictish into Gaelic with
slight phonological adaptations.

Since the sample given is a fair reflection of the total body of
names in this category, a satisfactory explanation is needed for this
phenomenon of numerous Pictish-Gaelic hybrids amongst the modern
Pit-names. Some of these Gaelic specifics may, of course, be translations
of earlier Pictish elements; indeed, a few of them undoubtedly are, but
the number is too large to make part-translation the only explanation.
It is much more likely that the Pictish word *pett* was borrowed and
applied by the incoming Gaelic population as a convenient toponymic

18   Pictish Class II symbol stones: symbol-bearing cross-slabs sculptured in relief

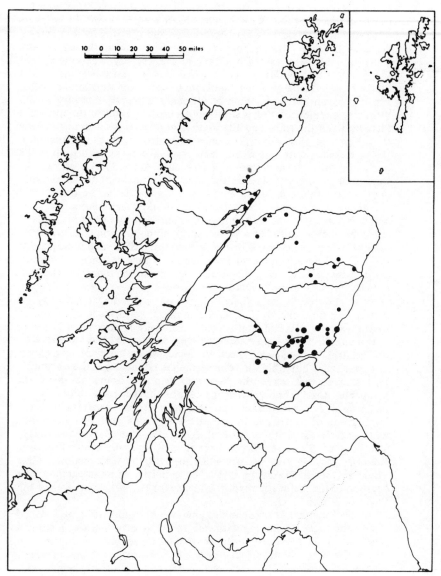

Symbol-bearing cross-slabs sculptured in relief

• Single slab

● Two or more slabs

generic while seemingly also current for a while in everyday speech, so
that Modern Gaelic *Peit Chraoibhe* 'tree share' for Pitcruive PER and
Peit nan Saor 'artisan's share' for Pettinseir MOR should not be regarded
as part-translations but as names which were created *in toto* by speakers
of Gaelic. Both processes — part-translation and use of *peit* from *pett* by
Gaels — became possible approximately from the ninth century onwards, notably after the fifth decade of that century, when the king of
the Scots, Kenneth MacAlpin, crushed Pictish resistance and united
Pictland and Gaelic-speaking Scotland to form the kingdom of Alba,
and it is anachronistic to think of Pitlochry, Pitcaple, Pittenweem and
Pitgaveny as 'Pictish', i.e. as survivors from the period of the historical
Picts between the third and the ninth centuries; it is much more likely
that these and most other *Pit*-names originated in, let us say, the ninth
to the eleventh centuries when Gaelic gradually established itself in the
north-east, first in a period of bilingualism when Pictish and Gaelic
were spoken side by side in the area. It is difficult to gauge what
implications this conclusion may have for the dating of the symbol
stones, but there may be a chronological pointer here. Since the word
pett was used and borrowed by the Gaels only in those parts of Scotland
in which they superseded a Pictish-speaking population, a distribution
map of names beginning with *Pit*- is therefore still a valid indicator for
the area of Pictish settlement in Scotland, as long as it is not taken for
granted that all surviving *Pit*-names were actually coined by the Picts
themselves; very few of them probably were.

It is also to be remembered that, just as in the archaeology of
material culture, the stuff linguistic archaeology is made of is subject
to the vagaries of accidental survival, and there is no way of knowing
how many *Pit*-names have gone completely unrecorded and are therefore
not available as evidence. There are some, which have not survived to
our own times but which have nevertheless left traces in the documentary sources that serve the Scottish historian. Some of these are
mappable, others are not sufficiently identifiable geographically to allow
inclusion in our distribution map. It is, however, not expected that this
small group of names and others which may have been lost altogether
would have created any surprises if they had been available to us today.
The map of *Pit*-names, as we have it (and we must thank Professor
Kenneth Jackson for first providing us with the first version of this
visual aid in 1955), can be said to be definitive as a cartographic expression of the major toponymic evidence for the settlement area of the
linguistic (Celtic) Picts.

A small number of original *Pit*-names may be hidden behind some of
the Gaelic names beginning with *Bal*- in the area outlined as historical
'Pictland'. It is known for instance, that in those parts of this area, in
which Gaelic is still alive today or has only recently become obsolete,
the Gaelic equivalent of map names beginning with *Pit*- begins with
Baile. Pitfour SUT, for instance, is *Baile-phùir* in Gaelic, Pitkerrie ROS
is *Baile-chéirigh*, Pitlochry PER is *Baile Chloichrigh*, and the nearby
Pitcastle and Pitarrick are referred to by Gaelic speakers as *Baile
a'Chaisteil* and *Baile an Tarraig*, respectively. Pitglassie ROS is in

Gaelic *Baile a'Ghlasaich*. For Pitmaduthy ROS Gaelic has both *Pit mhic Dhuibh* and *Baile mhic Dhuibh*. For how long these parallel names have existed side by side, is difficult to say. They are, of course, a phenomenon which has been a feature of bilingual situations wherever they have occurred throughout the ages (see pp. 53-55 above), but the fact that the map-makers saw fit to include the 'Pictish' rather than the Gaelic names seems to indicate that the Gaelic equivalents in *Baile* may be a comparatively recent development of, let us say, the eighteenth or nineteenth centuries. Certainly the *Pit*-names have continued in the respective English traditions, possibly because of the strong backing by a written tradition, rather than an oral one, as in the case of the Gaelic names. It is said that Gaelic speakers replaced *peit* by *baile* because of the potentially obscene, or at least suggestive, connotations of the former word in Gaelic; be that as it may, and there is a good deal of plausibility in this argument, the replacement of *peit* or *pit* by *baile* implies a certain amount of knowledge on the part pf Gaelic speakers as to the function and meaning of *peit* (from Pictish *pett*) as a generic, while it should also not be ignored that the creativity of *baile* as a toponymic element must have been considerable when the replacement took place so that the not to be underestimated forces of analogy must have been at work, too. Whether such replacements did also happen earlier than the last two centuries or so, cannot be decided at present, as the documentary sources appear to be silent on this point; there is, to the best of the writer's knowledge, no recorded instance of a *Pit*-name being changed to a *Bal*-name between, let us say, the twelfth and the eighteenth centuries. Potential substitutions must, however, be reckoned with.

In connection with this knotty, though onomastically exciting, subject of *Pit*- names, there is now available what has to be regarded as one of the most positive extensions of place-names studies in Scotland in recent years, and one which, it is hoped, will spark off many imitations and improvements. In 1968, G. Whittington and J. A. Soulsby published 'A Preliminary Report on an Investigation into *Pit* Place-names', in which they stated the results of an examination which they, as geographers, had undertaken of the *Pit*-names of Fife and the adjacent parts of Angus, analysing each individual site so named, with a view to gathering information about 'the preferred habitat of the Pictish people'. Since, as should be more than apparent in the pages of this book, names are more than words and consequently not the sole property and baili-wick of linguists, any attempt which treats their extra-linguistic qualities is welcome after their long confinement to servitude as raw material for the elucidation of the history of language. A geographer's interest in names is natural and potentially particularly helpful in this respect, and the Whittington-Soulsby systematic investigation has proved to be not only refreshingly new but also exceedingly productive, in its emphasis on names as indicators of preferred habitat.

The investigators state that, because of their specific preferences in the choice of habitation sites, the Picts generally did not favour the coastal zone and also avoided the floors of river-valleys, and that because of the largely coastal area below and the adverse exposure conditions above, *Pit*-names are almost entirely distributed between an altitude of 50 and 650 feet. Altitude, while of importance, was, however, a factor in the preferred choice of habitation sites primarily in relation to other factors, some of them caused by altitude itself. While the distance of one *Pit*-name from another varies between ¼ and 3½ miles, indications are that, in an economy based on an advanced farming system, the settlement pattern was a clustered rather than a random one. Loamy soils, often developed from the till of the volcanic rocks, as well as calciferous sandstone, where till-covered, proved particularly attractive to the Picts, especially when the chosen sites also provided shelter and good drainage. A southerly component in the aspect of the site and protection from the direction of the most frequent strong winds were therefore found desirable in the choice of sites which tended to be located on the sides of eminences which rose steeply behind the site, while providing a gentle slope in front which would promote the natural drainage of the soil. Defence, on the other hand, does not appear to have been an important consideration in the selection of sites. The Picts, or more accurately, the coiners of our *Pit*-names, consequently emerge as inland people who would prefer to settle on loamy soils in well-sheltered and well-drained positions — positions which are just as desirable today as they were a thousand years ago but the availability of which is certainly much more restricted as far as the modern settler is concerned.

As Whittington and Soulsby have shown, there is certainly nothing haphazard, hasty or primitive about the choice of habitat revealed by their study of the sites to which *Pit*-names are attached, and their folk-cultural response to this natural habitat is embedded semantically in the specific (second) elements of these names which would merit closer study from that point of view. It would also be interesting to find out, whether the local conditions in, let us say, Aberdeenshire, Perthshire or Ross-shire are similar enough to permit the Picts equivalent preferences and choices and what these habitation sites are like when the preferred conditions did not exist. What are the extremes which the creators of our *Pit*-nomenclature would tolerate? The student of Scottish place-names is grateful to the Scottish geographer for taking this new approach and for opening up these avenues.

If we accept the view — and there is no reason why it should prove unacceptable to anyone now — that the distribution of *Pit*-names is more or less identical with the settlement area of the historical Picts, then we are in a position to search for other *p*-Celtic place-name elements which might also be termed Pictish because they also occur within the boundaries of Celtic Pictland as outlined by *Pit*-names. As Jackson showed 20 years ago, there are at least five toponymic generics which meet these requirements: *carden, pert, lanerc, pevr,* and *aber.* Others, which might also qualify, are, for one reason or another, too ambiguous to be used as definite evidence in this context, mainly because they have either been adopted as loanwords into Gaelic or are indistinguishable from other elements. Of the five generics listed, only one corresponds closely in its distribution to that of *pett*: *Carden* (cognate with Welsh *cardden* 'thicket') is contained only in names which. occur within the area in which *Pit*-names are found, the only 'outlier' being Cardross D N B (*Cardinross* in 1208-33) which is nevertheless still north of the Clyde. The main representatives of names containing *carden* are Carden(den) F I F, Fettercairn A N G, Kincardine F I F, I N V, K C D, P E R, R O S,.Kincardine O'Neil A B D, and Pluscarden M O R, whereas in Cardno A B D, Cardny P E R, Cairney P E R, and Cairnie A B D *carden* is combined with the Gaelic suffix *-ach* or its locative. There seems to be little doubt therefore about *carden* being both linguistically and geographically Pictish, within a Scottish context.

When it comes to an evaluation of the linguistic affinities of the other four generics, matters become more complicated, in so far as none of them occurs exclusively in what we have defined as Pictish territory on the basis of the distribution of *Pit*-names. Indubitably they are also Pictish, but since they are also found south of the Forth-Clyde line and, in some instances, in Welsh and Cornish place-names, what linguistic situation does their geographical scatter imply, especially in relation to the *p*-Celtic place-name evidence of southern Scotland? The chief terms normally employed in the designation of the kind of *p*-Celtic spoken in the Scottish south before, and for some time after, the arrival of Angles, Norsemen and Gaelic-speaking Celts have been British, Brittonic, and Brythonic, stressing the linguistic unity of that language with the other *p*-Celtic dialects spoken at the time in England, Wales and Cornwall, from which modern Welsh and Cornish, as well as Breton, are derived. Since Kenneth Jackson's suggestion that the most appropriate term for the *p*-Celts of southern Scotland would be Cumbrians, and for their language Cumbric, is, however, preferable, the term Cumbric will be used here to refer to the non-Pictish, non-Gaelic Celtic language spoken in southern Scotland in the Dark Ages and Early Middle Ages.

Just as Pictish was the language of the political kingdom of the Picts, so Cumbric had its political associations, in its case mostly with the fortunes of the kingdom of Strathclyde which, with its roots likely to have been in the older territory of the Damnonii, from the seventh century onwards had its eastern boundary — and indeed that in the south and south-west — largely shaped by the activities of the Angles and the strength or weakness of Northumbria. Landmarks in this respect would be: (*a*) the acquisition of the Cumbric kingdom of Rheged by marriage about 635, putting an Anglian wedge between the Cumbrians of Stathclyde and the Solway; (*b*) the siege of the fortification on Edinburgh Castle rock in 638 which must have been a decisive stage in the displacing of the Votadini (Gododdin) by the Angles on the eastern flank of Strathclyde, in what later came to be called *Lothian*: (*c*) the defeat of the Picts by the English between Avon and Carron in 711; (*d*) the establishment of an Anglian bishopric at Whithorn about 720, and the annexation of Kyle by Eadbert in 750 (or 752); (*e*) Eadbert's victory (with the help of the Picts) over Strathclyde and his subsequent defeat in 756; (*f*) the dynastic struggles and virtual anarchy in Northumbria in the second half of the eighth century; (*g*) the

sacking of Lindisfarne by the Norsemen in 793 heralding the age of
Scandinavian influence and power; (*h*) the disintegration of Northumbria
in the ninth century under the impact of Danish, and later Norse,
forces.

The ninth century also witnessed the emergence of the new combined
kingdom of Dalriadic Scots and Picts in the north, after Kenneth
MacAlpin's victory over the last king of the Picts in 840. In 870
Dumbarton feels the scourge of the raiding Norsemen, but the Cumbrians of Strathclyde are able to extend their territory to the south,
possibly as far as 'the Rere or Rey Cross at the western edge of Stain-
more Common in the North Riding of Yorkshire', according to Barrow.
From then onwards the various peoples of Scotland are inextricably
linked in their destinies, whether in harmony or in discord. In 920
Britons (Cumbrians), Scots, and Angles submit to Edward the Elder,
then in 927 to Athelstan who, only seven years later, defeats the King
of Strathclyde and in 937 becomes the victor at Brunanburh over
Scots, Cumbrians and Norsemen. In 945 Edmund, King of Wessex,
commits Strathclyde to Malcolm I, King of the Scots, after harrying
and overrunning it first. After invading Lothian and killing the Scottish
king in the course of the invasion in 971, the Britons do homage to
King Edgar at Chester in 973, the same year in which Edgar cedes
Lothian to the Scottish King Kenneth, an event which Barrow has
described as 'the recognition by a powerful but extremely remote
south-country king of a long-standing *fait accompli*'. Cumbria is again
raided by an English king, Ethelred the Unready, in the year 1000, and
after losing Lothian, or part of it, after a disastrous expedition into
Northumberland in 1006, Malcolm II, King of the Scots, with the help
of Owein, King of Strathclyde, defeats the Earl of Northumbria at
Carham, virtually gaining confirmation of the cession of Lothian. After
Owein's death – at the battle or soon after – Malcolm is in a position
to place his own grandson, Duncan, on the throne of Strathclyde, and
Duncan, in his turn, becomes king of a country which includes the
whole of what we now know as Scotland, apart from the land held by
the Scandinavians.

Although it is difficult to determine when Cumbric place-names were
first created in Scotland, the topographical references in the early
classical writers (the tribal names *Novantae* and *Epidii*, the latter with
Epidion Akron, the Mull of Kintyre; and the place-name *Carbantorigon*
in Galloway) make it clear that *p*-Celtic was indeed the language spoken
in Roman, and pre-Roman, times in that part of Scotland in which
Cumbric later developed. For our purposes, the settlement names used
as the basis of the distribution maps (Maps 19-21) are likely to have
been mostly created some time during the period of the historical
Cumbrians, i.e. between the fifth and eleventh centuries AD.

The extent of the area in which Cumbric was spoken is best visualised
against the background of place-names beginning with *cair* 'fort' and,
with certain limitations, those containing *tref* 'homestead, village'. In
Cumbria, in contrast to Wales, *cair* probably did not refer to anything
as awe-inspiring as a military fortification, but rather meant a stockaded

19   Cumbric names containing *cair*

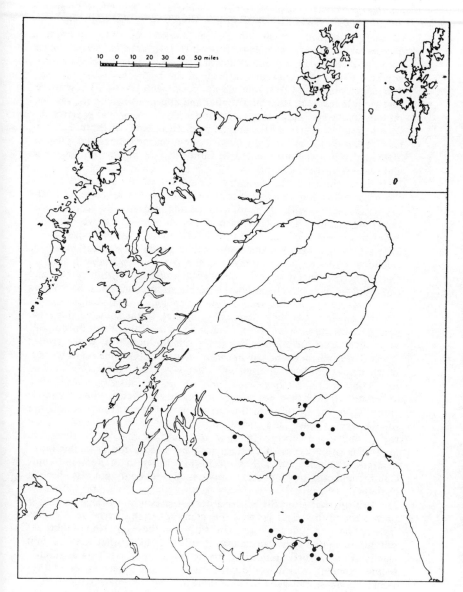

●   Name containing *cair*

farm or manor-house. Represented on Map 19 are names like *Cramond*
MLO (*Karramunt* 1166-1214; *Caramonde* 1178-9) which is 'fort on the
(River) Almond', here actually referring to a Roman station; then
Caerlanrig ROX (*Carlanerik* 1610) = *caer lanerch* 'hamlet in the glade',
Carfrae BWK and ELO, 'hill farm' from Welsh *bre* 'hill', and also
Cathcart RNF, for which the spelling *Kerkert* of 1158 indicates a
derivation *Caer Gart* 'hamlet or fort on the (River) Cart'. The English
material includes such Cumberland names as *Carlisle* in which *caer* is
prefixed to an older *Luguvalium* 'place of the Luguvalos', *Cardew*, containing Cumbric *du* 'black', and *Cardurnock* 'pebbly farm', These three
and the other examples from Cumberland appear to be late for various
reasons and were, according to Professor Jackson, probably 'given by
British immigrants from Strathclyde who reoccupied Northern Cumberland in the tenth century'. In *Carrick* NTB, on the other hand, OE *wīc*
'dwelling' was apparently added to Cumbric *cair*, making the linguistic
and ethnic sequence Cumbrians > Angles, quite clear.

In their almost exclusive distribution south of the Forth-Clyde line
these names undoubtedly reflect the kingdoms of Rheged and Strathclyde, the latter with its capital at Dumbarton and its ecclesiastical
centre in Glasgow. The occurrence of *cair* in place-names was possibly
wider in the south of Scotland than here depicted, but the word is very
difficult to distinguish from some other elements in areas in which
Gaelic was spoken later, intensively and for a considerable length of
time. On the other hand, the absence of *cair*-names from Carrick and
Galloway may have chronological implications, since, as *tref*-names
prove (Map 21), Cumbric was definitely spoken in that region. In this
connection, it is well worth remembering that, to the south of our area,
names beginning with *cair* do not occur again until the Welsh borderland
is reached (Caradoc HRE which is *Cayrcradoc* in 1292), Wales proper
(Cardiff, Carmarthen, and the like), and Cornwall (Cardinham, Kerrow).
Welsh names for English cities like *Caer Wysg* for Exeter, *Cair Ceri(n)*
for Cirencester, and *Cair Ebrauc* for York are, of course, in a somewhat
different category, but not totally irrelevant. Why this type of name is
absent from the English north-west, south of Cumberland, and how the
gap between Carlisle and Cardiff, so to speak, is to be interpreted are
real problems, especially in view of the fact that while there are
numerous other types of Celtic place-names to be found in this intermediate area, *cair*-names only occur in the south of Scotland (plus
Cumberland) and in Wales and Cornwall, but seemingly not elsewhere in
the north of Britain.

Their absence from the Scottish north-east is not as problematic as it
may seem at first sight because the many *Keirs* and *Kiers* of that area
have not been included on our map. Although these and some others are
potential candidates as *cair*-names, it is just as likely that they contain
Gaelic *cathair* 'fort'. Indeed, there is no pointer, such as a *p*-Celtic
second element, which would with some persuasion suggest *cair* rather
than *cathair* as the generic, and there is considerable justification in
regarding the *cair*-map as providing a glimpse of the Cumbric language
area. In this respect, *cair* serves the same function for Cumbric as *pett*

20   *P*-Celtic names containing *aber, pren, pert, lanerc* and *pevr*

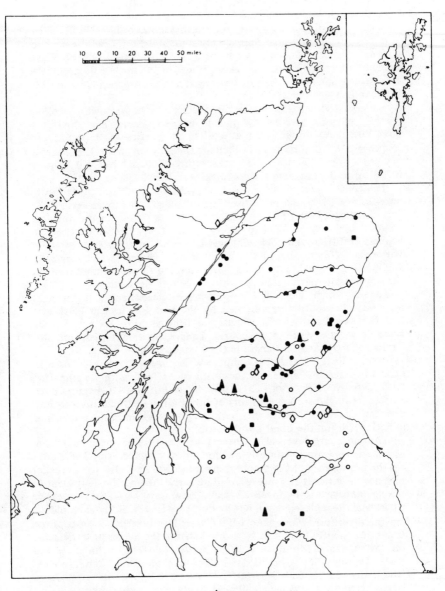

● Name containing *aber*   ▲ Name containing *lanerc*

○ Name containing *pren*   ◇ Name containing *pevr*

■ Name containing *pert*

for Pictish, and their almost complete mutual exclusion makes them especially valuable as important markers of Cumbric and Pictish, both linguistically and territorially. Any *p*-Celtic place-name generic occurring exclusively south of the Forth-Clyde line may now confidently be called Cumbric, just as any such generic only found north of that line may be designated as Pictish, but, as has already been noted, any place-name elements which are in evidence on both sides of the line are by definition creating a problem, particularly with regard to the linguistic relationship between Pictish and Cumbric.

Elements with a predominantly 'Pictish' distribution which belong to this category have been shown to be *pert, lanerc, pevr,* and *aber* (Map 20); these are joined by at least three generics which occur more frequently in Cumbria than in Pictland: *penn, pren* and *tref.* There are, of course, other generics but a brief scrutiny of these terms will be quite sufficient to demonstrate the complexity of the situation.

The generic *pert* 'wood, copse', as evidenced by Welsh *perth* 'bush, brake, copse', is found in Pictish territory in such names as Perth PER, Pert and Logie Pert ANG, and Larbert STL, as well as in the now lost names Perthok ABD and Perthbeg BNF; it appears in Cumbria in Pappert Hill DNB and LAN, Pappert Law SLK, and Perter Burn DMF. The main difference lies in the fact that this element, which originally applied to a natural feature, was never elevated to a settlement name in the south, while having survived only as such in the north.

Lanerc, which in Welsh is now *llanerch* 'clear space, glade' is in its northerly distribution represented by the two Lanricks in Perthshire and the two Lendricks in Angus and Kinross-shire. Its best known example in the south is, of course, Lanark LAN, but there are also Caerlanrig ROX and Barrlanark in the Glasgow area.

Pevr 'radiant', beautiful' (compare Welsh *pefr*) is primarily used in descriptive stream-names, in the north in Peffery, with Strathpaffer, ROS, *Peforyn* or *Paforyn* (1247, now Silver Burn) ABD, Paphrie Burn ANG, and in the second elements of Inverpeffer ANG and Inverpeffray PER 'Peffer-mouth', and in the south in two Peffers in East Lothian and in Peffer Mill (on the Braid Burn) MLO.

The most controversial of these four elements has been *aber* 'confluence, river-mouth', since it was for a time claimed as a Gaelic term by the proponents of the theory that Pictish was *qu*-Celtic (or Goidelic) and not *p*-Celtic. It is, however, quite clearly the *p*-Celtic equivalent of Gaelic *inbhear* (as in Inverness INV, Inveraray ARG, and Inverewe ROS), and the replacement of one by the other is very nicely exemplified by the older form *Haberberui* 1290 for modern Inverbervie KCD. *Aber* occurs frequently in Pictish territory, often in the names of settlements on the mouth or confluence of major water-courses, as in Aberdeen ABD 'Don-mouth', Arbroath ANG 'Brothockmouth', Aberfeldy PER, Abernethy PER, and Abertarff INV. In Cumbria its occurrence is restricted to a few names like Aberlady ELO, Aberlosk DMF, and the now obsolete Abermilk in the same county, and Abercarf LAN. For *aber,* therefore, a preponderantly north-easterly distribution is distinctly evident, the implication being that it was employed more productively in the naming of places by the Picts than by the Cumbrians, as far as the *p*-Celts of Scotland were concerned.

Of the three generics which can be said to have primary Cumbric connections, *penn* 'end, head' (Welsh *pen*) is probably the one which corresponds most closely in its distribution to that of *cair*, making it truly Cumbrian in Scotland. Only the eighth-century form *Peanfahel*, recorded by Bede for Kinneil WLO and showing substitution of an earlier *p*-Celtic *penn* by its Gaelic cognate *ceann*, gives us any hint that *penn* may also have been in toponymic usage in the heartland of the Picts. The Gaelic form is first recorded in such twelfth-century spellings as *Cenail*, *Kinel*, and *Kynnele*, and it is, of course, possible that Gaelic *ceann* may have been substituted for *penn* in other names, for which our written sources do not provide any documentation for such a substitution, but, as in the case of Gaelic *baile* for Pictish *pett*, it is extremely doubtful whether one has to reckon with any large-scale replacement, particularly in names in which this would have involved a process of part-translation. The fact that Gaelic *ceann* is cognate with *penn*, whereas *baile* and *pett* are not generically or even semantically related, lends only slight support to the substitution theory. Like *cair*, *penn* is consequently to all intents and purposes confined to Cumbria; it even shares with *cair* its absence from most south-westerly parts of the country. Examples of place-names containing *penn* in southern Scotland are Pennygant Hill ROX, Penmanshiel BWK, Penvalla PEB, Pencaitland ELO, Penicuik MLO, Pennel RNF, and Penpont DMF.

Like *penn*, *pren* 'tree' (Welsh *pren*), must originally have referred to a natural feature, perhaps conspicuous individual trees which could be seen from afar or were of significance in the locality in which they stood. Human settlements growing up near such trees would later adopt such tree names, and now the word appears in place-names either uncompounded or with a qualifying element which can be an adjective or the genitive of a noun (Map 20). In its uncompounded form it is found as *Pirn* PEB (near Innerleithen) and *Pirn* MLO (Stow parish) which is *Pryn* in 1463 and *Pyrn(e)* in 1489 and 1490, indicating the late fifteenth century as the time in which metathesis from *pryn* to *pyrn* took place. *Pren* plus an unknown suffix seems to be the basis of *Pirnie* ROX (near Maxton), *Pirny Braes* ELO (Pencaitland par.), *Pirniehall* DNB (Kilmaronock par.), as well as the Perthshire *Pairney* and *Kinpurnie* in Angus. In the examples from north of the Forth-Clyde line Gaelic *-ach* in the meaning 'place of' may be the ending. Colour adjectives qualify it in Prinlaws FIF which stands for *Pren las* 'green tree' and Primside ROX which, as the *Prenwensete* of the Melrose Liber is *pren wen* 'white tree' with the late OE *sete* 'seat' added to it. Surely it may be inferred from this that Primside only came to refer to human habitation after having passed into Anglian mouths. We may also have a glimpse here of a slight difference between Cumbric and Welsh, two dialects which are normally very close to each other, for in Welsh the word *pren* 'tree' is masculine and one would therefore expect unmutated forms like *pren glas* and *pren gwyn* for our two names which are not justified by the evidence before us. Nouns in the genitive seem to have been added to the word, in cases like the beautifully sounding modern name *Primrose* BWK, MLO, FIF which is to be interpreted as *pren ros* 'tree of the moor', *Barnbougle* WLO which in the fourteenth century is *Prenbowgall*, *Parbogalle*, and *Pronbugele*, spellings which stand for *pren bugail* 'herdman's tree', and *Printonan* BWK which according to earlier name forms (*Printanno* 1652 and *Prentonen* Retours) appears to contain Welsh *tonnen* 'sward, bog'. In *Traprain* ELO (*Trepren* 1335), *pren* forms the second element after *tref* 'a homestead'. None of these places is terribly important and none of the evidence is very early. One has the feeling that these Cumbric names were adopted by the Angles only after a considerable period of co-existence, and if one wanted to point to an area in which Cumbric may have survived longest in the Border Counties and the Lothians, one might like to single out the not very accessible, hilly district in upper Midlothian which is now known as the Parish of Stow where, apart from the *Pirn* already mentioned, there are *Pirntaton* and a now obsolete *Pirncader*, forming a very noticeable little cluster of three. It is also of interest to note that the *Pirny Braes* are in *Pencaitland* parish, where *pren-* and *cēd* might refer to the same wooded area. Somewhat surprising is the location of such *pren*-names as Barnweill in Craigie AYR (*Berenbouell* 1177-1204, *Brenwyfle* 1306), and the unidentified *Brenego* and *Roderbren* (so 1177-1204), associated with Enterkine in Tarbolton AYR, and *Prenteineth* (twelfth century), associated with Loudoun AYR. Apart from this westerly cluster of examples from Ayrshire, *pren*-names are absent not only from the regions covered by the two important kingdoms of the northern British, i.e. Strathclyde and Rheged, but also from the place-nomenclature of England where it does not seem to have been recorded. Their major distribution is in that part of Scotland in which ancient writers placed the Romano-British tribe of the *Votadini*, whose capital was probably on Edinburgh Castle Rock, the *Gododdin* or 'Men of the North' of Welsh poetry. It would, however, be rash, though tempting, to label a feminine *pren* 'tree', as evidenced by this group of place-names, Votadinic. *Pren*-names, despite their main location south of the Forth-Clyde line, are seen occurring in 'Pictish' territory, for instance in Perthshire, Fife and Angus, and are therefore, even more than *penn*-names, not exclusively Cumbric.

In contrast to *penn* and *pren*, the element *tref* must have referred from the beginning to human settlement. It is still current in Modern Welsh, usually with loss of the final consonant, in the meaning of 'town, home', and it is also a prolific place-name element not only in Wales but also in Cornwall. A map of Scottish names containing *tref* should accordingly provide a picture of the location and survival of Cumbric village names during and since the Anglian occupation (Map 21). In this context, it is assumed that 'homestead' or 'village' rather than 'town' was the meaning of our generic at the time when it was most productive as a toponymic element.

It can be seen at a glance that the distribution of *tref*-names differs essentially from that of those containing *pren*, *pen* and *cair*. Names with *tref* as a first element are exclusive to the south of the Forth-Clyde

21   *P*-Celtic names containing *tref*

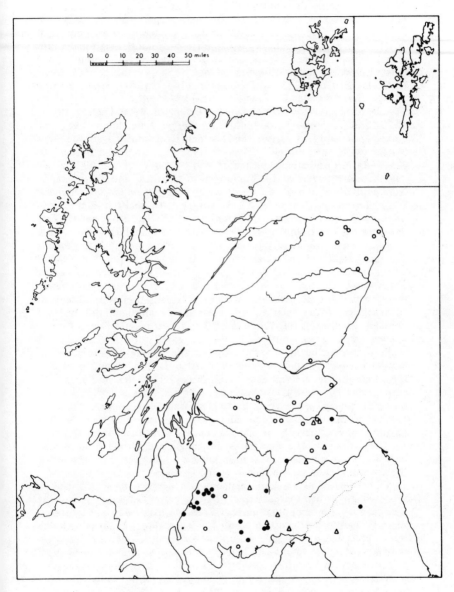

● **Name containing** *tref*   ○ **Name containing** − *tref*

△ **Name containing** *tref yr* −

line, with those followed by the definite article *yr* plus noun apparently
of a more easterly distribution than those in which neither the present
nor the historical forms do imply such usage.. However, this first
impression is deceptive, for it has been impossible to plot a number of
'lost' names in Carrick and Kyle unquestionably containing the definite
article which, incidentally, is always *yr*, or rather [ə̄r]. Some of the
better-known examples of names belonging to this category are *Tranent*
ELO (*Trauernent c.* 1127, *Treuernent* 1144, 1150) = *tref yr neint*
'village of the streams'; *Traquair* PEB (*Treverquyrd c.* 1124; *Treuquora*
1153) 'village on the (river) Quair'; *Trabrown* BWK (*Treuerbrun c.*
1170) and *Trabroun* ELO, both from *tref yr bryn* 'hill village', and
Terregles KCB (*Travereglys* 1365) which is obviously *tref yr eglwys*
'village with the church'. The two names across the border are
Triermain in Cumberland, on record as *Treverman* from 1169 onwards
and therefore *tref yr maen* 'homestead of the rock' and *Troughend* in
Northumberland the old forms of which − *Troquen* 1242, *Trequenne*
1279, *Trehquen, Troghwen* 1293 − appear to make it identical in
origin with *Torquhan* MLO (*Torquhene* 1593) in Stow parish, *Troquhain* KCB (*Trechanis* 1467, *Troquhane* 1590) and *Troquhain* AYR
(*Treu(e)-chane* 1371, *Troquhan* 1511, *Torquhane* 1506), showing
the same rounding and velarisation of the vowel in the first element
which is also found in names like *Tralorg, Traboyack, Tranew,
Tradunnock, Troax,* (all in Carrick) apart from the ones already
mentioned. This is, presumably, due to labialisation and subsequent
vocalisation of the final voiced [v] in *Tref-,* although this has not
operated in all cases (cf. *Triermain* CMB, *Trailtrow* and *Trailflat* DMF,
Terregles KCB, etc.).

From a distributional point of view the picture is valid for both
Scotland and England, for the only other isolated instance of this
formation between Cumberland and Wales is *Treales* in Lancashire,
emphasising the close relationship between Cumbria and Wales, in this
case particularly between Strathclyde and Wales, for it appears from our
map as if this type of name must have flourished in the Cumbric
kingdom of Strathclyde for many a century after the Border Counties
and the Lothians had become thoroughly anglicised, although there must
have been a good deal of Gaelic influence on the western seaboard of
the kingdom, especially in Galloway and Carrick.

As far as *tref* as a second element is concerned names formed in
this manner disturb the pattern set by those in which the generic is the
first part of the compound-name; for, as the map (Map 21) indicates,
there is, in the north-east, a considerable number of names in which
tref is preceded by the specific, unless it is assumed that they contain
the Gaelic cognate *treabh* (evidenced in no more than a couple of Irish
place-names) rather than Cumbric (?) *tref.* The detailed toponymic
material which follows illustrates the complexity of the issue:

(*a*)   *Names with p-Celtic first elements:*
Cantray, Gaelic *Cantra* INV (with Cantraydoune NAI, Gaelic *Cantra an
Dùin, Cantradoun* 1468), possibly from **canto-treb-* 'white settlement';
Menstrie CLA (*Mestryn* 1261; *Mestreth* 1263, *Mestry* 1315, *Menstry*

1392), probably *maes-dref* 'plain-settlement'; Niddry WLO (*Nudreff* 1370, *Nudry* 1392, *Nidre c.* 1542), Niddrie MLO (*Nudreth* 1140, *Nodrif* 1166-1214, `Noderyf* 1264-6, *Nudreff* 1296), Longniddry ELO (*Nodref, Langnodryf* 1315-21, *Loungnudrethe* 1380-81, in *Langnudre* [*de Langnodryffe*] *Robert I*), all probably from *newydd* 'new', although obviously influenced by the Gaelic cognate of the same word, *nodha*; Ochiltree AYR (*Uchiltrie* 1406, *Wchiltrie* David II), Ochiltree WIG (*Uchiltre* 1506), Ochiltree WLO (*Ockiltre 1211-14, Ouchiltre* 1282, *Uchiltre* 1382) all clearly corresponding to Welsh *Ucheldref* 'high settlement'; Soutra MLO (*Soltre* 1153-65, *Soltra* 1458-9, *Sowtre* 1473), from Welsh *sulw tref* 'steading of the wide view'; Trostrie KCB (*Trostaree* 1456, *Trostre* 1527), Troustrie FIF (apparently no early record), from *traws tref* 'thwart settlement'.

(*b*)   *Names with Gaelic first elements:*
Capledrae FIF (*Capildray* late 12th), possibly from Gaelic *capull* 'horse', Clentry FIF (*Easter and Wester Clintrayes* 1653), (?) Clenterty BNF, Clinterty ABD (one in Newhills: *villa de Clentrethi, le Crag de Clentrethy,* (?) *Clenterret* 1316, *Clyntreys* 1367, *de duabus Clynteys (sic), de Clyntreys, apud Clyntre* 1368, *de duabus Clyntrees* 1372, *de Clintreis* 1329-71, *litil Clyntree* 1381, *Clentre* 1382, *Clyntree* 1430, *Bishopis-Clintertie* 1649; one in Aberdour: *Clintertie* 1556), probably from Gaelic *claon* 'sloping squint', although synonymous with *claointe* with -*erie* as the termination of a stream-name has been suggested; Fintry STL (*Fyntrif* 1225, *Fyntryf* 1225-70, *Fyntre* 1464), Fintray ABD (*Fyntrach* 1175, *Fintreth* 1180, 1490), Fintry ABD (*Meikle Fyntra* 1375), Fintry ANG from Gaelic *fionn* 'white'; Fortree, Fortry ABD (there are several others on record with early spellings such as *Fortre* 1540), Fortrie (2), Fortry BNF' (example spellings, *Fortre, Fortrie* David II), apparently a Gaelic form of Welsh *gor-dref* 'big stead'; Moray MOR, Gaelic *Moireabh* (*Murebe* 1032, *Muireb* 1085, *Moreb* 1130), from Gaelic **Moirthreabh* Early Celtic **mori-treb-* 'sea-settlement'.

(*c*)   *Names in which the first element could be either p-Celtic or Gaelic:*
Rattray PER (*Rotrefe* 1291, *Rettref* 1296, *Rothtref* 1205), Rattray ABD (*Rettre* 1170, *Retref* 1274, *Ratreff* 1460), Rattra KCB, either from Welsh *rath* or Gaelic *rath* 'a circular fort'.

(*d*)   *Doubtful names:*
Coulaghailtro ARG (*Coulgalgreif* 1511); Muchtre ARG (so 1554, 1619), now apparently lost. Watson considers that 'if these are genuine instances of *tref*, the term must have come to Kintyre from Ayrshire'. Halltree MLO (*Haltre* 1483, *Haltrie* 1587, *Holltree* 1654), Dixon suggests a hybrid name consisting of OE *heald* or ON *hallr* and *tref.* If correct, this would be a remarkable formation.

    The first fact which clearly emerges from this survey is that the linguistic groupings (*a*) and (*b*) roughly correspond to geographical divisions which means that the material is not as homogeneous as it first appears to be. No example in the area in which *tref* occurs as a second element, shows a Gaelic first part unless the three Niddries in the Lothians with their *No-* forms can be said to exhibit at least traces of one. On the other hand, *p*-Celtic first elements — with the exception of the rather poorly documented Cantray on the Inverness-Nairn border — only sporadically cross the Forth-Clyde line to the north, leaving the field to Gaelic first components, i.e. to names of the Fintry-type. The possibility of the Gaelic cognate *treabh* as the second part of these names is rather ruled out because of the scarcity of this word as a place-name element in Ireland (it also seems to be totally absent elsewhere in Scotland), and for semantic reasons. Part-translation is therefore the most likely explanation for some of these names, as seems to be proved by the entry in the Register of the Great Seal, '*terras et baroniam de Cantres vulgo vocat. Fintries in parochia de Kingeduard*' (1634, similar in 1625) which makes it very likely that the original name was some-thing like **can-dref-* < **canto-treb-* 'white settlement'. As in the case of the many *Pit*-names in this area, however, the presence of numerous Gaelic elements is in all probability due to the majority of the names, in this category, having been coined in a Pictish-Gaelic bilingual period in the ninth and tenth centuries, or even a little later. The Fintry-type name would in this respect parallel the Pitlochry model (see p. 156).

Whatever the correct explanation in each individual case, the fact remains that *tref* was used extensively as a second element in place-names in the Scottish east and north-east, from Fife to Moray (or even Nairn), largely in the same region in which *Pit*-names occur. Since the Gaulish tribal name *Atrebati* 'settlers' contains the same element, this is by no means surprising, if one considers the claim for the special link of Pictish with Gaulish. The name Moray, Gaelic *Moireabh*, from some-thing like early Celtic **mori-treb-* 'sea-settlement' would further sub-stantiate such potential links. It remains slightly puzzling why, if *tref* was also Pictish, it does not occur as a first element in Pictland. Perhaps the reason is that *pett* was usefully and satisfactorily fulfilling that morphological function while, to the best of our knowledge, not occurring as the second part of a compound and therefore leaving the field to *tref*. In this way, the two generics might be regarded as complementary — only north of the Forth-Clyde line, of course.

What, then, is the picture which emerges from an examination of the distribution patterns of the major *p*-Celtic place-name elements in Scotland? Descriptively, the answer is that we have one element, or possibly two, which are exclusively attested in so-called 'Pictland': *Pit-* and *carden*. We have another two which are practically restricted to 'Cumbric' territory: *cair* and *penn*. Then there are several which occur both north and south of the Forth-Clyde line, sometimes more commonly in the north like *aber*, *pert*, and *pefr*, sometimes with greater emphasis in the south, like *pren*, sometimes with a fairly even distribution like *lanerc*. Finally, one important word, *tref*, is exclusive to the south when used as a first element, and occurs both south and north of the Wall when employed as a second part, in the south always in combination with a Cumbric word, in the north mostly with a Gaelic first element. All these words, apart from *pett* are also to be found in Welsh place-names.

The conclusion reached on the basis of this brief and incomplete survey of toponymic material is that, although there are features which appear to separate Pictish from other insular *p*-Celtic languages and perhaps even associate it with Gaulish, there is other evidence which demonstrates with some weight that Pictish was not as different from Cumbric as these other place-name elements might suggest. Probably Pictish, although not simply a northern extension of British (or Cumbric), should rather be called a dialect of Northern Brittonic or of Brittonic in general, and not a separate language. This tentative conclusion does not disregard the fact that Bede in his *Ecclesiastical History*, i.e. at a time 'when the Pictish nation was still very much alive', speaks 'of Pictish as a fourth language distinct from Gaelic, Brittonic and English' (Jackson) but it takes cognisance of a place-name (already mentioned) which the same Bede in the same source (1.12) tells us is Pictish: *Peanfahel* (now Kinneil) near Abercorn. This is a hybrid of *p*-Celtic *penn* 'end' and Gaelic *fal*, Gen. *fail* 'wall'. By the beginning of the eighth century, therefore, Pictish did use general Brittonic words and was under the initial influence of Gaelic. Whatever Bede's criteria for Pictish as a language different from Brittonic or Cumbric, as well as Gaelic and English, may have been (and this may after all only have been a difference of degree), there appear to be several other qualities, lexical as well as phonological, which do link Pictish not unexpectedly quite closely with Brittonic, both the Cumbric of Scotland and the Welsh and Cornish of Wales and Cornwall. In fact, one suspects that its separateness has perhaps been rather overstressed. The place-name evidence certainly appears to point towards the direction of closer links, while at the same time bearing witness to the considerable complexity in the relationships amongst the various *p*-Celtic languages in Scotland and elsewhere in Britain.

In concluding this account of *p*-Celtic place-names in Scotland, a possibly misleading impression may have to be corrected. The method adopted in most chapters of this book makes considerable use of certain significant place-name generics as a means towards establishing the several linguistic strata involved and the settlement areas of the people who were the speakers of those languages. Such an approach has the tendency to ignore individual place-names, frequently of major settlements, which belong to the strata concerned but cannot easily be 'typed' and categorised, in the way in which names containing the same generic can be grouped together. Consequently there are not only sizable gaps in the nomenclature treated, but the reader may also be left with the impression that either the place-name scholar is not interested in such individual names or such names cannot be handled satisfactorily. It is therefore well to remind ourselves that the kind of name we have in mind can indeed be utilised in the establishing of linguistic strata; there is certainly no difficulty in fitting such names, if adequate documentation is available and an acceptable etymology possible, into established strata. Particularising this general statement, the following names, for example, belong to the same Cumbric stratum as *cair*, *tref*, *pren*, *penn*, etc.:

Melrose ROX (in Bede *Mailros*) represents *Moelros* 'bare Moor'. Peebles PEB (*Pobles c.* 1124, *Pebles c.* 1126) must be based on the plural of Welsh *pebyll* 'tent, pavilion' as it shows an English plural in its anglicised form; Cumbric *cēd* 'wood' is seen in Dalkeith MLO (*Dolchet* 1144, *Dalkied* 1142, and *-keith, -keithe, keth-, -kethe, -ketht, -keyth, -ket* as later medieval variants) whose first part appears to be Old Welsh *dol* 'meadow, valley', while *cēt*, of course, also appears in Bathgate WLO (*Batket* 1153-65, *Batchet* 1165-70) 'boar wood', and Pencaitland ELO; Ancrum ROX, situated on a bend of the river *Ale*, perfectly describes its situation as its early forms testify (Latin *Alnecrumba c.* 1124, *Alncromb c.* 1150) which point to Welsh *crwm* 'bent' (adjective) or 'bend' (noun) as the second part — 'Alnebend'; Renfrew RNF (*Reinfry c.* 1128) can be compared with Welsh *rhynfrwd* 'point of current'; and Glasgow LAN and Linlithgow WLO contain the same last element, an earlier form of Welsh *cau* 'hollow'; the former, which is recorded as *Glasgu* in 1136, is composed of *glas* and *cau* 'green hollow', whereas the latter is a compound of *llyn, llaith* and *cau* 'lake in the moist hollow'. Lanark LAN (*Lannerc* 1187-89) has, of course, already been mentioned in connection with Cumbric *lanerc*. It is intriguing to note that, with the possible exception of Peebles, not one of these names originally referred to a human settlement or structure; they are all transferred to such from their primary designation of natural features. This transfer was possibly effected after many of these names had been adopted by the incoming Angles who would no longer understand the original meaning but only their approximate location. As settlement names, most of these examples are therefore probably not Celtic, although Glasgow must have referred to some kind of human habitation in Cumbric times.

Definitely connected with human settlements and activities, on the other hand, are Eccles BWK (*Eccles c.* 1200, *Ecclys c.* 1220, *Hecles* 1297) 'church', Eccles DMF (*Eklis* 1494) 'church', Ecclefechan DMF (*Eggleffychan* 1296, *Egilfichan* 1425) (?) 'little church', and Ecclesmachan WLO (*Egglesmanekin* 1207, 1218, *Eglismauchin* 1540) 'church of St Machan'. These are from Early Welsh **eglēs* (Welsh *eglwys,* Cornish *eglos*) 'church', rather than Gaelic *eaglais*. If St Machan was a disciple of St Cadoc of Llancarvan and therefore contemporary with Kentigern, the name Ecclesmachan cannot be older than the seventh century AD. The others may be of similar age.

9
Pre-Celtic Names

The group of names mentioned at the end of Chapter VIII serves a useful function, in so far as it draws attention to the fact that, the farther back we move into the early history and prehistory of Scotland, the more likely we are to encounter a scarcity, or even total lack, of original settlement names proper. What has survived from these early periods, however, is a sizable number of names of natural features, and amongst these particularly of river-names. Water-courses have at all times played important roles in the lives of human beings, as life-sustaining sources of water and of fertile alluvial soil, as means of communication, as obstacles, as boundaries, as objects of religious worship, etc. Major rivers in particular have always been known far beyond their catchment areas, even to people who had no personal acquaintance with them. It is therefore only to be expected that their names should have had a special power of survival when names of other natural features did not. Names of water-courses, more than any other kind of place-name, have, because of their transmission from language to language, frequently involving three or more different linguistic strata over a long period of time, tended to become semantically opaque lexical terms, not containable, with meaning other than their onomastic denotation, by the vocabulary of any one language. It does not follow from this that stream-names were never lost nor that all water-courses have been named since the very beginning of human settlement. In fact, numerous name-changes can be documented to have occurred, and some of the smallest and/or most remote streams may never have had a name until recently.

If, then, the names of the larger and more important water-courses are the most durable of all types of place-names and if, further, the fertile valleys of the larger rivers are likely to have been settled first, whereas the tributaries and smaller streams, especially in hilly and mountainous country, might have seen permanent human settlement only centuries, or perhaps even thousands of years, later, it would appear to follow that the names of the larger rivers should go back to the earliest 'stratum' of settlement and therefore also to the earliest language spoken, whereas the tributaries and smallest burns would preserve evidence of later linguistic invasions. This is, of course,

not to be seen as a mechanical hierarchy which could never be inter-
fered with, for we have noted that names can be lost or replaced and
also that the earliest settlers did not always restrict themselves to the
most fertile and most accessible valleys. As a general rule, however,
such a conclusion would seem to be acceptable.

One could test this assumption in almost any part of Scotland but
within the context of our enquiry one sample area must suffice:
Glenlivet in upper Banffshire which through extensive field-work this
writer knows very well (see Table III). The oldest name in this little
catchment basin should obviously be the name of the main river, the
Livet itself, and there is no doubt that this name — which is pronounced
something like 'Leevet' locally and means 'full of water' or perhaps
'flooding' — either belongs to a very early Gaelic type of name or may
even be pre-Gaelic Celtic.

The Livet's main tributaries from its confluence with the Avon
upwards, are, on the left, Burn of Tervie, Burn of Nevie, Allt Dregnie,
and the Suie Burn; and on the right, Allt a'Choire, Culraggie Burn,
Crombie Water, Blye Water, and the Kymah Burn. Every single one of
these is basically Gaelic, although the burns of Tervie and Nevie have
now names which go back to a period of bilingualism when the English
language first reached this Gaelic-speaking part of Scotland. Allt Dregnie
and Allt a'Choire have preserved their Gaelic element *allt* 'burn', and
the latter even its Gaelic spelling, but in other cases the English
words *burn* and *water* are probably translations of their Gaelic pre-
decessors *allt* and *abhainn*. However, even if they are not, they show
quite clearly how English is overlying Gaelic.

At the head of the Livet there is the Little Livet, which again could
be a part-translation from Gaelic or an English innovation, but it is
significant that the thoroughly English names Back Burn and Fore
Burn appear at the very top of the glen, as the names of the two head-
streams of the Suie Burn, whereas the Gaelic equivalent *Cul Allt* 'back
burn' is found as the name of a tributary of the Blye Water. At the
other end of its course the Livet falls into the Avon (or Aven or A'an)
which itself is a tributary of the Spey, and although nobody has so far
suggested any definite etymologies for either of these, they appear to
take us at least one step, perhaps even two steps, farther back into
linguistic history. The chronological sequence would therefore be Spey
— Avon — Livet — Crombie — Burn of Tervie — Suie Burn — Back
Burn. Of course, the Suie Burn does not fall into the Burn of Tervie, and
the latter does not join the Crombie, but the linguistic stratification is
nevertheless very closely related to the geography of the district, on the
one hand, and the relative size of the water-courses on the other; and
there is no evidence in this corner of Scotland at least, that would
contradict the basic assumption of this argument.

Further support of this interpretation comes from the meanings of
the names concerned, for research has shown that the earliest river-
names normally simply refer to qualities of the water itself, or perhaps
to the shape of the water-course, whereas later names often incorporate
the names of neighbouring features or refer to the geographical situation

Table III

The River Livet and its Tributaries

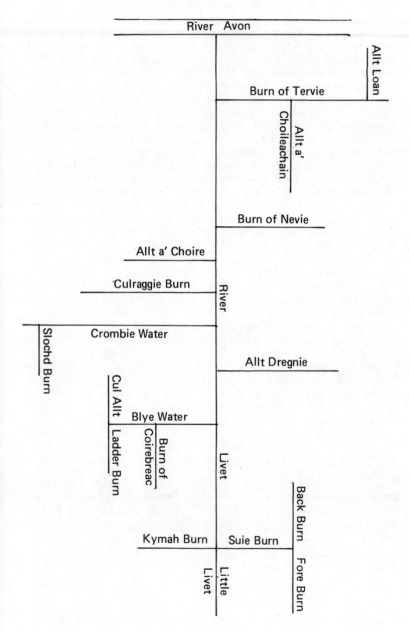

of the stream, or the like. The names in the catchment area of the Livet bear out this theory very well indeed, for the name Livet itself does, as we have seen, simply mean something like 'full of water'. The Crombie Water would be an example of a name stressing the shape of the water-course, for, based on the Gaelic word *crom* 'bent', it means 'winding (river)'. Names like Suie Burn, Burn of Coirebreac, Ladder Burn, Slochd Burn, Allt a'Choire etc. are based on names of other geographical features nearby (Suie equals Gaelic *suidhe* 'seat', *Coire breac* 'speckled corrie', *Ladder* equals *leitir* 'slope', *slochd* equals *sloc* 'hollow', *coire* 'corrie'). Back Burn, Fore Burn and Cul Allt are indicative of the situation of the streams concerned, the latter being the Gaelic equivalent of 'Back Burn'. It is unlikely that the difficult or obscure names in this area would, if acceptable explanations could be found, in any way upset this structure of meaning.

Proof of stream-names as markers of relative chronology within a certain catchment area, however large or small, could be provided over and over again from many parts of Scotland, perhaps not always as neatly as in the case of Glenlivet, but nevertheless convincingly. In practically all instances, if the river chosen is only large enough, one would ultimately end up with an Early Celtic or even pre-Celtic name, as in the cases of Avon and Spey, names which are of considerable antiquity predating the arrival of any Gaelic or Germanic (English and Scandinavian) settlers in this part of the country, indeed in the whole of the country. As such linguistic fossils, these two names and others like them are perhaps even more important toponymic raw material than any of the names we have encountered so far. Antiquity is, of course, not an onomastic virtue in itself; even the most modern and seemingly most pedestrian name usually has an exciting story to tell and is full of fascination for the onomastician; but since more recent periods normally have well-documented written traditions and several other more conventional sources for the elucidation of linguistic (and settlement) history, later geographical names are, more often than not, additional rather than unique and irreplaceable evidence, in the way in which the earliest discernible strata of the Scottish river-nomenclature are singular and without parallel; indeed, they are all there is to give us any information whatsoever about the language or languages which may have been spoken before even any Celts ever set foot in Scotland. In that sense, antiquity is a virtue.

As is to be expected, the main difficulty lies in finding a method and criteria which will enable us to distinguish between the earliest Celtic river-names and those of any potential pre-Celtic stratum, because both nomenclatures were created in the linguistic pre-history of this country and are not referred to in any written record until centuries after they had been coined. For that reason, it will be helpful to parade briefly a particular morphological type of early Celtic, presumably *p*-Celtic, Scottish river-name which will give us some notion as to what to expect in those early days, in the first few centuries AD or even BC; for it is more than likely that most of these early Celtic names of water-courses predate the group of *cair-*, *pren-*, *penn-*, *tref-*names which we discussed at length in Chapter VIII as representatives of the Cumbric stratum. They may also be older, although perhaps overlapping with such names as Melrose, Peebles, Bathgate, Glasgow, etc., which were originally names of natural features before being (also) turned into settlement names.

There are two main reasons for ascribing this particular type of river-name to a relatively early age: (1) Whereas practically all the names discussed so far, whether English, Norse, Anglian, Gaelic, Cumbric, or Pictish, have been compound names, formed through the combination of two (or sometimes more) simple words which we have called generics and specifics, or just 'elements', this early river-nomenclature consists mostly of names which were formed by the addition of a suffix (or suffixes) to a so-called 'stem', a morphological process to which the closest, but not identical modern English parallels would be 'complex' words like *hair-y, small-ish, total-ity, fair-ness, tight-en,* and the like. This principle of name-formation ceased to be productive, and was gradually replaced by compounding, in the early phases of Celtic Scotland, and there appears to be, on the Scottish map, no *primary* settlement-name which was created by this morphological process at any time by non-Celtic languages. (2) From a semantic point of view, the names in this category refer largely to qualities of the water-course itself, and not to its surroundings. This is also a sign of an early nomenclature, at least within the relative chronological framework of the Scottish hydronymy.

Of the several kinds of formation, perhaps the most instructive in this context are names ending in *-ona*, not only because they are fairly numerous but also because the chief word for river in modern Celtic languages (Welsh *afon*, Breton *auon*, Gaelic *abhainn*) is one of them (the Banffshire *Avon*, already quoted in connection with the structure of the stream-nomenclature of Glenlivet, seems to be non-genuine example, on the other hand, which only conformed in spelling by analogy at a later date). In the make-up of these names, the ending *-ona* has to be broken down into the suffix *-no/-na*, preceded by the thematic vowel *-o-*, which indicates that the names originally belonging to this category were derived from *o*-stems. As the following list shows, this was no longer necessarily the common basis when the early Celtic river-names were created in Scotland, and it is therefore possible to distinguish three classes of names in *-ona*, according to the base to which the ending is suffixed:

(1) *The basis is a Celtic adjective or noun which is an o-stem:*
*Dēuonā from **Deiuonā* < **deiuo-s* 'god, divine person', Old Irish *dia*, Welsh *duw*, Old Cornish *duy*, etc. (Don ABD); compare the neighbouring *Dee* from **Dēu-a*.
*Dubona from **dubo-* 'black', Old Irish, Old Welsh *dub*, etc. (*Devon* PER, *Black Devon* FIF).
*Labaronā from **labaro-* 'talkative', Old Irish *labar* 'talkative', Welsh *llafar* 'language' (*Lavern Burn* DMF, *Levern Water* RNF, *Lowran Burn* and *Louran Burn* KCB); compare the river-name **Labarā*, now, for instance, the *Burn of Aberlour* BNF.
*Lemonā from **lemo-* 'elm', Middle Irish *lem*, Gaulish *Lemo-, Limo-*

(*Leven* (a) INV/ARG, (b) DNB, (c) KNR/FIF).

Līmonā from **līmo-* 'flood', Welsh *llif*, Cornish *lyf* (Lyon PER); cf. the river-name **Lima*, now Lyme (DEV and DOR).

(2) *The basis is a Celtic word, formed with the element -to-/-tā, usually from a verbal root.*

*Brutonā from **bru-to-*, Old Irish *bruth* 'glow, rage', Old Welsh *brut* 'animus', Welsh *brwd* 'hot', Indo-European root **bhereu-* 'to boil' (*Burn of Brown* INV/BNF).

*Iektonā from **iek-to-*, cf. Welsh *iaith* 'language' (**jekti-*), Indo-European root **iek-* 'to talk' (*Ythan* ABD).

*Lektonā from **lik-to-*, Welsh *llaith*, Breton *leiz* 'moist', Indo-European root **leg-* 'to drip, to ooze, to dissolve' (*Leithen Water* PEB).

*Nektonā from **Niktonā *nik-to-*, Old Irish *necht*, Sanscrit *nikta* 'clean', Indo-European root **neigu-* 'to wash' (*Nethan* LAN).

(3) *The basis is not an o-stem:*

*Abonā from Old Irish *ab* (**abā*) 'river', Indo-European root **ab-* 'water', river'; identical with Welsh *afon*, Cornish, Breton *auon*, Old Irish *abann*, Gaulish *Abona* (*Water of Aven* ABD/KCD, *Avon* STL — WLO, *Avon Water* LAN, *Evan Water* DMF).

*Katonā from Gaulish *Catu-*, Gaelic *cath*, Welsh *cad* 'battle, fight', Here *-onā* must have been regarded as the ending, cf. *Inverhadden Burn* PER.

Kunonā from Old Irish *cu*, genitive *con* 'dog, wolf', Welsh *ci*, Breton Cornish *ki*; Indo-European **kuuṓ(n)*, genitive **kunos*. Formed from the oblique case or from the compositional form of the stem (*Conan* ROS).

(4) *The basis has not been established with certainty:*

*Ambonā, from the reduction grade **m̥bh-* of the Indo-European root **embh-/ombh-* 'moist, water', as seen in Gaulish *ambe* 'rivo' (*Almond* WLO and PER).

*Kalonā, or possibly **Kalaunā*, frequently connected with the root **kel-* 'to shout, cry, sound', found in Irish *cailech*, Welsh *ceiliog* (**kaljākos*) 'cock'. In this context, a nominal root is probably preferable to a verbal one, and one might think of **kal-* 'hard', well evidenced in Old Irish, Middle Irish *calath, calad*, Welsh *caled* 'hard' and in our many rivers called *Calder* (**Caleto-dubron*). Examples in Scotland are *Calneburne* ELO, *Kale Water* ROX, *Caddon Water* SLK.

A feature, which is worth drawing attention to, is the way in which names in *-onā* frequently parallel names in simple *-ā* from the same stem, as, for instance, in: **Abonā* (Avon) — **Abā* (Awe), **Dēuonā* (Don) — *Dēuā* (Dee), **Labaronā* (Lavern, etc.) — **Labarā* (Burn of Aberlour), **Līmonā* (Lyon) — **Līmā* (Lyme). This *-no-/-nā* suffix also combines with other suffixes in the formation of names. A fuller account of the whole scope of this early Celtic river-nomenclature would make us aware of what one might be tempted to call a whole 'structural system' of such suffixes and suffix combinations. The meaning of these names is never dependent on their endings, apart from the determination of gender which is usually feminine. This fact has to be stressed, since it has at times been claimed that the *onā*-ending in particular implies a river-divinity of some kind, in the way in which *Damona* 'the divine cow' and *Epona* 'horse-goddess' are Gaulish goddesses. Especially *Abonā* has been connected with a Sumerian word *ab* 'cow', to form the name of a goddess 'the great cow'. It is worth reiterating here that there is no reason to believe that *Abonā* means anything but 'river' as stated above, although *-ona* does also serve in the formation of names of divine beings, and although *Dēuā* and *Dēuonā* mean 'goddess', a meaning which is provided by the stem, not the suffixes. Similarly the claim that the river-name Clyde, which also belongs to this early stratum and is recorded by Tacitus as *Clota*, derives from the name of a river-goddess, 'the cleansing one', is probably without foundation. Clyde is much more likely to have been a primary river-name. We are not denying that there was Celtic river-worship, but it should not be assumed for rivers whose names permit a straightforward 'profane' explanation.

River-names of the *Abonā* or *Clota* type take us back to what must have been the very beginnings of Celtic settlements in Scotland and the question now arises whether there is any toponymic information at all about the pre-Celtic linguistic stratum or strata in Scotland. It has already become clear that a search for name material which may have survived from such an early age — somewhere between 500 and 1500 BC, let us say — is most likely to be successful amongst the names of water-courses, especially the larger ones, and it is here that one has to look for potential pre-Celtic candidates. However, whereas with regard to all the names discussed so far we have had obvious points of reference outside Scotland — for English in England, for Scandinavian in Norway and Denmark, for Gaelic in Ireland, for Cumbric and Pictish in Wales, Cornwall and the Bretagne, as well as in continental Gaul — similar references do not immediately offer themselves for any pre-Celtic linguistic stratum, and apart from naturally seeking points of prehistoric contact in the geographic neighbourhood rather than in distant lands, researchers were kept guessing for a long time.

Until the 1950s it had almost always been taken for granted that with regard to the settlement sequence in the British Isles, pre-Celtic would be synonymous with non-Indo-European, and therefore the Phoenicians, the Berbers, and the Basques had been favoured to fill that slot, although an Eskimo-related circumpolar culture had also been considered. Most of the proposals put forward had been based on rather extravagant theories, however seriously advanced, and their main weakness had lain in the scarcity of suitable linguistic, primarily onomastic, material on the one hand, and the lack of clear points of reference on the other. It is always difficult to interpret a small body of obscure names when one does not know what to look for, while labouring within the confines of the 'law' which says that the more obscure the name, the more exotic and bizarre the explanation. Only once had a systematic attempt been made to ascribe a group of pre-Celtic river-names in the British Isles to an Indo-European people, i.e. when the late Julius Pokorny declared these to be Illyrian, in conjunction with his investigation of the linguistic affiliations of the 'Urnfield People'. However, since it was most unlikely that any single linguistic people could ever possibly have covered so vast an area the notion had to be refuted that, as part of an almost Europe-wide expansion, the Illyrians had once intensively settled the British Isles.

This, however, did not preclude the Indo-European nature of much of the material Pokorny had used, and by the middle of the 1950s a number of scholars had become aware of the possibility (in Professor Jackson's words) 'that some place-names in Britain which have an Indo-European look but are not clearly either Celtic or Germanic may be due to non-Celtic Indo-European elements among the prehistoric immigrants to these islands'. By Indo-European, of course, is meant that large family of languages that is extensively spoken from India to Ireland, as well as in the Americas, Australia and Africa as a result of settlement by speakers of Indo-European languages, mainly from Europe. All the languages mentioned so far in connection with the history of Scottish place-names belong to that family.

For the purposes of this enquiry the question therefore is: Are there Indo-European river-names in Scotland which, because of their phonological development, their morphological base, or derivative elements, their likely meaning, and their geographical situation, are presumably neither Celtic nor Germanic? In order to answer this question, it will not be enough to scrutinise only those names for which an ascription to any Celtic or Germanic language has never been attempted or for which no convincing etymology has ever been suggested, for such obscure names would form a miserable little group, largely providing hopelessly barren etymological material. It will also be necessary to look critically at a number of names for which vaguely satisfying derivations have already been advanced, mainly before the possibility of non-Germanic or non-Celtic Indo-European origin was ever considered. The River *Cart*, tributary of the Clyde, has, for example, sometimes been referred to as Gaelic *caraid* 'a pair' on account of its two branches, the Black and White Cart, and sometimes to Irish *cartaim* 'I clean' or Welsh *carthu* 'to cleanse'. It is, however, difficult to see what morphological relationships the river-name *Cart* might have to these two Celtic verbs or how a river might be called 'a pair', and it is therefore necessary that a name such as this be re-examined as a potential candidate for pre-Celtic Indo-European origin.

The main potential body of material to be examined in this way consists of those river-names which are recorded too early, or are on geographical grounds not likely, to be Germanic but for which Celtic origin is, for one reason or another, at least doubtful. A good example in this respect is the river-name *Farrar* which together with the river *Glass* forms the river *Beauly* in Inverness-shire. Theoretically, practically any of the languages known to have been spoken in Scotland might have created this name, for it runs through what is now English- and Gaelic-speaking country, lies on the southern edge of the former Norse settlement area, and is also situated in former Pictish territory. However, a number of these possibilities are immediately eliminated once it is noted that the name was first recorded as *Varar* by Ptolemy 150 AD, a date which, owing to Ptolemy's likely sources for the names he mentions in Britain, may in fact be pushed back even further. Such an early date — whether A D 150 or earlier is almost immaterial — does not permit us to consider any kind of Germanic origin. It also, to all intents and purposes, excludes Pictish, since A D 200 is usually taken to be the beginning of the 'historical' Pictish period, and it can hardly be Gaelic because the first Gaelic-speaking settlers are known to have come to the Scottish Dalriada in the fifth century and probably did not reach the banks of the Farrar until a century or two later. This leaves three potential origins: (a) non-Pictish *p*-Celtic, (b) pre-Celtic Indo-European, and (c) pre-Celtic non-Indo-European. Perhaps it might be more appropriate to label (b) and (c) *non*-Celtic rather than *pre*-Celtic but the simultaneous existence of a Celtic and a non-Celtic population in this particular part of Scotland on the fringe of the Highlands 1800 to 2000 years ago is difficult to imagine and has never been seriously suggested on the basis of any other evidence, despite the known non-Celtic ingredient in Pictish.

Most scholars recognising that the initial F- of the modern name Farrar is a Gaelic adaptation of the original initial sound, seem to have decided on a non-Gaelic Celtic derivation although they are by no means agreed as to the etymology of the name. MacBain, for example, suggests a root *var* 'crooked' and is also said to have linked the name with Latin *varus, varius*. Watson, commenting on this etymology, thought that a meaning 'winding, bending' would be quite appropriate as regards the last part of its course at present'. Nevertheless he takes the meaning of this river-name to be obscure, stating at the same time that '*var*- is not uncommon in E[arly] Celt[ic] names' and that 'the formation resembles that of the Gaulish river Arar'. The trouble with this whole proposal, which looks so convincing on the surface, is that Latin *varius* probably does not derive from an Indo-European root *var* (or rather *uer*- 'turn, bend') but from *uā*- 'asunder, especially to bend apart, turn' and is therefore not suitable as a cognate. However, even if one discards the Latin parallel one is still left with a root *uer*- which does not occur in its abstract form but only in numerous extensions. It would consequently be difficult to envisage an -*ar*- formation from such an unextended root. As to Watson's statement that '*var*- is not uncommon in early Celtic Names', he must have had in mind the list of names mentioned by Holder in his *Alt-Celtischer Sprachschatz*. It has been shown since the publication of that great work 80 years ago that many of the names on that list are not Celtic, perhaps not even Indo-European.

Before comment is made on this whole matter in a more general way, it should be mentioned that Mackenzie, who also thinks of *Farrar* as a Brittonic name, compares it with 'Welsh gwâr "gentle"', with the *ar* (river) termination'; that Nicholson similarly proposed *Vo-arar* 'gentle stream'; and that Johnston, after citing MacBain's link with Latin *varius* and completely misunderstanding Watson's suggestion, proposed that 'this is one of our rare pre-Celtic names; cf R. Var, S.E. France, in Strabo *Ouaros*, which is Basq. *uar*, "thick, muddy water"'. Let it

suffice to say that the notion of a compound name at this early stage
is a highly improbable one, even if there were such ready-made bases as
ar 'river', *vo* 'gentle', or *arar* 'stream' of which we have no knowledge.
Also the exact way in which a modern Welsh word — *gwâr* which, by
the way, usually means 'tame, civilised' these days — can be linked with
an Early Celtic '(river) termination' is not at all clear. I am therefore
inclined to take neither Mackenzie's nor Nicholson's suggestion very
seriously. Johnston's idea of a pre-Celtic non-Indo-European name
cannot of course be rejected out of hand, especially since he quotes as a
continental parallel a name which has all the potential qualities of being
cognate with *Farrar*. The chief objection to Johnston's proposal of a
connection with Basque, however, lies in the fact that the very name he
uses as evidence from France is not very likely to be Basque at all but
rather belongs to a western Indo-European stratum, and that not only
for distributional reasons. Because of this inherent weakness in
Johnston's argument and because Basque has never been convincingly
demonstrated to have been a force in the linguistic history of the
British Isles, Basque origin of the name in question is not likely.

Returning to the possibility of an Early Celtic root *var-*, voiced by
MacBain and Watson — always the most reliable sources with regard to
Celtic place-names in Scotland — one has to concern oneself with the
phonological shape of this potentially Celtic morphological element. It
contains the vowel *a* which, as even the most fleeting perusal of an
etymological dictionary will show, never had a very large part to play
in the phonemic shape of Indo-European roots and stems, whereas *ĕ*, *ŏ*
and *ə* abound. It later appears in many Indo-European dialects, usually
developed by some sound-change, spontaneous or conditioned, from
some other original vowel. The continental pre-dialectal Indo-European
hydronymy, to which further reference will be made shortly, stands
out, in this respect, for the frequency with which *â* occurs in both stems
and their morphological extensions in the river-names ascribed to this
hydronymy is quite noticeable. This is understandable in the cases of
names which have passed through the mouths of speakers of Germanic,
Illyrian or Lithuanian since a change from Indo-European *ŏ* to *ă* is a
characteristic of these three languages within the area in which these
early Indo-European river-names are said to occur in Europe, anyhow.
Indo-European *ŏ* remains *ŏ* in Celtic, however (except for a small
number of conditioned changes in later Celtic dialects), and Celtic has
therefore to be regarded, together with Italic and Venetic, as a kind of
'border language' within this European group of languages. Normally
Celtic short *ă* cannot be explained from Indo-European short *ŏ* nor can
a sequence like -*ar*- be said to have originated in the reduction grade *ŗ*
because this would have become *ri* in Celtic. Since an Indo-European
root *u̯er-* 'to moisten, to wet' is, however, the most likely base of this
name and since many early river-names derive from a nominal *o*-stem
rather than a verbal *e*-stem there is hardly any way in which *Var-* can
be considered to be Celtic, except if one accepts Lewis and Pedersen's
argument that 'in Brit. *o* appears as *a* due to unrounding after original
w'. This, however, even if acceptable as a conditioned sound change, is

by no means clear with regard to its chronological place and may well be later. As the first record of Farrar is, as we have seen, also too early to be Germanic and as the river does (despite Pokorny) not run through Illyrian or Lithuanian territory, *Farrar* cannot be explained through ascription to any of the individual western Indo-European languages. Its 'Indo-European-ness' can nevertheless hardly be denied, and it must therefore be explained as belonging to category (b) of the three possibilities, i.e. it must be regarded as a non-Celtic Indo-European name.

This phonological contrast of pre-Celtic Indo-European *ă* versus Celtic *ŏ* is also the most useful criterion in the detection of potential candidates for the stratum under discussion. Indeed, in a way it is the only reliable evidence, since any potentially Indo-European formations from the normal grade of an Indo-European root, i.e. the *e*-grade, cannot be distinguished from their Celtic counterparts. There may consequently be other non-Celtic Indo-European river-names in Scotland (and in Britain) but these are impossible to sift out, and the only reasonably certain group consists therefore of those which undoubtedly contain a short *ă*. This does not mean that one has to rely on this criterion alone, for only when, in addition to this phonological evidence, both stems and suffixes can be shown to be good Indo-European morphological material, is one entitled to think of a river-name in the British Isles as potentially Indo-European. This is certainly the case with *Farrar* (from *Varar-[is]*) because both the nominal *o*-grade *ųor-* of *ųer-* 'to moisten' and the *r*-extension are well-proven Indo-European elements, and because it also has such European counterparts — with different derivational suffixes — as *Vara* (Liguria), *Varia* (France; now *Vaire* and *Veyre*), *Varantia* (a tributary of the Danube; now *Woernitz*); consequently there seems to be little doubt about its Indo-European origins.

The river-name *Farrar* has been paraded in so much detail not only because it provides a good opportunity for demonstrating the methodological principles (and problems) involved, but also because the arguments used here in connection with establishing a name as non-Celtic Indo-European apply just as much to any of the other names which might be ascribable to this stratum. Obviously, a decision is more difficult if there is no recorded form early enough to prove a name to be pre-Germanic but even in those instances other reasons might make Germanic origin an unrealistic possibility.

In the presentation of relevant material appropriate reference must be made to parallel names outside Scotland, not only in the rest of Britain but also on the European continent, for if there were indeed Indo-Europeans in Scotland before the arrival of the Celts, this is no longer a purely Scottish matter and one which can only be fully understood within a wider European context. Without such wider geographical framework, it would be extremely difficult, if not impossible, to establish the nature of this early Scottish hydronymy of about 3000 years ago. Because of the age of this nomenclature, frequently tentative rather than definitive linguistic ascription will have to be made without discrediting the ascription altogether. In some cases, a fuller account and argument will have to be provided than in others, depending on both the name in question and the documentary evidence available.

One Scottish river-name, which may well belong to this pre-Celtic Indo-European category is, *Adder*, as contained in such modern names as Blackadder, Whiteadder, Edrington, and Edrom. It is on record thus:

Blackadder (river rising in the Lammermuirs and joining the White-adder near Allanton in the parish of Edrom BWK; length *c*. 20 miles): *Edre c.* 1050 (12th cent.) *Edrae, ibid.*

Blackadder House BWK (on the right bank of the river in the parish of Edrom): *Blaccedre* 1095-1100, *Blakeder* 1296, *Blacheder* 1325, *Blakedre* 1330, *Blacader* 1541.

Blackadder (surname of local origin, derived from the name of the estate and house); the early spellings are from Black's *Surnames of Scotland:* Adam of Blacathathir (1477), Charles Blakater (1486), Robert Blackader (end of 15th cent.), Rolland Blaykatter (1521) = [?]) Roland Blackadyr (1524), Thomas Blacater (1557).

Whiteadder (river rising in the parish of Whittingehame ELO, flowing into the Tweed not far from Berwick; length c. 34 miles): *Withedre* 1165-1214, *Witedre* 1214-49, *Witeddre* 1231, *Quhitewatter* 1542.

Edrington BWK (the ruins of Edrington Castle are on the left bank of the Whiteadder about five miles from Berwick; Edrington House is on a small tributary of the same river): *Hadryngton* 1095 (15th cent.), *Hoedrinton* 1095-1100 (15th cent.), *Edringtoun* 1309, *Ederington* 1330.

Edrom BWK (village on the right bank of Whiteadder Water; also parish name): *Edrem* 1095 (15th cent.), *Ederham* 1095, 1095-1100, 1138, *Edirham* 1248, *Heddreham* 1248, *Hederham* 1263.

In this list the estate name Blackadder is obviously a secondary development from the river-name, and the distinctive epithets *black* and *white* must have been previously added to an existing name applying to two water-courses joining each other to form one. This does not necessarily mean that the water of the Blackadder is indeed blacker than that of the Whiteadder as the usual reference to define colours in these two adjectives may not be intended here. They simply serve as two opposing distinguishing marks as, for instance, also in *Black* and *White Cart* RNF, or *Black* and *White Esk* DMF; this kind of distinction may also be made when two rivers bearing the same name flow quite near each other, as in *Findhorn* and *Deveron* which contain as first elements the Gaelic colour adjectives *fionn* 'white' and *dubh* 'black', as later additions to identical original names. The surname *Blackadder* is even one stage further removed from the river-name as it is derived from the secondary estate name and not direct from the name of the river. Because of its detachment from the locality from which it stems, and its migrations, it is perhaps not admissible as the same type of evidence as the river and settlement-names. Presumably the name Whiteadder never produced a surname because it never applied to a settlement.

Edrom, as most of the old forms testify, is a compound of the river-name and Old English *hām* 'homestead', a word which became obsolete as a productive place-name element not long after the Angles first reached Scotland. It is therefore one of the earliest English place-names in Scotland and may be translated as 'village on the (River) Adder' (see p. 76 above). In *Edrington* the river-name is compounded with Old English *-ingtūn*, a combination of the connective particle *-ing* with *tūn* 'enclosure, enclosed place'. Meaning 'farm associated with (River) Adder', it is another very early English name in this area (see p. 73). Both these names must have been coined before the distinctive adjectives *black* and *white* were added to the river-name(s).

As far as etymologies so far advanced for the name of the water-course are concerned, we can dismiss as irrelevant the proposed derivation from Gaelic *eadaradh* 'a division' and the suggestion that it perhaps simply means English *water*. Not only would it be wrong to expect a Gaelic river-name of such importance in this region, but the word *eadaradh* is also phonologically and semantically unsuitable; and the equation of *Adder*, or the like, with *-water* is a late medieval invention as the recorded form *Quhitewatter* for 1542 shows. The two derivations which must be taken seriously both consider the river-name to be of English, i.e. Anglian, origin. One of these takes the earliest form *Edre* to be the same as OE *ǣdre*, *ēdre* 'a vein, a water-course'. The other, objecting that this word is not probable for a stream so relatively important as the Adder, suggests that the name, if English, should be derived from an adjective found in Old High German *ātar* 'quick' and in the adverbs OE *ǣdre*, Old Saxon *ādro*, Old Frisian *edre* 'quickly, at once'. This would translate the river-name as meaning 'the swift one', but the objection in both these cases must be that there is no justification for assuming an original English long vowel. The occasional *-dd-* spellings in the early forms, like *Whiteddre* and *Heddreham*, decisively point to a short stem-vowel as a necessary point of departure. Therefore, instead of being of English origin, the Adders must have been among the very first Scottish rivers whose native name the earliest Anglian settlers learnt and on whose banks they settled.

Their most plausible etymological connection is with a group of names for which a suitable *Indo-European* root exists, i.e. **ad(u)-/*adro-* 'water-course'. As an appellative, the *u*-stem occurs as Avestan *adu* 'water-course, stream, canal', and in onomastic usage in *Adua*, now *Adda*, a tributary of the Po in Northern Italy; *Adula*, a tributary of the Tirza in Latvia, **Adula*, now Odla, a river near Odelsk (Poland), and **Adulia* (Attula 807), now *Attel*, a tributary of the Austrian Inn. The corresponding formation in *-ro-* (a parallel well-known in Indo-European morphology) is only found in names, like *Adra* in *Attersee* and *Attergau* (*in pago Adragaoe* 788) in Upper Austria; *Adrana* (Tacitus) and *Adrina* (800), now *Eder*, a tributary of the Fulda in Hesse, with *n*-extension; **Adrina*, later *Ederna*, *Ethrina*, a lost river-name near Gandersheim (Germany); **Adara* (*Odera* 940, *Adora* 968), now the river *Oder* which flows into the Baltic on the German-Polish border.

As far as Adder is concerned the oldest form of the last mentioned name, the *Oder*, would provide the most suitable starting-point, for **Adara* would presumably become known to the Anglian seventh-century invaders in its Primitive Cumbric form **Aðar*, subsequently

beçoming Old English **Ader* with initial *A-* remaining before the *a* of
the following syllable, substitution of *-d-* for *-ð-*, and subsequent
weakening of the − in English − unstressed vowel in the second syllable.
Similarly a feminine *iā*-stem **Adaria* would undergo lenition of the *-d-*
(**A ðariā*), show final *i*-affection (**A ðeriā̆*), loss of final syllable (**A ðer*),
and internal *i*-affection (**E ðer*). As such it would be borrowed into the
Anglian dialect in which substitution of *-d-* for *-ð-* would take place as
in **A ðer* > **A der*. This would be followed by lengthening of the stem-
vowel in the open syllable in the nominative, and no lengthening in the
oblique cases of the singular, resulting in **Adre* and **Edre*, from where
short initial vowel also spread to the nominative, producing the doublet
*Edder and *Adder*. The geographical distribution of cognate names on
the Continent, together with a convincing etymology based on an
Indo-European word meaning 'water-course' and the formation from
well-known Indo-European morphological material, seems to weigh
heavily in favour of this etymology, and, if this view is acceptable,
Adder would be an identical equivalent of the name of one of Europe's
most important rivers, the *Oder*, both deriving from **Adarā*. It is
difficult to decide whether *Edre, Edder-*, etc. are the result of a parallel
formation **Adariā* − perhaps for the Whiteadder, whereas **Adarā*
originally meant the Blackadder, or simply two slightly different
formations for the same name − or whether the *E-* should or must be
explained differently. Not all the problems concerning this name have
therefore been solved but perhaps a beginning has been made by
providing an acceptable etymology.

The next name to be considered would be

Ale Water (river rising in south-east Selkirkshire and joining the
Teviot near Ancrum **ROX**): *Alne* 1176.

Ancrum **ROX** (village on the right bank of the Ale Water in the
parish of the same name): *Alnecrumba c.* 1124, *Alncromb c.* 1150,
Alnecrum 1296, *Allyncrom* 1304.

Allan Water (river rising in the Ochil Hills **PER** and entering the
Forth near Inverallan **STL**): *Alun* 12th century; (*Strath*)*alun* 1187.

Inverallan **STL** (transferred from the confluence of the Allan with
the Forth to a location half a mile south-west of Bridge of Allan):
Invalone, Inviraloun from 1375; *Inneralloun Moss* 1579.

Both river-names are ultimately traceable to an original form **Alauna*,
itself a *-no-/-nā* extension of **Alaunā*, a *uā*-formation from the Indo-
European root **el-/ol-* 'to flow, to stream'. The nominal base *ol-* appears
to have created a Western Indo-European **al(a)* 'water' which can be
seen in such river-names as *Ala* (Norway), *Aller* (Germany) from
*Alara, *Elz* (Germany) from **Alantia*, *Yealm* (Devon, England) from
*Alma, *Aumance* (France) from **Almantia*, etc. The Scottish **Alauna*
itself has its closest identical equivalents in several English river-names
such as the River Alne **NTB** (*Alaunou c.* 150), Ayle Burn **NTB** (*Alne*
1317), the River Ellen **CMB** (*Alne* 1157-99) with the place-name
Allerdale (*Alnerdall c.* 1060) and a number of names in the south of
England, Wales and Cornwall. On the continent, *Alauna* and *Alaunium*
are recorded as settlement-names, in addition to a tribal name *Alauni*

and others. **Alauna* appears to have been a very popular or fashionable name to call rivers by and Scotland must have shared in that popularity. Its meaning is obviously something like 'the flowing one', probably a synonym for 'stream'. Possible further candidates in Scotland might be Allan Water ROX, a tributary of the Teviot, the Ale Water BWK which flows into the Eye Water, the River Alness ROS which enters the Cromarty Firth near the place of that name (*Alenes* 1227), and the Allander Water STL, a tributary of the Kelvin, but the lack of appropriate documentation leaves some doubt about their linguistic origins.

A different extension of **Alaua*, this time with an *nt*-suffix may well be

Allan ROX (river rising in North Roxburghshire and flowing into the Tweed near Melrose): *Aloent* 12th century, *Alwente* 1153-65.

Its geographically closest identical equivalents are the river-names Allen NTB (*Alwent* 1275), Alwin/Alwyn NTB (*Alewent* 1200), and Alwent Beck DRH (*Alewent* 1235). This has been said to derive from an early Celtic *Alo-vinda* 'bright-stoned one', but a pre-Celtic **Alaventa* would seem at least as satisfactory etymologically. What might make such antiquity doubtful, on the other hand, is the fact that all the names in question apply to relatively small water-courses, and there is therefore no certainty about this proposed derivation. **Alaua* itself occurs, by the way, in *Alaw* (Wales) and the *-allow* of Porthallow CNW.

Another candidate for pre-Celtic origin would be the name of the *Ayr* (river rising in Muirkirk parish and flowing 38 miles into the Firth of Clyde at Ayr AYR): *Ar* 1177, *Are* 1197, *Air c.* 1300.

If the Gaelic name for the town of Ayr — *Inbhir-áir* 'Ayr-mouth' — reflects an original long *ā*, it would be difficult to determine whether the river-name is early Celtic or pre-Celtic, since the main phonological criterion for pre-Celtic Indo-European origin, short *ă* versus short *ŏ*, would no longer apply. It might of course still be pre-Celtic but for different reasons. As it is, however, not at all unlikely that the original form of the name had a short *a*, identity is probable not only with the English Oare Water SOM (*Ar* 1279), but also with the Ahr, a tributary of the Rhine in Germany, the *Aar*, flowing into the Oude Riju near Leiden (Belgium), the *Ahre*, a tributary of the Nuhne (Germany), the Spanish river *Ara*, and others. **Arā* 'water-course' would be from **orā* 'flowing movement', the Indo-European root being **er-/*or-* 'to cause to move, to stimulate'. Apart from a basic **Arā*, there are numerous names, in both Britain and Europe, formed by a variety of suffixes, and it is just possible that the *Armet Water*, a tributary of the Gala Water in Midlothian, and that whole group of names consisting of the *Earn Water* RNF, *River Earn* PER, *Strawearn Burn* PER, *Auldearn* (now a place-name) NAI, as well as the River *Findhorn* INV/NAI/MOR and *Deveron* ABD, belong here, but the evidence is too scanty to make a final judgement.

The name *Farrar* INV has already been discussed at length (p. 181), the derivations advanced so far for the name *Cart* RNF have been declared unsatisfactory (p. 180). At present, it is difficult to determine whether the latter is of pre-Celtic rather than Celtic provenance, a fate which the name *Cart* shares with *Carron*, the name of six Scottish rivers in Ross-shire (2), Banffshire, Kincardineshire, Stirlingshire, and Dumfriesshire. Both *Cart* and *Carron* can with confidence be derived from the Indo-European root **kar-* 'hard, stone, stony', with obvious reference to the quality of the beds of these water-courses! While *Cart* may ultimately go back to **Karentī* or **Karentia* (for which there are parallels in the Gloucestershire *Carrant*, as well as the river-names *Carad* in Ireland and *Cheran* in Savoy), *Carron* derives from **Karona* or **Karsona*. Its limited geographical distribution suggests that there may have been an equivalent noun in the early Celtic or pre-Celtic dialect of northern Britain, meaning 'the stony one', or a regional connotative name. The fact that *Cart* and *Carrant* have potentially pre-Celtic equivalents on the Continent makes it likely that the Scottish and English river-names, as well as *Carron* are Indo-European but not Celtic. Unfortunately, the sparse written documentation for five of the Carrons obscures their early history, but for the Stirlingshire river of this name, situated as it is on the border between Highlands and Lowlands, between Pictland and Anglian territory, in comparatively close proximity to the Scottish capital, there is a much fuller record not only from Scottish sources (*Caroun* c. 1200, *Carun* 13th century) but also from English and Irish ones. In a later addition to the annal for AD 710 in the Anglo-Saxon Chronicle the phrase *betwux Hæfe and Cære* occurs, in reference to the Linlithgow Avon and the Stirlingshire Carron; of this a copy is extant, made about 1100 of an original dating to approximately 950. The same phrase appears as Latin *inter Heve et Cere* in Henry of Huntingdon's *Historia Anglorum* (1125-30). There is also in the Trinity College Ms. of the Irish *Annals of Ulster* a reference to the events in which Domnall Breac was slain in Strathcarra in AD 641: *in bello sraith Cairuin*. The language is seventh century or a little later, and the name here appears in the genitive. There is confirmation of this in the Irish phrase *i catha sratha Carun* in the fourteenth-century copy of the *Annals of Tigernach*. If the consistent spellings with only one *-r-* mean anything at all, they probably favour the original **Karona* rather that **Karsona*, which would presuppose a development *-rs-* to *-rr-*.

As for five of the *Carrons*, lack of really early documentation also is a drawback with regard to the river-name *Nairn* which flows into the Moray Firth at Invernairn and has given its name to a town and county. The place-name is recorded as *Invernaren* 1189-99, *Invernaryn* 1204, and the relevant Gaelic names are *Abhainn, Inbhir,* and *Srath Narunn.* The name in all probability is identical with the early form *Narōn* of the river-name Narenta in Illyria, deriving from an Indo-European root **ner-* 'dive, cave, submerge', the *o*-grade of which, **nor-*, would give us the base **nar-* we require. There are several European river-names derived from this root, amongst them the *Naraïs* in France, the *Narasa* in Lithuania, and the *Niers*, a tributary of the Maas.

In contrast to the names discussed so far, apart from *Farrar*, the next one is clearly an early name, as it is mentioned by Ptolemy around AD 150 in the genitival form *Nabarou*. This is in reference to the Naver (river issuing from Loch Naver and flowing 19 miles through

Strath Naver into Torrisdale Bay not far from Invernaver SUT): *Strathnauir* 1268; *Inernauyr* 1378, *Innvyrnavyr* 1401.

If it were not for the written record of the second century AD which probably reflects a much earlier source, one might conjecture that the original form of the name was *Nabaros*, but the lateness of the documentation would not have allowed us to be certain. By the same token, Ptolemy's references to Farrar and Naver show that even comparatively short rivers – the former is 25 miles long, the latter 19 – did have names 2000 or more years ago, names which have survived several linguistic changes since then. *Nabaros* is undoubtedly from the *o*-grade of the Indo-European root **nebh-* 'moist, water, mist, cloud'. Other early river-names from the same root would be Nevern PEM (**Naberna*), Naab (tributary of the Danube) from **Nobhā*; as well as the ancient *Nabalia* and *Nablis* on the continent while a Celtic river-name from the *e*-grade **nebh-* is *Nevis*.

An uncertain candidate for pre-Celtic provenance is

Ness (river issuing from the northern end of Loch Ness and flowing 7 miles into Moray Firth at Inverness INV): *Nesa*, genitive *Nis* 700, *Nis* 1300, *Inuernis* 1171-84.

Presumably the sound development has been *Ness*, from **Nessos* or **Nessa*, from **Nestos* or **Nesta*, from **Nedtos*, **Nedta*, meaning 'stream, river', from the Indo-European root **ned-* 'to wet, flood'. Identical equivalents would be *Nestos*, two river-names in Thracia and Dalmatia, and *Neste* (from *Nesta*), a former river-name in the Pyrenees. There are also other stream-names formed with different suffixes from the same root. No decision is possible on a phonological basis, but the geographical distribution of this name-type indicates that it was not purely Celtic, and that we may therefore consider common earlier origin for the names in Celtic countries as well as Thracia and Dalmatia. This argument is not conclusive, of course, and *Ness* will have to remain doubtful as a pre-Celtic river-name.

We are on much firmer ground with regard to:

Shiel, Gaelic *Seile* (1) (river issuing from Loch Shiel and flowing 3 miles to the sea at Loch Moidart): *Sale* 7th century. (2) (river issuing from Loch Cluanie and flowing into Loch Duich at Invershiel ROS): *Glenselle* 1509, *Glenschale* 1574, *Innerselle* 1571.

As **Salia*, both these names are part of a large hydronymic family derived from the Indo-European root **sal-* 'stream, flowing water, current'. Identical equivalents are the English river-name Hayle CNW and the obsolete English stream-names *Hail* (?), *Hayle* and *Haill*, the Spanish rivers *Sella* and *Saja*, two French rivers *Seille*, all on record as *Salia*. In addition, several continental river-names, from Hungary to Norway, were originally *Sala*, *Salma*, *Salantia*, etc. It would be difficult not to acknowledge that these names cannot have been created by any one language, like Celtic, for example, and pre-Celtic origin is almost inevitable.

A river-name which might also well belong to this category is:

Shin, Gaelic *Abhainn Sin* (river issuing from Loch Shin and joining the river Oykell at Invershin SUT): *Shyne flu* 1610, *Inverchyn*,

Innerchen 1203-14, *Innershyn* 1570, *Inershin* 1610; *L. Shyn* 1570, *L. Schin* 1583, etc.

If a derivation **Sindh-nā* 'river' (an *n*-formation **sindhn-* from an oblique case of the Indo-European **sindhu* 'river') is acceptable, *Shin* would be identical with the German river-name *Sinn* (a tributary of the Frankische Saale) and cognate with *Shannon* (Ireland), *Sinnius* (Italy) and *Senne* (Brabant). Even if such a derivation is somewhat awkward morphologically, there is no real alternative to thinking of *Shin* as a pre-Celtic name, as all attempts at providing it with a Celtic, particularly Gaelic, etymology have failed.

Finally, there is a morphologically complex and geographically widespread group of names of which the *Thames* is the main representative in Britain and which in Scotland has derivatives in the names *Tain* ROS (originally a river-name), *Water of Tanar* ABD, *Glentanner Water* SLK, *Teviot* ROX, and, very likely, *Tay* PER. The Indo-European root for these and numerous other names in England and on the Continent would be **tā-, tə-* 'to melt, to dissolve, to flow'. From a different form of the same root are formed the *Tyne* ELO and its larger Northumbrian namesake. Since none of the criteria developed for a distinction between Celtic and pre-Celtic apply here, one cannot come to any decision with regard to the linguistic origin of this sizable family of names. It is, indeed, possible that both the Celtic and the pre-Celtic Indo-European strata are involved in the creation of these names, for there is no reason why 'water-words' used by an earlier stratum should not also be productive in a later one. Whatever the situation and the ultimate verdict may be, at present such names as *Tain, Tay, Teviot,* and *Tyne* cannot be included in the pre-Celtic category, nor can they confidently be called Celtic.

This, then, is the evidence for what must be regarded as the earliest recognisable stratum of geographical names in Scotland. As a result of their investigation, the following points emerge:

(*a*) There are river-names in Scotland which cannot be explained as Celtic but which, although too early to be Germanic, are very likely Indo-European.

(*b*) Many of these names are identical with names elsewhere in Britain and on the Continent. While in quite a number of instances complete identity is found, in others common stems are combined with common derivative morphemes, fitting well into a general pattern.

(*c*) There are quite a few names on the fringe of this set which, mostly for phonological reasons, cannot be ascribed with the same certainty to this pre-Celtic Indo-European stratum. Some of these may indeed belong here but cannot be distinguished. Others may be Celtic.

(*d*) It would be wrong to regard the names in question as part of a 'system'. The more flexible term 'network' seems to be much more appropriate.

While the first three points sum up the arguments already advanced in this chapter, the last is offered more in response to criticism expressed over the years, not so much perhaps in relation to the thesis of a pre-Celtic Indo-European river-nomenclature as such but rather to what appeared to be a highly structured 'system' of stems and suffixes in a variety of different combinations; and criticism there certainly has been. It is perhaps also fair to say that it has not been directed primarily or mainly at the situation as outlined for Scotland or Britain, but predominantly at the idea of a pre-Celtic, pre-Germanic, pre-Italic, pre-Illyrian, pre-Venetic, pre-Baltic Indo-European river-nomenclature in Europe, an idea first proposed and subsequently supported and worked out in many publications by the late German Indo-Europeanist Hans Krahe who coined the term 'Old European' for this particular stratum. His extensive investigation of the pre-historic river-names of Europe, as well as of other lexical material, led him to the conclusion that such a pre-dialectal linguistic situation existed in central, northern and western Europe around 1500 BC, before any of the Indo-European dialects listed above had become fully-fledged independent languages. Although he never said so in so many words, Krahe was quite clearly not thinking of a stratum without chronological depth, just as it would be impossible to think of it without geographical distribution, but his critics have, on the whole, overlooked this assumption and have preferred to see it as an over-structured static 'system'.

What has been asserted in the last few pages is that Scotland and Britain share that 'Old European' river-nomenclature, and that, therefore, when the Celts first arrived in Scotland, there were already people present who, as immigrants from Europe centuries before them, had introduced an Indo-European language to the British Isles. Although such a notion is controversial, there is no real alternative which would explain convincingly the presence of names that are clearly Indo-European in character but cannot be called Celtic or Germanic.

Further back we cannot go at present. This does not mean that there are no names left on the Scottish map which may be pre-Indo-European or at least non-Indo-European. Major river-names like Tweed, Spey, Ettrick, and others, have never been explained satisfactorily, and several island names in the Hebrides also appear to be old but have so far escaped explanation. If these are non-Indo-European, we do not have the key to their linguistic affinities. Similarly, there are other Scottish place-names for which nobody has ever offered an acceptable etymology, but obscurity and opacity are not synonyms for antiquity, and it would be wrong to assume that every unexplained name is by definition old. For the time being, we simply have to acknowledge that we do not know what lies linguistically beyond the 'Old European' — the pre-Celtic Indo-European — stratum of river-names. Maybe some future student of Scottish place-names will be able to offer a solution to that linguistic puzzle. We wish him or her luck; the establishment of an 'Old European' stratum has been difficult enough.

Index

This index includes all place-names which are discussed in the book or which are used to illustrate certain points or to substantiate certain arguments. Names mentioned only in connection with geographical locations have been omitted.

Roman type indicates that the name is in use today, whereas historical forms are in italics. An asterisk (*) before a name means that, as listed, the spelling is hypothetical, and single quotation marks around a name imply that this name exists only in oral tradition.

of SHE 63

Haarsal (South Uist) IN V 108
Habost (Lewis) R OS 94, 97
Haddington ELO 73
Haddingtonshire ELO 48
Hail (river) GLO, HNT 189
Hailisepeth BWK 116
Haill (river) CNW 189
Haithwaite CMB 104
Hala MLO 19
Halkerston MLO 30
Halltree MLO 169
Hamar, Keen of SHE 63
Hamara Field SHE 108
Hamarifield, Burn of SHE 57
Hammermen's Close (Edinburgh) 49
Hanby LIN 114
Handforth CHE 79
Handwick ANG 5, 79, 81
Hanover Street, (Edinburgh) 50
Happisburgh NFK 73
Harperwhat DMF 103, 104
Hartaval (Barra) IN V 108
Hassington BWK 25, 73
Hastie's Close (Edinburgh) 49
Haversay (Hebrides) 97
Hawick NTB 4, 79
Hawick R OX 3-6, 78, 79, 81
Hayle (river) CNW 189
Haythwaite Y ON 104
Head of Gutcher SHE 63
Head of Mula SHE 63
Heatherwick ABD 5, 79
Heatherwick NTB 79
Hebrides 54
Hedderwick ANG 5, 79, 81
Hedderwick BWK 5, 79, 81
Hedderwick ELO 5, 79, 81
Heishival (Vatersay) IN V 108
Heithat DMF 104
Helensburgh DNB 52
Hellisdale (South Uist) IN V 95
Helmsdale SUT 95, 136
Henken, Geo of SHE 63
Heriot MLO 12, 18
Hermiston MLO 30
Hermiston R OX 30
Herston ORK 90
Hestam (North Uist) IN V 97
Hestaval (Lewis) R OS 97
Hevdadale SHE 95
Heylipoll (Tiree) ARG 94
'Highlandman's Umbrella, The'

(Glasgow) 51
High Street (Edinburgh) 49
Hill of Gutcher SHE 63
Hiltly WLO 18
Hoathwaite LNC 104
Hoglibister SHE 94
Holm of Skaw SHE 63
Holsas, The Burn of SHE 63
'Holy Corner' (Edinburgh) 51
Horasaid SUT 92
Horse Wynd (Edinburgh) 49
Hosta (North Uist) IN V 90
Houlland SHE 98
Hourston ORK 90
House of Fetterkarne KCD 60
Housetter SHE 91
Houstry, Burn of CAI 57
Hove, Bull of ORK 64
Howatstone MLO 29
Howthat DMF 103, 104
Hoy, Water of ORK 61
Humbie ELO 113, 114
Humbie FIF 113, 114
Humbie MLO 113, 114
Humbie RNF 113
Humbie WLO 113, 114
Humby LIN 114
Hunsta SHE 90
Hutton BWK 38
Hutton DMF 38
Huxter SHE 91

Illieston WLO 30, 115
Ingleston DRH 116
Ingleton Y OW 116
Ingliston MLO 116
Ingoldisthorpe NFK 116
Ingoldmells LIN 116
Ingoldsby LIN 116
Inkster ORK 91
Innse Gall 54
Inverallan STL 186
Inveraray ARG 164
Inverbervie KCD 164
Inverewe R OS 164
Inverhadden Burn PER 178
Invernairn N AI 188
Invernaver SUT 189
Inverness IN V 49, 164, 189
Inverness-shire IN V 49
Inverpeffer ANG 164
Inverpeffray PER 164
Invershiel R OS 189
Invershin SUT 189